TRINITIES
to
ENNEAGRAMS

TRINITIES
to
ENNEAGRAMS

FINDING YOUR IDENTITIES
AND LIFE STAGES

Allen David Young, PhD

Library of Congress Control Number:		2017913042
ISBN:	Hardcover	978-1-5434-4614-2
	Softcover	978-1-5434-4613-5
	eBook	978-1-5434-4612-8

KJV
Scripture quotations marked KJV are from the Holy Bible, King James Version (Authorized Version). First published in 1611. Quoted from the KJV Classic Reference Bible, Copyright © 1983 by The Zondervan Corporation.

Any people depicted in stock imagery provided by Thinkstock are models, and such images are being used for illustrative purposes only.
Certain stock imagery © Thinkstock.

Print information available on the last page.

Rev. date: 12/04/2017

To order additional copies of this book, contact:
Xlibris
1-888-795-4274
www.Xlibris.com
Orders@Xlibris.com
763772

Contents

Acknowledgments xi

Introduction xiii

1   Cosmic Circles for All Time 1

   The Circle of One 4

   Dualism and the Law of Two (Two Diagrams) 6

   Trinities, the Enneagram, and Law of Three (Diagram).........7

   Three Triangles in the Circle of Nine Points (Diagram)........10

   Three Triangles in the Enneagram 10

   Signs and Stages of Development 11

   The Zodiac as Enneagram Signs (Table) 15

   Cyclical Time and Change...16

   Individuation 18

2   Trinities 20

   Trinity Principles from Different World Views (Table) 23

   Trinity Groups Psychologies (Table) 23

   Trinity Cases 24

   Taoist Trinity..30

   Hindu Trinity..31

   Planet Symbols Trinity 32

   Holistic Healing Trinity..33

   Mental Science Trinity..33

3   Enneagram Signs in the Zodiac...36

   Numbered Enneagram Signs in the Zodiac (Diagram) 38

   One, The Initiator..38

   Two, The Guide 39

   Three, The Contestant 40

Four, The Romantic 41

Five, The Innovator...42

Six, The Skeptic 43

Seven, The Seeker..44

Eight, The Defender...45

Nine, The Mediator 46

The Trinities among Soul Types...47

4   Nine Types and Planets...49

Planet Types 51

Planets (Table)..53

Trinity Forces and Stages in the Planets (Table) 54

The Reformer Type, Mercury..55

The Helper, The Moon 57

The Achiever, The Sun 59

The Individualists, Neptune 61

The Investigator, Uranus 63

The Loyalist, Saturn 65

The Enthusiast, Jupiter 67

The Challenger, Mars..69

The Peacemaker, Venus 71

Manifesting the Types 72

Finding Your Type..75

5   Signs and Type Associations..76

Enneagram Signs Through the Zodiac 77

Trinity Groups 78

Trinity Forces and Stages (Table) 79

Enneagram Type and Sign Associations (Table) 80

Enneagram Types

The Enneagram Letters 83

Enneagram Letter Groups (Table) 84

Enneagram System Features 85

The Enneagram Typology (Diagram) 86
The Signs and Cycles..87
The Ego and Soul Personality..89
Cycles of Becoming 90
Life Stages and Cycles by Enneagram Sign (Table) 91

6   Sign, Type, and Stage Traits 93
Sign, Type, and Stage 1..95
Sign, Type, and Stage 2..99
Sign, Type, and Stage 3..101
Sign, Type, and Stage 4..104
Sign, Type, and Stage 5..107
Sign, Type, and Stage 6..110
Sign, Type, and Stage 7..112
Sign, Type, and Stage 8..115
Sign, Type, and Stage 9..118

7   Sign and Type Pair Meanings.....................................121
Compatibilities Among Types, Signs, and Cycles................122
Sign and Type Compatibilities (Table)...............................123
The Enneagram Typology (Diagram) 125
Pairs with One, Initiators or Reformers 125
Pairs with Two, Guides or Helpers....................................130
Pairs with Three, Contestants or Achievers 134
Pairs with Four, Romantics or Individualists......................138
Pairs with Five, Innovators or Investors 141
Pairs with Six, Skeptics or Loyalists 144
Pairs with Seven, Seekers or Enthusiasts 146
Pairs with Eight, Defenders or Challengers........................147
Nine-Nine, The Mediators or Peacemakers........................148

8   The First Third of the Life Cycle 149
Life Stage and Cycle Awareness 150
Living from Birth to Age Twenty-Seven............................152

The Initiator Cycle 153

The Guide Cycle 155

The Contestant Cycle..161

9   *The Middle Third of the Life Cycle* 166

The Romantic Cycle 168

The Innovator Cycle 173

The Skeptic Cycle 178

10   *The Last third of Life and Beyond* 184

The Seeker Cycle...186

The Defender Cycle 191

The Mediator Ages..196

The New Life After Eighty 202

The Second Initiator Ages 203

11   *Name and Letter Types* 210

The Alphabet and Enneagram 211

Enneagram Letters by Group....................................212

Letter Stages and Cycles around the Zodiac (Diagram).......213

The Initiator and Reform Type Letters—AJS 215

The Guide and Helper Type Letters—BKT..................217

The Contestant and Achiever Type Letters—CLU 218

The Romantic and Individualist Type Letters—DMV.......219

The Innovator and Investigator Type Letters—ENW 221

The Skeptic and Loyalist Type Letters—FOX..............222

The Seeker and Enthusiast Type Letters—GPY 223

The Defender and Challenger Type Letters—HQZ 225

The Mediator and Peacemaker Type Letters—IR 226

Trinity Forces and Stages in the Alphabet (Table) 228

Missing Letters in a Name..228

The First Letter in a Name 230

The Birth Name or Authentic Personality 233

Names and Personality Changes 236

Related Bibliography 239
Index 243
The Nine Stages of Manifesting 247
From Four to Three Seasons 250
Life Events, Stages, and Your Biography 253

Acknowledgments

This book is an outgrowth of my 1987 unpublished manuscript based on numerology and titled *The Nine Stages of Life, Work, and Personal Development*. Since that manuscript was the inspiration for the new enneagram directions presented in this book, I am grateful for the knowledge numerology has contributed to its contents. I am grateful for the many astrology book authors, teachers, and clients I have had the opportunity to learn from and counseled over the years.

I would like to thank Ernest Holmes and the teachings of the Science of Mind philosophy for my understanding of the trinity. I would like to thank the numerous spiritual and intuitive counseling clients who allowed me to serve them over the past three decades, the congregants and visitors I served in my role as minister at the Illuminata Center for Spiritual Living over the past ten years, and the invaluable support from Centers for Spiritual Living. As a new student to the enneagram, I believe my outsider status has helped me view this spiritual tool and system of types in expanded ways.

Introduction

This book is about trinities or the Law of Three and how they unify the universe and allow us to reveal all its hidden mysteries. The Law of Three is a basic metaphysical principle that was newly discovered by G. I. Gurdjieff, though he claimed it has ancient roots. This principle states that any new arising throughout the universe is the result of three independent forces—active, receptive, and mediating—and that without these forces, there is no legitimate change or growth in nature. The Taoist trinity of yang, yin, and the Tao is a mirror image of the Law of Three. When there's a deadlock or duality, the only way to a graceful resolution that satisfies both parties is the third or unifying face of the trinity.

The enneagrams is a spiritual tool and system of personality types based on trinities and the Law of Three. Trinities and enneagrams give a clear understanding of ourselves and those who are important to us. Like the Law of Three, the ancient enneagram, rediscovered and adapted for modern use by Gurdjieff, has become popular since the 1980s. They represent specific nondual perspectives and ways of knowing and recognizing the unity of being. Enneagram authors do not divide the types into binary categories, such as yang and yin, four directions, or eight types. They are divided into three categories or trinities, such as body, mind, and soul; beginning, middle, and ending; affirming, denying, and reconciling; and inspiration, power, and harmony. For instance, the Inspiration types and names are one, four, and five, or

The Reformer, The Individualists, and The Investigator respectively; the Power types are three, six, and eight, or The Achiever, The Loyalist, and The Challenger; and the Harmony types are two, seven, and nine, or The Helper, The Enthusiast, and The Peacemaker. Instead of paired opposites, we have the interaction of three energies that create a whole new realm of possibility that greatly benefits people in the personal, interpersonal, and social spheres of human existence.

Oscar Ichazo was the person who originally put the enneagram system together as it is widely understood nowadays, but the enneagram is not limited to the form he created. The system has gone through several transformations throughout its history, and its types have mostly been developed in isolation from its original source. In this work, the enneagram applications and the trinities within them are a modern synthesis of many ancient wisdom traditions. Trinities give a straightforward way to understand the whole, and in this work every enneagram contains six trinity arrangements. Enneagrams are essentially a more detailed, complete, and advanced version of trinities. In addition to the enneagram types based on ego-centered personality preferences, you will find nine enneagram soul types based on the astrology signs given to you by your soul and the cosmos at birth. The enneagram signs represent your essence or soul's eternal personality, and form the starting point of the recurring annual stages and nine-year development cycles throughout the human life span. Finally, the nine enneagram letter groups identified from the cycle of alphabet of letters presents an additional opportunity, along with your birth sign, to understand what your name reveals about the essence of your soul.

The enneagram has roots in several wisdom traditions, including Christianity, Judaism, Islam, and astrology, the world's oldest system of psychological types. Although most authors give no source for the origin of enneagram types, the nine types and the nine-astrological planet types are essentially the same. Each system has a common source, but they have been developed in isolation from one another. Like the astrological planet types, enneagram types represent nine nearly identical and distinct human types. Both planets and types are motivational forces and carriers of energy. While there are some differences between planet types and enneagram types, the simplicity and elegance of the enneagram makes it much easier to understand than astrology. Even though astrology is the oldest system of psychological types in the world, I believe that creators of the enneagram kept their source hidden because astrology was no longer reputable as a system of psychology.

Trinities and the Law of Three allow situations to unfold at a higher level of consciousness but do not produce uniform results for everyone because people operate at various levels of awareness. For instance, those who seek solutions through the power of the father-mother-child trinity and its variations, such as the trinities of seeds, earth, and plants or active, receptive, and reconciling forces, will benefit according to what they can allow themselves to truly receive. Those who affirm new goals, plant seeds, or put forward ideas always have a relationship to the womb, growth, producing earth, or receptive hearers. Reliable results follow when these two parts of the trinity are bound together, and when they are not, things don't work out well. The following two cases should explain this point.

If I plant seeds in an area with too much or too little sunlight or water and not enough good earth or in an area taken up by too many weeds, it is unlikely that a healthy plant or any plant will grow. When I plant seeds in good earth and do not follow up with the right care needed for growth, I have essentially walked away from the relationship between seed and soil. Since seeds planted in good conditions have the best opportunity for growth at the outset, such conditions should be sought before planting takes place. If the seeds represent ideas, the adverse conditions could symbolize situations where the ideas are heard but where the hearer is too distracted by other things to focus on getting the ideas developed. In both situations, good outcomes call for having good conditions at the outset and sticking with the trinity relationship among father, mother, and child long enough for the desired growth to take place. This trinity connection is necessary for individuals, between individuals in partnership, or in groups who want to resolve such problems.

Throughout this work, you will see the term *trinities* rather than *sacred trinities* because the term *sacred trinity* refers to a combination of divine and human characteristics as seen in the Holy Trinity from Christianity of father, holy spirit, and son. The term *trinities* or *trinity* is interchangeable with the Law of Three, which may or may not include divine and human traits. The sacred or Holy Trinity is a theological concept discussed among religious types who are empowered to do so. While this trinity is of little interest to most people and not really understood, it is a personification of the Law of Three.

The creation of enneagram signs in this work is adapted from the twelve astrology signs. They were created by dividing the 360-degree zodiac into nine forty-degree signs, each containing parts of two complimentary opposite astrology signs. For example, the first sign contains Aries and part of Taurus but is neither sign by itself, the second sign contains both Taurus and Gemini but is neither sign by itself, and so forth. The two signs make up a "proactive" and "receptive" trinity pair, and the enneagram sign creates the third trinity force by uniting the opposing signs. The meaning of these trinities is like the meaning of the nine enneagram types but not identical. While enneagram types describe one's egocentric personality and way of being, enneagram signs are based on one's birth date and time and reveal their immortal soul-centered personality. I use the term *soul-centered personality* because the enneagram sign is given by the cosmos at birth and considers the hidden qualities in things, in individuals, and in one's soul. Because the date and time of birth can never be duplicated, each person is an original creation, seed, and literally one of a kind.

Although Gurdjieff did not present a model of the enneagram or explain how the system works, he taught that the enneagram must be thought of as a system in motion and that a motionless enneagram is a dead symbol. The enneagram becomes a system in motion and reveals more of its insights with the addition of nine signs and stages of development through the life cycle introduced in this work. Stages and cycles of development exist, and they are adapted to the enneagram because the earth's movement around the sun has been taking place with regularity since the beginning. In its annual journey around the sun, the earth spends about forty days in each enneagram sign, and every birthday year represents a new one-year stage in the nine-year cycles that are recurrent through the life cycle from birth to age eighty-one.

In this work, the nine stages and life development cycles are named after the enneagram signs. The first third of life from birth to age twenty-seven is represented by the affirming or active forces of the trinity and the desire to initiate action. There are three nine-year trinity cycles in the first third of life. In the first or beginning cycle from birth to age nine, children often start projects and often lose interest without finishing them. Those in the second or middle cycle of these early years from nine to eighteen experience unlimited possibilities and difficulties in dealing with concrete reality, and those in the third or ending cycle from ages eighteen to twenty-seven develop an interest in seeing the big picture and work to make the best of everything. The middle third of life from ages twenty-seven to fifty-four represents the denying or receptive forces of the trinity and the desire to preserve and sustain their involvements. The most obvious characteristics of these years in the life cycle is persistence, the desire for practical results, and learning to reason things out before acting. The last third of life from ages fifty-four and beyond is represented by the reconciling or mediating forces of the trinity and the desire for self-discovery, change, transformation, and adaptation. These qualities make them easygoing, tolerant, free-flowing, and introduce an increased interest in highly personal relationships with others.

Enneagram signs and planets are at the center of all letters, words, forms of thought, measurement, explanation, analysis, growth, and existence. The movement of the earth around the sun and the nine planets are not only the origin of enneagram types and signs but also of the enneagram letter groups and stages contained in the three cycles of letters. The first cycle containing the letters from A to I is followed by the second cycle containing the letters from J to R and the third cycle containing the letters from S to Z. While planets and the numbers they represent remain in the background, they are always present and a source of power.

This book comes to an end with the introduction of enneagram letter groups and examples that give readers a tool for understanding the personality revealed by names. The birth name is a tremendous symbol of consciousness. The importance of one's original name is identical to that of the exact date and time of birth in astrology—both are given and tied to the birth moment. There are few personality maps that reveal as much information as the birth name. They function to help spell out one's unique mission in life and further define what can be built or produced by the individual. Even though name changes do not replace one's birth name, they modify the way we are seen and our projected egocentric personality.

The first of three short sections added after the Related Bibliography presents my understanding of the inner observation process in nine steps. These steps are universal and should help you to better understand the objective measures of the enneagram personalities, soul types, and cycles. It is my aim to help bring about this understanding by presenting the roles played by the nine subjective steps that take place from conceiving in the beginning to manifesting results in the end with all forms of imagery, visioning, concentration and meditation.

The second section presents an explanation of the transition from the twelve-months and twelve zodiac signs to the nine-enneagram signs and types. This section comments on the transition from oneness to duality and presents a table of the forces and stages among the enneagram types.

The third section presents biographical questions for you to reflect on many of the past events in your stages of life by age. By recording many of these events you can view them in an informational and entertaining manner that can help you gain insights into the personal meanings of your history and future.

1

Cosmic Circles for All Time

For things to reveal themselves to us,
we need to be ready to abandon our view about them.

— Thich Nhat Hanh

Everything has a purpose, a time, a measure, and a season. Scientists and nonscientists agree that we can't ignore numbers in nature. Finding purpose in life is questioned by many people as they ponder the reasons for their existence. The meaning of your birth date represents the cosmic theme of your purpose in life, your authentic self, and the ongoing process or personality of your soul. In this work, the nine stages the earth travels through in its annual journey around the sun and through the seasons represent the personality of the soul. While the four seasons and twelve zodiac signs are well-known divisions of the annual cycle, the numbers one through nine offer a zodiac map based on nine enneagram signs. The first sign is associated with the early part of spring, and the last or ninth sign is associated with the last part of winter. The earth-sun or cosmic relationship does not represent the actual soul itself but rather, our way of being and those aspects of our nature that are most positive and radiant like the sun. Your birth date and time is a map of your cosmic goals and ambitions based on the universal principles represented by the nine single-digit numbers one through nine.

In most cases, your enneagram sign is determined by your birthday alone. When it's not clear whether your birth date falls at the beginning or end of a sign, your exact time and place of birth can be used to clear things up, or you can see yourself as being influenced by both signs. The enneagram sign identifies the position of the sun, the nature power within you, your purpose in life, your life path or destiny, what you came here to learn, challenges to grow through, and insights into your natural talents. The enneagram signs present the nine cosmic spring-to-spring life paths or soul personality types as part of the cosmos. The cosmic qualities present when we are born are completely unique to everyone. They are not chosen by us, and they cannot be reconstructed. They are like a cosmic egg, laid by the cosmos and hatched at birth, and they become the basis of all that follows throughout our lifetime. In addition to describing the personality of your soul, your cosmic-given enneagram sign makes the starting point of the annual life stages and nine-year life cycle over the course of your lifetime. The enneagram signs give meaning to every letter of the alphabet and the names they have come together to represent.

The origin and meanings of numbers from one to nine are defined by their relationship to the circle or whole when it is divided into three equal parts. Before we get to the existence of three and its meaning, we need to explain the meanings of one and two. The circle, the whole, and one share much of the same meaning. All things are contained in zero, a symbol for the nothingness of spirit, and the nothingness of spirit is contained in all things. Even though zero is a symbol of the soul or transcendent and not a number, one is contained in zero, and zero is contained in one. The difference between one and zero is that zero is infinite and that one is a mixture of the infinite and finite. One is the beginning of manifestation, and zero is the unknown potential or concept of manifestation before anything about the manifestation is known. The mother of one is the infinite cosmic clock that gives birth to every moment in time, and every moment contains the DNA of that moment's entry into existence.

The source, the blueprint, the egg, and seed are all represented by one. One is the recognition that all life and all possibilities are contained within it. All creation is contained in one, all life is one, and all life is whole, perfect, and complete before anything comes into being. Because the infinite contains all of one and one contains access to all the infinite, one contains the whole. Every individual and all things come into being through one. All manifestations are bodies of ones. All words, thoughts, and ideas that convey the conscious understanding of things are represented by one. Without one, there is no beginning, no existence, and no life. The closest thing to zero is one, and one stands between zero and two. Just as zero is the source of one, one is the source of two. When the egg hatches, when the circle or whole is divided into two parts, one becomes two.

The division of one circle into two parts gives us the basic meaning of two, which represents the beginning of duality, oppositions, and relationships between two sides, such as spirit and matter, yang and yin, and so forth. The relationship between zero and one is like the relationship between one and two in the sense that each pair shares some qualities of the other. Just as one is the source of two, two is the source of three. When one and two give birth to three, the third force comes into existence to neutralize or reconcile the unresolved forces of one and two.

In this work, the universal order of the trinities, nine forces, and stages given here are associated with the enneagram signs, types, letters of the alphabet, names, and stages or cycles of development. The numbers one, two, and three represent the beginning stages of all cycles of any size, the youthful years in the life cycle from birth to about age thirty, and the enneagram signs and types that are most associated with youth are Types One, Two, and Three. The numbers four, five, and six represent the middle stages of all cycles, the middle adult years in the life cycle from about age thirty to sixty, and the enneagram signs and types that are most associated with mid-life development are Types Four, Five, and Six. The numbers seven, eight, and nine represent the completion stages in all cycles, the golden years in the life cycle from about age sixty to ninety, and the enneagram signs and types that are most associated with wisdom are Types Seven, Eight, and Nine.

Though it's true that we traditionally celebrate the beginning of spring on March 21, astronomers and calendar manufactures alike now say that spring starts one day earlier, March 20, in all North American time zones. In the northern hemisphere, the spring equinox takes place in the USA, Central America, Canada, Europe, Asia, and North Africa. In the southern hemisphere, the spring equinox takes place in Australia, New Zealand, South America, and Southern Africa. In the southern hemisphere, January is the seasonal equivalent of July in the northern hemisphere and vice versa.

In the wheel of the year, the sun is a symbol of love, the Christ Principle and the universal spiritual force whose nature is forever giving and expanding. The sun's visual journey through the course of the year signifies a stage or cycle of life which has been understood by people throughout the world. The spring equinox is the time in the earth's annual cycle around the sun in which day and night are equal in length before the days finally start to get longer after the dominance of darkness, during winter, and life springs forth from death. The spring equinox stands upon the points of balance, upon which everything pivots in its motion, in the universe, in the cycles of the seasons, and within ourselves.

Dividing the 360-degree zodiac circle or any circle or simply one living whole by any of the single-digit numbers one, two, or three allows us to understand the characteristics of the nine single-digit numbers as personality types and stages of life. The relationship among the three trinities and trinity parts of a circle reveal the characteristics of enneagram numbers.

The Circle of One

Any circle, point, or thing is represented by the number one. One remains one if it's not divided. Everything represented by this number tends to act in ways that represent its perspective—a kind of "what you see is what you get" expression. One is not given to second-guessing or being in competition with the various parts itself. Rather than compete against itself, one represents the undivided circle, the whole and united energy that has not yet separated itself into two or more parts. One is the easiest number to understand because it represents a unified personality. Ones derives their motivation from within and represent the whole. They have a tough time acknowledging others as distinct or separate and naturally assume that others are much the same way. In this sense, one represents focus, single-mindedness, action, and self-projection.

Traditionally, the number one contains the essence of both odd and even and represents unification, indivisibility, agreement, and coming together. Cyclically, it represents beginnings, seeds, eggs, renewals, returning to the beginning, and the union or conjunctions of two planetary energies. Though the symbolic meaning of one may not be apparent, this number is associated with the beginning of awareness and the manifest universe. One contains the whole, the awareness of wholeness, and all there is of the one life or thing. All life is an incarnation of one spirit, one universe or cosmos, and when we take our attention off oneness, we take our attention off ourselves. *The Law of One states that we are all one, one with all, and there is no division.* This law tells us that everything is one, and there is no separation. It tells us that the center of your universe is right where you are, that you are the seed of its unlimited potential, and that there is no limit to how much you can grow.

The circle depicted below, on the left side, with the point in the center is a symbol of the totality of all the energy in the cosmos. Like creation itself, it is eternal and infinite. It is a perfect shape, for it has no beginning and no end and contains within itself the potential of all creation. The point in the center is the symbolic beginning of the cosmic egg where the infinite becomes the finite. The Tao-like symbol on the right depicts the divided circle and shows that yang or the light side contains the potential beginning of yin, and the dark side contains the potential beginning of yang.

 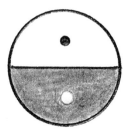

Dualism and the Law of Two

When we divide a circle or whole by two, we get two halves and a situation where we are caught in the middle of duality and two completely opposing tendencies. The result of ½ = .5 tells us that two has an unchanging connection to the finite world or forms—the physical universe. Two represents the emergence of life into the form of matter and material evolution. Two is often experienced as the need to form cooperative partnerships and deal with the constant challenges around personal relationships. The real challenge among the oppositions represented by twos is the conflict between misunderstood external and internal factors and between thinking and feeling. Traditionally, this opposition brings wisdom. While one represents unity and focus, two points to separation and distance between individuals and one's goals and purposes. While one is independent, two seeks out others, is aware of others, and helps others to mirror its own internal struggles. Those represented by two who have not mastered the opposition energy become apparent victims of the conditions and people around them. *The Law of Two, of dualism, states that reality consists of two opposing powers or elements often taken to be mind and matter, good and evil, or yang and yin.* Both conflicting powers exist as ultimate first causes.

Two is associated with a line of two halves of a circle, relationships, conflicts because of the externalization of one's conscious awareness and the pulling apart or separation of one. Two is the dyad and represents the division of all things into two realms: yang and yin, light and dark, heaven and earth, internal and external, the first and second half of life, etc. This number points to struggle whenever you refuse to allow changes to take place or experience situations where changes cannot readily take place. The two sides are in a deadlock, and there is no way out besides compromise or one side overpowering the other. Both potential outcomes lead to unsatisfactory conclusions. With two, the goal is to recognize that both sides and energies are within and must be allowed to exist. This goal cannot be attained without a third perspective. When there's a deadlock in life, the only way to a graceful conclusion that satisfies both parties is with a third viewpoint that allows the situation to unfold at a higher level of awareness. While those on the path represented by two may or may not be significant in the world at large, they experience and often master important psychological and spiritual lessons.

Cyclically, two represents the repolarization of one's awareness and the peak of a cycle. Division of the circle into three gives birth to nonduality or the shaded trinity as depicted in the diagram here.

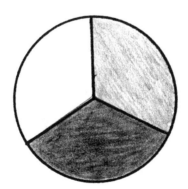

Trinities, the Enneagram, and Law of Three

Dividing the circle into three parts or points reveals the power and meaning of the Law of Three. The division of the circle or whole into three parts represents the beginning of trinities and all triangular relationships, such as father, mother, and child; conscious mind, creative mind, and manifestations; yang, yin, and the Tao; light, matter, and energy; and so forth. By dividing the circle or whole into three parts, we get three triangles and trinity principles. Because the result of ⅓ = .33333 . . . goes on forever into infinity or the nonphysical universe, three has an unchanging connection to the infinite, and there is no precise measure of ⅓. Since trinities are infinite, they are symbolic of the principle of spirit and the process of spiritual evolution. Three brings harmony and balance to two and implies energy patterns that are not driven to change or progress.

Each third of the circle contains the basic meaning of the trinities. Among the nine points on the circle, G. I. Gurdjieff saw the first trinity as consisting of points one, four, and seven which are associated with three affirming forces; the second trinity consists of points two, five, and eight, which are associated with three denying forces, and the third trinity consists of points three, six, and nine, which are associated with three reconciling forces. Affirming forces deal with what we see as the right and best approach to doing things. This approach is considered good and one that should be pursued. Denying forces deal with what we see as the wrong and worst approach to doing things. This approach is considered bad and one that must be resisted. Neutralizing or reconciling forces calls for taking a step back to observe what is going on and consider the relationship between the first two forces. This approach aims to bring the solution to the opposites, which has been there all along, into view.

When represented in groups of three enneagram signs around the circle from one to nine, we have signs one, two, and three in the first group; signs four, five, and six in the second group; and signs seven, eight, and nine in the third group. These groups represent recurring stages of the beginning, middle, and ending forces. In addition, they can be understood as the personal, social, and universal stages of development. The Law of Three is a basic metaphysical principle that was made popular by G. I. Gurdjieff, though the teaching of the three forces is at the root of all ancient systems. *This principle states that any new arising throughout the universe is the result of three independent forces—force one is affirming, active, positive, or motivating; force two is denying, negative, passive, or receptive; and force three is reconciling, facilitating, mediating, or invisible—and that without these forces, there is no legitimate change or growth in nature.* The widely known Taoist trinity model of yang, yin, and the Tao is a mirror image of the Law of Three.

Unlike the change, growth potential, and conflict that comes with two, three is rather passive and does resist conflict. The power of three or the triangle is associated with the emergence of new possibilities and has been traditionally assumed to be extremely beneficial. The triangle and three are symbols of good luck, psychological comfort, and the easy flow of energy into established channels of expression, by nature, three points to creative talent and the urge to accept others, ourselves, and situations.

Traditionally, the number three represents understanding through the principle of reconciling opposites around a common source, growth, goodness, and ease. Three is a symbol of the expansion of one's horizons and consciousness and implies inherent abilities or gifts, cyclically, three points to both the expansion and attainment of equilibrium of an activity. Unlike the opposing energy of two, the energy of three results in reconciliation. Things seem to fall into one's lap, proceed with minimum effort, and work out of their own accord under the influence of trinities. The existence of trinities gives birth to all nine points on the circle. Its existence allows for the creation of points four through nine and all things on earth.

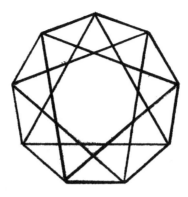

Three Triangles in the Circle of Nine Points

Three Triangles in the Enneagram

Dividing the circle into the three trinities or triangles as shown in the diagram above gives us nine equal points or forty-degree segments. The last single-digit number, nine, is an expression of the spiritual reality of completion and preparation for a new beginning with one. In most mystical cosmologies, nine is the number of human potential, commonly expressed through the experience of spiritual unfoldment. They indicate the end results of stages and cycles of development and what life produces in the long run. The enneagram or nine indicates the level at which complete fulfillment is possible as a condition for emergence into an altogether new and higher realm of being. However, nine is no more than an end for those who have not consciously absorbed enough of the pre-nine experiences to move onto the next level. Like the end of winter or the life cycle, the final stage indicates development of one's ability to digest additional information for one's spiritual and evolutionary growth.

Traditionally, the number nine represents the end products of life, endings, and completion in general. In Hindu astrology, the nine forty-degree divisions of the circle are said to describe what life produces in the long run and in one's needs and capacities in relationships, especially marriage. Since ancient times, various cultures have considered nine to be a very special and sacred number. Nines or nonagons are about knowing a deep soul level that helps us overcome restrictions. Cyclically, this nine represents completions and preparations for a new beginning. It marks the introduction of new wisdom and the responsibility of using that wisdom.

Every enneagram can be understood as consisting of six primary trinity arrangements and three creative trinity arrangements that can represent the whole in other ways. The first three primary trinities represent the beginning, middle, and completion segments of the whole circular journey or cycle. The second three trinities represent the affirming, denying, and reconciling forces within the whole. In addition to the primary groups, the number of other trinity arrangements of the whole is unlimited, creative, and inspiring.

Signs and Stages of Development

The birth date is the starting point of the zodiac-based enneagram signs. Enneagram signs, like astrology signs, identify one's soul personality and potential. Throughout this work, ennead-based signs are defined by the nine stages that the earth passes through as it moves around the sun every year. The lifelong stages of development from one to nine are based on the earth's movement through nine enneagram signs around the sun from birthday to birthday. Like the twelve zodiac signs, the nine numbers represent myths of humanity in a connected pattern that reflect how humans and the nonphysical universe interact. In their entirety, the nine numbers symbolize the cosmic wheel, and the individual stage numbers represent personal characteristics from one to nine. Like all cycles, the enneagram stages of development are a form or structure of time. They are the context in which change takes place throughout the human life span.

The recognition and celebration of a birthday or solar revolution is well established. The meaning is usually read in terms of what the sun means for an individual birth date. All existence is structured by time, and all activity takes place in time. Within a lifetime, there are nine recurring nine-year cycles and nine annual cycles within each nine-year period. Cycles are not a repetitive sequence of events. Although the pattern of unfoldment from the beginning to end of a cycle repeats itself, the contents of a cycle are never repeated. The interrelationship among cycles describes the total uniqueness of each moment and at the same time links them together in a universal rhythmic order. Astronomy provides us with the data for the nine single-digit cycles from one to nine, and astrology interprets these data regarding the processes of life on earth and particularly within the individual.

Each person is born to express in as pure a way as possible the promise contained in their birth year and birth date. As the physical center of our solar system and symbolic center of who we are, the sun is the most enlightened part of a person's identity—the part that contains the essence of the lessons learned in all previous lifetimes, which is brought forward into this life as a natural, basic, effortless main feather. It is the dynamic inner light of an individual's nature and has a decidedly masculine connotation. Since the solar system is maintained by the sun, this central light symbolizes the self—the purpose and direction of an individual's existence. The symbolic meaning of one's spiritual potential can be seen by looking from the earth (the human point of view) to contemplate the timing of their relationships to the sun or center of the solar system (the soul's point of view). This relationship and place within the nine phases is represented by the year of birth in general and the birth date.

A cycle, being a whole activity, contains a beginning, a middle, and an end, and there are recognizable stages of development as it unfolds. As soon as a particular moment is identified as being part of the cycle, it becomes closely related to both the beginning and the end of that cycle. Any specific moment within a cycle is considered part of a working-out of the impulse that began the cycle and is directed toward the purpose of that cycle. In this sense, all moments within a cycle stretch back to the cyclic roots and at the same time forward toward the cyclic seed. Every moment in time is a part or phase of an all-encompassing whole and has its essential meaning only regarding this whole. Every apparently separate unit is involved with and participates in every other unit within the time span of a cycle. The entire cycle is implicit in every moment of it. The birth date marks the beginning of the grand or fixed cycle of life—the life span itself. The one-year and nine-year cycles within the life span do not refer essentially to outer events or to forces external to the individual but to stages of growth of the personality.

The cosmic year on Earth starts with the spring solstice, which usually comes every March 20. In a minority of cases, the actual solstice may begin on March 19 or March 21. Just as the cosmos reveals itself each year in the path of the earth's journey around the sun, all individuals who reveal the process of enlightenment do so in the events of their lives. Throughout the world, the spring equinox is a time of confrontations between the forces of darkness and light. This is represented by the dark half of the year on one side of the spring equinox and the light half of the year on the other side. The struggle in the individual and in the world that pulls back and forth between the light half and the dark half symbolizes a universal principle in creation found in the cycles of cosmic time and human life. The solar or cosmic year reveals its unique version of darkness and light in creating movement through opposition and often struggle.

Everything in the world is dependent upon the symbolic properties of enneagram sign numbers. There are hundreds of different human characteristics, and each is represented by one of the single-digit numbers. Sign one represents the transition from the end of winter to the beginning of spring and stands as a symbol for newcomers, being first, determined, and cunning. Sign two is a symbol for cooperation and tends to be diplomatic and intuitive. Sign three represents movement from spring to summer growth and is a symbol of growth, thinking, and acting outside the box. Sign four represents individualism and interest in understanding and manifesting dreams. Sign five represents the transition from summer to autumn and stands as symbol for balance, change, quick thinking, and action. Sign six is a symbol for loyalty and tends to be unhurried and people oriented. Sign seven represents the transition from autumn to winter and stands as a symbol for consciousness, the pursuit of information, and analysis. Sign eight represents accomplishments and tends to be a visionary warrior. Sign nine represents completions and humanitarianism and seeing the big picture.

Every stage, phase, or cycle from one period to the next represents a change in the movement of an individual's life. Each cycle has its own special significance in one's growth. All types and cycles represent the natural process of change and progress in one's life. The forty-degree stage that an individual's birthday falls into, beginning with the first degree of the zodiac and ending at 360 degrees from one to nine, is their enneagram sign within the zodiac. Like a cycle, each type has a unique set of characteristics or personality that points to the primary areas of growth and change during the individual's lifetime. Every stage is a stepping stone to growing and learning. Like a class or program of study, the birth stage represents what the person is here to learn. The table that follows shows the relationship between the twelve traditional astrology signs and the nine enneagram signs from one through nine.

Since the nine signs or stages embody all the single-digit numbers—all the intellectual and emotional phases—they also symbolize the total creative process and the grand zodiac cycle of creation. The enneagram sign represents the area where an individual seeks to learn the lessons from inner and outer teachers. Every sign conveys one's perception of their work and attitude toward life. The lessons for all signs are taught by the people and situations that the individual interacts with.

The Zodiac as Enneagram Signs

Zodiac Sign Degrees	Birth Date	Enneagram Sign
0° Aries to 10° Taurus	March 20 to May 1	**One** *The Initiator*
10° Taurus to 20° Gemini	May 1 to June 11	**Two** *The Guide*
20° Gemini through Cancer	June 11 to July 23	**Three** *The Contestant*
0° Leo to 10° Virgo	July 23 to September 3	**Four** *The Romantic*
10° Virgo to 20° Libra	September 3 to October 14	**Five** *The Innovator*
20° Libra to through Scorpio	October 14 to November 23	**Six** *The Skeptic*
0° Sagittarius to 10° Capricorn	November 23 to January 1	**Seven** *The Seeker*
10° Capricorn to 20° Aquarius	January 1 to February 9	**Eight** *The Defender*
20° Aquarius through Pisces	February 9 March 20	**Nine** *The Mediator*

Birth dates a day before or after the dates given here should be checked to ensure that the birth date is aligned correctly within the 360-degree zodiac. For instance, the degree of a person's sun sign for their birth date on February 8 should be at least twenty-degree Aquarius to qualify for solar type nine; otherwise, the birth date will fall into the eighth sign. Fixed and exact divisions of the solar-based enneagram year into signs or stages will vary from one year to the next by very small amounts. Because of earthquakes, tidal coupling with the moon, and other disturbances, the earth's rotation, upon which our clocks depend, either speeds up or slows down by varying tiny amounts at irregular time intervals. Since the dates given in the table, The Zodiac as Ennead Signs or Types, could not be off by a day over the last century, birth dates that fall within a day of the signs' beginning or ending should be checked with an ephemeris to get the exact zodiac degree and then adjusted. For instance, the birthday on February 9 or 10 could, depending on the time of one's birth, fall in enneagram sign eight or nine. For any given year, you can look at the position of the sun for any month, day, or year by doing a Google search—"ephemeris for YYYY." Those who want the exact degree of their sun can google "free astrologychart.com" and enter the requested birth data.

Cyclical Time and Change

While measures of the circular concept of time are found in the East and in ancient Egypt, the measure of linear time is a Western concept. In this book, measures of time and the events or change that take place within it are circular. A clock, for instance, is not a time line but a circle for the simple reason that time does not begin or stop. Like a clock, days, seasons, and years measure circular time more accurately than straight lines. While segments of time can be measured, such as birth and death, time itself continues without beginning or end. With circular time, the beginning is not the beginning, and the end is not the end, but time is a continual cycle of beginnings and endings. The perspective of circular time tells us that the universe, all existence and all energy, has been eternally recurring and will continue to recur in individual forms an infinite number of times across infinite time or space. As times move on, you eventually return to the fixed point in space-time where you started. Because time and space are like two sides of a coin, the circular view of time can be applied to space as well. In this sense, the role of circles and cycles of time is described by the first law of thermodynamics, which states, "Matter cannot be created or destroyed, only transformed."

When you move in a straight line on the earth or in outer space, you will eventually end up in the same place as you started. Throughout the universe, there are an infinite number of circles, some small and some large. The most obvious of these extremes is the orbits of electrons around protons and the nine planets we observe from the earth, which appear to go around the earth in our solar system. The repeating intervals of time, whether seconds or billions of years, can also be represented by a circle. The history of humankind is the interlacing circles of generations of people who live and die and nations that rise and fall time and time again. In fact, the earth circles the sun, the moon circles the earth, and entire solar systems rise and fall through creation and destruction.

There are many definitions of time, yet time doesn't really exist, and what we know about it is strange. Even though measures of time are everywhere, there's just the eternal now. Despite this reality, we pay attention to measures of time because they help us organize, regulate, and better understand our lives and affairs. Even though most events in the world happen in cycles of time, we also use linear time, psychological time, time in our cells and body, etc. Because we don't notice time when we stop paying attention to it, it often appears that time is flexible and personal. The presentation of stages, cycles, and types in this book are intended to help us pay closer attention to our movement through time in relation to how things have always been.

People believe that time begins, goes forward, and ends (the Western concept), and they also understand that as time moves on, they must return to the fixed point or time of their beginning. The fixed point of one's beginning is their date and time of birth or enneagram sign. The meaning of this sign is a benchmark that never changes and may be used to expand one's understanding of their potential and soul personality. The meaning of one's recurring stages and cycles in life can be understood in greater detail by contemplating their relationship to the fixed and potential parts of life.

Time and change are psychological concepts that function like day and night. Time and change are not the same thing, though you can't have change without time, and you can't have time without change. Where there is time, you must have three types of change. The first type occurs as the birth of an individual or event and may be understood as the nonchanging. This kind of change is a starting point, contains the characteristics of its beginning, and cannot be duplicated. Even though we may return to this time and place in the cycle, e.g., the birth date, things will not be the same. The tendency for individuals to specialize in expressing only this part of the whole or their potential comes about because the first type is the most familiar, preferred, and dominant. The second type of change is cyclic. In cyclic change, life presents and manages changes that we must adjust to. Being in touch with these cyclical changes, like the seasons, allows us to be healthier in body, mind, and soul. The third type of change is governed by the law of karma, cause and effect, or karmic. This kind of change is equivalent to Newton's third law, which states that *for every action or force, there is an equal and opposite reaction.*

Although we have some control over the third kind of change, we do not control the first and second types of change. Our birth sign, personality, and stages or cycles of life are given by the cosmos, and we must live with them and the opportunities they present. They all determine how we receive information from the world and the soul. Whether any of these changes will strike us as desirable or undesirable will depend upon whether they are carrying out what we have in mind.

Individuation

The term *individuation* was created by Jung to describe his theory of attaining wholeness. Individuation is the process of unifying all aspects of our diverse personality. The process aims to integrate conscious and unconscious personality traits and types. The journey toward individuation or wholeness requires that we remain open to unfamiliar personality types. Because all enneagram personalities and relationships live within the whole and are one with the whole, we can choose to receive and express the whole at any time. The degree to which we receive and express the whole is the degree to which we attain health in our personality and relationships. The enneagram model and the recurring trinities within in it offer opportunities to experience and embrace all personalities and dualities throughout the entire cycle of life.

People come into and move through the stages of life with enormous potential to fully embody all enneagram personality types. Those who move through the stages and cycles of life receive countless opportunities to learn about and embrace diverse personality types. Those who make the conscious choice to adopt the nine personalities move beyond individual differences and no longer fit any one category. With time and the practice of adopting all personalities, there is no dominance of any ego-preferred type. The types that remain unconscious are the secure source of much of our thoughts, feelings, and behavior. They influence us in ways that are more powerful because of being hidden, avoided, and unexpected. The idea of unconscious types derives from the simple observation in daily human life—there is material contained in our minds that we are not aware of most of the time.

Awakening to the gifts and forms of the enneagram types requires learning, and this learning takes time. As we release our beginning personality and embrace other personalities as needed, we grow and change. When we can shift our beginning personality from "one of nine" to "nine of nine," we go beyond our beginning and become individuated or whole. The individuation process integrates one's conscious and unconscious attitudes toward all types, and in the end, the "nine of nine" individual is awakened to all forms of expression. These individuals can step out of the "one in nine" box and into the realm of being fully available to serving the soul.

2

Trinities

The first fundamental law of the universe is the Law of Three.
Every phenomenon is the result of simultaneous action of
three forces—the positive, the negative, and the neutralizing.

— P. D. Ouspensky

Three is the most important number among the nine single-digit numbers. All creation uses the power of the Law of Three forces to create—active, passive, and mutual or neutral. The number three and trinities help explain the relationship between the nonphysical and physical universe, how physical forms are created, and refer to a broad range of nonphysical characteristics—psychological and philosophical—such as behaviors, cycles of development, actions, and modes of perception. Stages one, two, three; four, five, six; and seven, eight, nine respectively identify the first, second, and third trinity groups in the nine-fold development cycle. Within the first, second, and third trinity groups, we have recurring beginning, middle, and ending stages. Over the complete circle of nine stages, conflicts between stages in the first and second trinity groups are reconciled by stages in the last trinity group. Conflicts between the first and last stages are resolved by the middle stages, and conflicts between the last two stages are reconciled by the first stages. Examples of this trinity can be found in models of human behavior built upon the relationship among the child, adult, and parent aspect of life and in models of the relationship among the first, second, and last of the life cycle.

The beginning of the three trinity groups (personality types, signs, and cycles of development) are the *affirming* forces—one, four, and seven—which represent the experience of creations, beginnings, making things happen, self-activation, and the tendency to counter outside pressures with their own initiatives. The middle points of the three trinity groups are the *denying* forces—two, five, and eight—which represent the experience of being in control, making things stable, managing, sustaining what has already been created, and the tendency to both resist outside pressures and avoid changes. The last stage of the three trinity groups are the *reconciling* forces—three, six, and nine—which represent the experience of self-discovery, transformation, the exchange of ideas and observations, applying what has already been created, and the tendency to adapt to outside pressures by shifting the course of events toward their desired direction.

In the Law of Three that governs trinities, reconciling is not the synthesis but the mediating principle between the other two. The three forces working together dissolve gridlocks and move everything into a new playing field. Identifying the numbered groups for enneagram signs, types, and related groups is useful in understanding the central nature of any individual's psychological makeup, cycle of development, interests, and how they approach life. These groups represent where you're coming from, where your consciousness is rooted, where you're going, and the mode of activity from which you derive your power. They also represent the three stages within the first, second, and third parts of every cycle of development

The *affirming* personality types—one, four, and seven—live in a state of excitement and inspired activity that must be maintained for them to stay healthy and happy. The *denying* types—two, five, and eight—live on the ground in the material world and embrace the practical aspects of life. The *reconciling* types—three, six, and nine— live in the realms of thought and relationships with other people.

Although the third force for all trinities is right beneath our noses in most situations, it is almost always not seen because we are attached to "either/or" thinking. When the Tai Chi symbol of the Taoist circle is divided into three equal parts, we get solid expressions of yang and yin and a mixture of the two. This view of the world suggests that *affirming* types contain more yang than yin, *denying* types contain more yin than yang, and *reconciling* types represent a balanced blend of yang and yin.

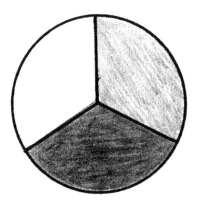

The *affirming, denying,* and *reconciling* forces are present in every new situation. Additional examples of this trinity are present throughout the *I Ching*, which teaches that change always involves going through a time of discontent and then splitting apart or releasing and then reconstruction.

The trinity concept of introverts, extroverts, and centroverts is present in the personalities of individuals and in the personalities of both social and collective groups.

> *At a football club, there's a holy trinity—*
> *the players, the manager, and the supporters.*
>
> Bill Sharkly

The list of trinity groups here identifies the main principles and level of awareness found in different world views and systems of the trinity (parts adapted from *Know Your Type* by Ralph Metzner).

Trinity Principles from Different World Views

Taoism	Yang	Yin	Tao
Christians	Father	Son	Holy Spirit
Hindus	Brahma	Vishnu	Shiva
Astrology	Cardinal	Fixed	Mutable
Physical Science	Transmits Light	Absorbs Light	Magnifies Light
Einstein	Light (c^2)	Mass (m)	Energy (e)
Mathematics	+	-	=
Mental Science	Conscious Mind	Forms, Effects	Unconscious
Planet Symbols	Circle	Cross	Semicircle
Letters	ajs/dmv/gpy	bkt/enw/hqz	clu/fox/ir
Human Beings	Mind	Body	Soul
Elements	Air	Earth, Water	Fire

The main personality and psychological traits expressed through the trinity related numbers are given in the following table.

Trinity Groups Psychologies

Affirming Types	*Denying Types*	*Reconciling Types*
1, 4, 7	*2, 5, 8*	*3, 6, 9*
Action	Stationary	Flexibility
Thinking	Sensing, Feeling	Intuition
Reason	Observation	Experience
Aggressive	Practical	Friendly
Beginning	Middle	Ending
Leading	Supporting	Coordinating
Creative	Conventional	Changing
Dynamic	Magnetic	Balanced
Independence	Attachments	Cooperation
Spirit	Matter	Karma
The Word	Reflection	Not Knowing

In every trinity, the power or Law of Three is fully present. In all cases, the duality represented by "two of three" is resolved by "three of three." Even though all members of the yang and yin groups mentioned above are naturally reconciled by the Tao group, it is also true that any arrangement of duality is resolved by the third trinity member. The law of three is fully present in the different world views of the trinity principles, trinity groups, and type characteristics. In addition to the items given in the tables above, the third force allows us to step back, watch, observe, and not get trapped in the unresolved conflict or deadlock represented by one-two sides. If there is no third point, the two forces must compromise, or one side simply dominates the other, but in each case, the solution is often unsatisfactory. The third force allows situations to get neutralized and unfold at a higher level of awareness. The illustrations that follow should broaden our understanding of the power of three in just about all areas of life.

Trinity Cases

Trinities exist because the Law of Three is the power behind everything in the creative process. About twenty-five hundred years ago, Pythagoras taught that everything in the universe has a three-part structure and that every problem can be reduced to a triangle. Along with trios and triads, three is the great mystery that unifies the universe and is the key to all hidden mysteries. Trinities and the law of three are different perspectives of a powerful divine principle and wholeness. The power of three is the basis of the Gospel, and the Gospel is a manifestation of the trinity in action. The trinity is a central part of every discipline that studies the human soul. The trinity and triangles are hardwired into the human psyche. The concept of trinities has been a part of our psyche for thousands of years and has appeared in creation tales, myths, religious writings, and holy text the world over. Trinities are an expression of life itself, the spirit, and God or the changeless reality in which we live, move, and have our being. Trinities are all about the relationship among the three sides of life, which all beings have in some form.

Each member of the trinity has special functions. For example, the life of all beings takes place within the threefold source of life: a masculine, feminine, and child face—not unlike the Holy Trinity and the trinities of the creative process, such as thoughts, law, and results; words, laws, and body; attention, energy, and manifestation; thoughts, feelings, and tangible forms; seeds, soil, and plants; and past, present, and future. Just as thoughts and feelings produce an outcome, father and mother produce children, and the attraction to and embrace of innovative ideas produce the birth of additional new ideas. In the world of science, the trinity consists of reason, observation, and experience.

The Creative Process in Science consists of the trinity of reason, observation, and experience. The scientific creative begins with a rational study of existing subject matter, which is often referred to as a literature review (the first force). This phase of the trinity determines what has already been done around subject matter to ensure that something new is being created. The second force is to allow for a period of incubation and openness to receive or observe new insights and information about the new creation. When the reasons and observations are united, new ideas are manifested and experienced (the third force).

Three Stages and Cycles in the circle of enneagram signs represent three recurring trinities that are apparent through the life cycle. The first represents the *Beginning,* signs one, two, and three; the second represents the *Middle,* signs four, five, and six; and the third represents the *Completion,* signs seven, eight, and nine. The three trinities are similar in that the first two points in each group are resolved by the third point. Thus, the early, middle, and last trinity stages are recurring versions through the circle.

Signs one, two, and three are archetypes of the *Beginning* third of life and human development, which deals with constructing one's self-concept, identity, perspective, and definition of who one is. They represent the experience of youthful, spring-like energy, being an individual, optimism, and learning new things. They represent the development of the individual, their personal relationship with themselves and others, and their basic role in society or service to it.

Signs four, five, and six are associated with the experience of standing in the *Middle*, between beginning and ending, start and finish, and young and old at the same time. These stages of development give us a clever idea of where we stand now, where we've been, and what we hope to achieve. Types four, five and six are associated with one's involvements with thoughts, things, and close relationships. They are the midlife stages for change and creating stability in ways of thinking and relationships with others.

Signs seven, eight, and nine represent the early, halfway, and concluding stages in the *Completion* chapter of the development cycle. Happiness among these types is tied to their goals and humanitarian causes, not to people or things. As a symbol, winter is associated with the end of the previous year and return of the light. Instead of days getting shorter, the winter equinox marks the beginning of the days getting longer. As a group, types seven, eight, and nine bring us the experience of thinking deeply about society and the universe, leading and directing society in some way, and educating or healing society. They point to letting the old go and giving birth to the new, the death of physical forms and the birth of the spiritual—being on God's side and giving oneself to life as much as possible. More than other stages, this stage is represented by Einstein's little-known equation, which says Ego = 1/Knowledge. This means that more knowledge leads to less ego, less knowledge leads to more ego, and the total of one's knowledge and ego is One.

Three Forces are apparent in the circle of enneagram signs. In the early third of the circle, the conflicting nature of the *affirming* sign one and the *denying* sign two is settled by the *reconciling* sign three. In the middle third of the circle, the opposing nature of the *affirming* sign four and the *denying* sign five is resolved by the *reconciling* sign six. In the last third of the circle, the opposing nature of the *affirming* sign seven and the *denying* sign eight is brought into balance by the *reconciling* sign nine. Conflicts between the first and second trinity groups or stages of development are reconciled in the third group or stage.

The Legal System of prosecution and defense is made legitimate when disputes are mediated and settled by a judge or jury. Prosecutors represent the first force that seeks to prove wrongdoing. The defense represents the second force that seeks opposing arguments that present a different outcome. The judge and jury represent the third force to settle the case.

The Serenity Prayer, popularized by Alcoholics Anonymous and other twelve-step programs, offers an illustration of the trinity. As the prayer says, "Grant me the serenity to accept the things I cannot change" represents the second force. "The courage to change the things I can" represents the first force. "And the wisdom to know the difference" represents the third force.

The Adulterous Woman story illustrates the power of three. Here, the religious authorities bring an adulterous woman before Jesus to get his "agreement" to stoning her to death, according to the law of Moses (the first force). If he "disagrees" to the stoning, he violates the law of Moses, which has clear rules (the second force). As they corner him and ask him to agree with the law permitting stoning for punishment, he replies, "He that is without sin among you, let him cast the first stone" (the third force).

Paying Taxes to Caesar or Honoring God is a story about Jesus being cornered by religious leaders in an apparent trap. When he tells those who question him to pay the tax (the first force) and honor God as well (the second force), his response is not expected. He breaks the "either/or" pattern of the answer imposed by traditional religious leaders by changing it to "both/and" and says, "Render to Caesar the things that are Caesar's and to God the things that are God's" (the third force).

The Christian Trinity origin of Father, Holy Spirit, and Son or simply father, mother, and child is as example of how any two faces of the trinity or God are in conflict until they are resolved by a third face. The masculine face represented by the father and feminine face represented by the mother remain in conflict until they are integrated by the child. God the Father is the intellectual or ethical self, God the Son is the physical or actual self, and God the Holy Spirit is the emotional or aspirational self. The apparent dynamic of the difference between the Old Testament view of God as a stern figure and the New Testament view of God as compassionate and loving predates Christianity. Jesus, the Son of God, was chosen to integrate the two sides in the religion established in his name called Christianity. In *Jung and the Lost Gospels* by Stephan A. Hoeller, sayings 71 and 78 in the Gnostic Gospel of Philip capture Jesus's pre-Christian Judaism message of uniting the masculine and feminine faces of God.

> At a time when Eve was in Adam, then there was no death: but when she was separated from him death came to exist. If completion shall occur again and the earlier state is attained, then death will be no more. (71)

> If the feminine had not separated from the masculine, she would not die with the masculine. This separation became the origin of death. Christ came, so that he might take away the separation which was there from the beginning and thus again reunite the two: and so that he might give life to those who dies while separated and make them one. (78)

Conflicts between the feminine face of God, which represents the holy spirit or soul, and the son or daughter face of God, which represents the world of forms or things made by words, are reconciled by the masculine face of God. The father or masculine side represents the intuitive realm of ideas and words. Father-son conflicts are reconciled by the mother.

The Trinity of Leadership Types is composed of enneagram types one, three, and eight in the *dominant* leadership group; types two, four, and six in the *amenable* leadership group; and types five, seven, and nine in the *servant* leadership group. The dominant leaders are aggressive and controlling and need to have the upper hand. They fight for what they want and move against whatever gets in the way of their plans and desires. The amenable leaders value relationships with others and exhibit the skill of listening, hearing, and understanding how others feel. Those in this group are inward leaning and idealistic, look for agreement and ways to support others, and often play the role of mediator. The servant leaders are optimistic and skilled at seeing new possibilities and reframing situations but appear relatively weak compared to the other two leadership groups. They are driven by vision, look within themselves to find fulfillment, and move away from whatever blocks or disturbs them.

The resolution of conflicts between any two of the three leadership styles is always found in the third style. Since two points represent different sides of a duality and set up a situation where one side tends to dominate or exclude the other, the establishment of the triangle, trinity, or third point always offers the possibility of a solution. When a conflict of styles arises between doers represented by dominant leader types and visionaries represented by servant leader types, the conflict is reconciled by the amicable approach to leading. For instance, I once witnessed a situation where several individuals wanted to create a body, mind, and spirit center. The first meeting was led by a visionary type who encouraged the group to develop a vision and mission for the center. After the visioning session, two thirds of the participants withdrew their interest because they were action-oriented doers who wanted to get things done. They felt more comfortable doing things in the realm of marketing and promotion rather than envisioning and planning. These people did not get on board until a plan was developed that they agreed with. Months later, when an amicable approach emerged between the aggressive doers and visionary servants, things began to move forward.

Planet Trinities that exist among the nine planets appear in many forms. The main trinity of affirming, denying, and reconciling forces includes Mercury, Neptune, and Jupiter as active and affirming planets;

the moon, Uranus, and Mars as receptive and denying planets; and the sun, Saturn, and Venus as mediating and reconciling planets.

Individuals represented by planets in the active group are independent, detached, and creative. Their attention is on communicating innovative thoughts and ideas and starting new projects, beginnings, and first causes. They are intuitive and idealistic types who want to be special and promote perfection. Those represented by planets in the receptive group are practical yet often face opposition from others and the established order. They put their energy into making things, creating forms, supporting the growth, safety, protection, and stability of themselves and others. They want to be needed, help others, understand things, and work against the outdated order. Those represented by planets in the mediating group are people-oriented, easygoing, and balanced and manifest harmony, cooperation, and unity. They are associated with expansion and want to succeed, be secure, reconcile opposing perspectives, and facilitate positive change.

Taoist Trinity

Yang and yin are concepts of duality that form a whole. Yang and yin are also the starting point for change. In Taoism, the trinity consists of yang, yin, and the reconciling force known as the Tao, which unites both together. Yang and yin are two halves that, together, complete wholeness. When something is whole, it is unchanging and complete. When the circle of wholeness is split into two halves, it upsets the equilibrium and whole and starts the process of both halves chasing after each other as they seek a new balance between them.

The yin components of the Tao are everything perceived by the senses, and the yang components are everything hidden from the senses. The English translation of yang and yin as "young" and "old," respectively, tells us that half of the universe is made of young energy and half of old energy. In daily life, the Tao is represented by the nation, yang by the government, and yin by the judiciary. The movement of energy toward light and matter has much in common with the movement toward yang or yin. Although yang and yin have differing natures, the differences between them can vary from almost completely identical to almost completely opposite. For instance, thinking contains more yang than yin, and feeling contains more yin than yang; intuition contains more yang than thinking, and sensing is more yin than feeling.

Hindu Trinity

In the Hindu trinity, Shiva is the place where opposites meet and all things come together in a balanced outcome. Shiva not only is the destroyer part of the trinity, which is necessary for re-creation, but also contains Vishnu, the preserver part of the universe, and Brahma, the creative part. Brahma is preoccupied with the task of creating things or bringing things into being. No matter how great any creation is, all creation leads to destruction and destruction to creation. Vishnu is the preserver of universal order and maintainer of reality or the world. Vishnu is most apparent in the lives of those who choose to follow the path of devotion and pursue material outcomes with an eye toward religion or spirituality. Shiva is the destroyer and anger aspect of the trinity that eliminates or corrects all mistakes, waste, and excess. Simply put, Shiva destroys the reality created by Brahma and maintained by Vishnu.

The destruction task of Shiva is an essential part of creation because without destruction, we cannot really create anything. Destruction is therefore an integral part of progress and change. We cannot experience the next moment or stage of development unless our experience of the present is replaced or rather destroyed by the experience of the next stage. Brahma, Vishnu, and Shiva are the triple gods of Hinduism, which are all considered manifestations of the same universal reality. For instance, just as some individuals play different mental and physical roles while performing different duties, God appears as the trinity in three different roles. These parts of the trinity perform different tasks and have qualities and energies that differ widely from one another and control different worlds.

Planet Symbols Trinity

The arrangement of the circle, cross, and semicircle give us the trinity of symbols that allow us to describe the influence of the nine planets plus the earth on human behavior. The circle is a symbol of light, energy, and motion and the source or father of all life that is always giving. The circle can be as small as a point of consciousness, a seed for a new beginning, or gigantic. It is the spark of life, the atom, and the cosmos. For Mercury, the circle between the cross below and the semicircle above identifies this planet as the messenger of light, the word that allows all beginning to take place. The circle is present in the symbols for Mercury, the sun, Mars, and Venus.

The semicircle is the container of life, the womb from which all life emerges, the unknown and transcendent. All life comes through and emerges from the element of water in a container represented by the semicircle. The semicircle is a member of the feminine family, whose yielding nature conquers the resistance and hardness of life. The semicircle represents feelings and emotional energy that connects and serves all life. It also represents the order and principles of law that govern life on earth.

The placement of the cross part of a planet represents the area of interest in the manifest universe. For instance, the cross as the lowest symbol represents the planet's foundation and takes its meaning and interest from the cross. In planets where the cross is the highest symbol, it represents the planets' aspirations. For example, the planets Mars and Saturn have the cross in the place of aspirations, and both planets are interested in material success. The cross brings a practical presence to any planet energy it relates to. The message of the cross is to look beyond appearances, such as making judgments based on first impressions or seeing only the tip of the iceberg. The cross is a symbol of the connection between spirit, the vertical line, and matter, the horizontal line, or between the divine and the human. The cross is found in every planet except the sun and moon. The cross is a symbol of the physical or visible universe, which takes its form from the formless semicircle.

Holistic Healing Trinity

The body-mind-soul trinity is popular among proponents of integrated healing. In this trinity, the enneagram types fall into three groups or centers. The body center is represented by types eight, nine, and one. They operate in the here and now based on gut feelings, instincts, physical conditions, and senses and need to be in control. The mind center is associated with types five, six, and seven. These types rely on the intellect, thinking things through, objectivity, analysis, and understanding and need silence to recognize the eternal presence. The soul center is associated with types two, three, and four. Soul types rely on their intuition, spiritual nature, the creative or unconscious mind, and extrasensory perceptions. They are identity oriented, concerned with the feelings of others and relationships, and need to be recognized by others. The body-, mind-, and soul-centered trinities are arranged around the enneagram circle in a unique way.

Unresolved conflicts between the body and soul must be reconciled by the mind. For instance, conflicts between one's feelings and intuitions about a situation must be resolved by objective thinking and understanding. Unresolved conflicts between the soul and mind must be reconciled by the body. For example, conflicts between one's intuitions and objective thoughts about a situation must be resolved by listening to their feelings and gut. Unresolved conflicts between the body and mind must be reconciled by the soul. Conflicts between how one thinks and feels about a situation must be resolved by their intuitive and spiritual nature.

Mental Science Trinity

The trinity model developed by Ernest Holmes in *The Science of Mind* provides a psychospiritual perspective of the trinity in relation to the whole. As seen in the diagram here, the trinity is viewed as a circle with three horizontal sections. The V-like symbol superimposed over the circle represents the ever-expanding energy of the universe. The diagram tells us that the energy of the universe is within and one with the trinity. This means that as the energy of the universe expands, the trinity expands. Let's talk about the components of the trinity model.

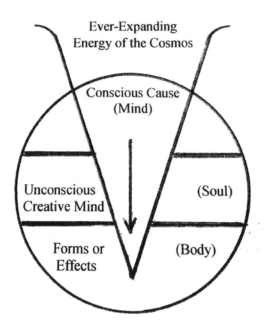

The upper section of the circle represents consciousness, the conscious mind, thoughts, Logos or the word, and what we know and want. This part of the trinity is analogous to what others call yang energy, the father, light, dynamic energy, and one's personality and independence. This model depicts the relationship between conscious thought and the middle section. Communicating with other people and with the divine mind or law takes place in the realm of conscious thought. All things are set in motion and begin with the word, and without the word, nothing takes place. In this stage of the trinity, people think about, pray for, ask, and look for what they want. When a person's conscious thoughts and intentions are not aligned with the law or creative mind, the results they seek will not be attained. Simply put, overlooking the creative mind is like ignoring the laws of life and manifestation. While most manifestations can and do take place without complete knowledge, their appearance only happens because of nurturing forces beyond our control. For instance, all have experienced unexpected outcomes from the law of karma or cause and effect.

This middle part of the trinity represents unconsciousness, the holy spirit or mother, the Tao, the soul, and the power of reconciliation. *The Science of Mind* calls this section of the model the subjective or creative mind, the law, the soul, the womb of existence, and maya. This section of the trinity is receptive to the thoughts and commands of the conscious mind, such as getting answers to questions from dreams, visions, and divination models and getting guidance on how to make things and attain success in concrete reality. Listening directly to the creative, deeper mind or will of God for guidance takes place when the conscious mind is relaxed, centered, and open to receiving information from this source. The conscious mind requests guidance and information from the deeper mind and often seeks help in manifesting one's desire. While the conscious and unconscious parts of the trinity within are always interacting, it takes time for each side to respond to the other in ways that make the most sense. For instance, it takes more time to manifest things and conditions than it takes to manifest information about one's perceptions about things.

The bottom section of the circle represents the body of the universe, effects, the world of things, forms, and results. This part of the trinity represents yin energy, the child, daughter, or son, and mass and physical conditions. The lower part of the circle is a symbol of concrete manifestation and the result of the interplay between the upper conscious realm of the circle and the middle unconscious realm. This part of the trinity is like the actual wood, roots, leaves, and bark of a tree. In terms of human life, individuals and the ideas they actualize are born onto the earth. The model tells us that things are an outward expression of thoughts or planted in the creative mind. The V-like symbol of expanding energy is the source of motivation throughout the universe that feeds all parts of the trinity. Like the sun, it represents the source of ever-expanding energy within thoughts, the womb of unconscious activity, and all material things.

3

Enneagram Signs in the Zodiac

Like vintage years of wine, we are born with the qualities
of the year and of the season in which we are born.

— C. G. Jung

Enneagram signs are based on one's birth date. Enneagram signs offer
the soul's view of the enneagram because they are given by the cosmos
and aligned with the zodiac signs from Aries to Pisces. Enneagram
signs and types share the same meanings but differ in that signs are
based on one's date of birth, whereas types are determined by one's
historical preferences and behaviors and reveal a person's ego-centered
personality. While enneagram signs reveal a person's soul-centered
personality, enneagram types are determined by surveys and trained
observers. Like the twelve thirty-degree zodiac signs, the nine forty-
degree enneagram signs reveal an individual's soul personality and
potential for self-expression.

The timing of the nine phases of the zodiac based on enneagram
signs and stages is based on the earth's cyclic rotations around the sun.
The enneagram sign describes the personality you were born into and
the stages and development cycles that all people experience in every
year of life. While the enneagram sign at birth is fixed for the duration

of one's life, the ever-changing stages and development cycles of signs can help you understand, create, and change the conditions of your life.

Although the enneagram type is chosen by the individual based on their historical preferences for approaching life, the choices and actions they pursue in life are related to their enneagram sign and stage of development. The nine signs that the earth travels through in its annual journey around the sun represent different faces of the soul's personality. The first face is associated with the early part of spring, and the ninth face represents the last part of winter. The earth-sun relationship represents those aspects of our soul's nature that are most positive and radiant like the sun.

The enneagram signs were created by dividing the 360-degree zodiac into nine forty-degree signs that each contain parts of two traditional astrology signs. Throughout this work, the enneagram signs around the zodiac replace the twelve signs in the astrology system with nine enneagram signs and cyclical stages of development. When the planets linked to enneagram types are aligned with the enneagram signs, they expand upon the sign's meanings. The two adjacent astrology signs that define an enneagram sign have a lot in common with the enneagram type, but there are some differences.

The relationship between astrology signs and Jung's psychological types is like the relationship between enneagram signs and enneagram types. In each case, the sign personalities are soul centered, and the type personalities are ego centered. Because there are twelve zodiac signs and nine enneagram signs, each enneagram sign is comprised of two zodiac signs. For example, the first sign contains Aries and part of Taurus but is neither sign by itself, the second sign contains both Taurus and Gemini but is neither sign by itself, and so forth. While the two signs oppose each other, the enneagram sign creates the third force or trinity by uniting the opposing signs. The meaning of these nine sign trinities is like the meaning of the nine enneagram types but not identical. While enneagram types describe one's egocentric personality and way of being, enneagram signs are based on one's birth date and time and reveal their soul-centered personality.

As seen in the chapter 1 table titled The Zodiac as Enneagram Signs and in the clockwise diagram given below titled Numbered Enneagram Signs in the Zodiac, each forty-degree enneagram sign contains parts of two zodiac signs. The first type in this diagram is numbered 0 to 1, the second is numbered 1 to 2, and so forth.

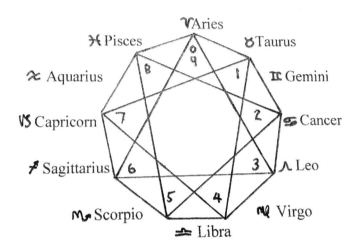

Numbered Enneagram Signs in the Zodiac

One, The Initiator

March 20 to May 1
0° Aries to 10° Taurus

The Initiator sign represents all areas of originality, writing, speaking, learning, commerce, and message giving and represents the beginning of understanding. As indicated by the planet Mercury, this sign governs the creation of things through the power of words. The chief function of this sign is to translate ideas and signs from one level to another, creating several different maps of reality for thinking, speaking, imagining, dreaming, and direct experience. The people of this sign have an excessive concern for details and can turn into nitpickers and perfectionists and replace actual experience with these concerns. They like to confront problems head-on and have exacting standards for themselves and others. They are self-righteous and seek perfection in their communications and the endeavors they support. The more advanced individuals of this type are associated with being down-to-earth and motivated to create practical manifestations.

Individuals born in the first enneagram sign have all the qualities of Aries and the added ability to give concrete expression to their endeavors, thanks to Taurus. Aries and Taurus are the first signs of the zodiac and are therefore linked to getting things started, beginnings, and confidence. The elements of fire and earth give this enneagram sign a steamroller approach to getting things done. The union between Aries the Ram and Taurus the Bull produces practical and assertive leader types who are self-confident and expressive. Unlike the risky and rash Aries, individuals of the third sign are reformers who have the potential to actively manifest themselves through steadiness, reliability, and productivity.

Two, The Guide

May 1 to June 11
10° Taurus to 20° Gemini

The Guide sign is associated with the moon, which represents the ability and interest to understand, attract, and serve others. They are focused on human relationships and are sensitive, tolerant, charming, and friendly. They want to be loved, appreciated, and connected to others and prefer to follow rather than lead. They are born communicators who love to converse with those who need extra attention and acceptance. They are known for being people pleasers and generous and spending a great deal of time trying to understand and explain their own and other people's emotions. These people combine intellectual, intuitive, conceptual, and psychic awareness to pursue concrete objectives. The second sign is a symbol of service, the highest good that life can offer. People of this sign don't understand the world by purely rational means; they understand through feelings and emotions. They have a fondness for comfort and ease, and the home is their center of interest and activity.

Taurus introduces a practical and down-to-earth quality of being aware of others as unique individuals to Gemini's natural ability to connect with others and explain things. The patient Taurus side slows down the flighty Gemini side and adds focus so that all options are considered before chasing after half-baked plans. The union between Taurus the Bull and Gemini the Twins makes for individuals with strong mental determination, persistence, and the ability to make in-depth observations. In addition to their ability to communicate in practical ways, they are a source of information and knowledge about many topics and good at writing. The Gemini influence in this enneagram sign wants to work on intellectual solutions, and the Taurus side wants to stick to one goal until it is achieved.

Three, The Contestant

June 11 to July 23
20° Gemini to 0° Leo

The third enneagram sign is associated with the sun, a symbol of the power, achievement, status, love, organization, and creative energy that enables all life to expand. The Contestant values family, close friends, and associates and sees them as the most important part of their foundation and existence. They are image conscious and identify with being the source and center of attention. They are charming, witty, creative, and multifaceted and have an interest in the new and fashionable. The people of this sign speak out often but remain silent when needed. The more aggressive individuals of this sign employ their powers of persuasion without any qualms to get their way, even though others might be hurt in the process. These people are intelligent, humorous, and optimistic and tend to control those around them. They are anxious to gain public favor, want status and applause, and attain success in the world without a great deal of effort on their part.

The third enneagram sign unites the qualities of Gemini and Cancer. Cancer is the beginning of a new cycle of evolution through the zodiac or summer, while Gemini concludes the old cycle or spring. Like the Guides, they are good communicators, cheerful, and knowledgeable. Unlike the Guides, they are doers and go-getters who express their ideas with greater emotional intensity. The Cancer part of the third sign brings out the emotions and sensuality hidden within, while the Gemini part helps Cancer rationalize their worst fears. The Cancer influence moves this sign to be at home, nurturing loved ones, while the Gemini influence moves them to be out and about in the world, spreading their message.

Four, The Romantic

July 23 to September 3
0° Leo to 10° Virgo

The fourth enneagram sign is represented by Neptune, the romantic planet and symbol of universal love, transcendent awareness, imagination, and deeper, more profound interpersonal relationships. Individuals of this enneagram sign have an enthusiastic approach to life and pursue fun-loving projects and romance up to the limits of what is possible. They are generous, inspire the affection of many admirers, and transcend any culture. Many of these individuals are stubborn and can stick with way-out and weird creative projects until they are completed. However, their gregarious nature often makes it difficult for them to stick with boring projects and routine activities. People of this sign tend to be artistically or musically inclined, embody the need to create, and possess the typical concern for others. They pay attention to the psychic aspects of life, including their own inner life, ideals, and values.

Individuals born in the fourth enneagram sign have the qualities of Leo and Virgo. Historically, Leo has been the personification of a romantic who loves to contemplate affairs or even intimate friendships with others. They want to have a fine balance between egotism and humility and between generosity and conservativism. They are susceptible to the sudden emotional ups and downs from Leo's loud nature to Virgo's silent nature. The Leo influence on this sign shows Virgo how to find a more joyful way of life, while the Virgo influence teaches Leo some discrimination to help them direct their energy in a more focused way. While the combination of the fire and earth elements give them a steamroller quality, as seen in the first sign, they also have an interest in the healing arts, helping others improve.

Five, The Innovator

September 3 to October 14
10° Virgo to 20° Libra

The fifth enneagram sign is represented by Uranus, the planet of the Innovator, creative thinking, and liberating individuals from the bondage of rigid patterns that need to change. Those born under this sign are most cerebral of the nine signs; they are less emotional, more objective, and analytical and have few self-conflicts. They are creative, spontaneous, and usually committed to something greater than themselves. They have a talent for detail, working with routines, and are known to be fair-minded problem solvers with a practical awareness of relationships. They are known to be levelheaded and independent thinkers but do not necessarily follow traditional logic to express their potential. They love justice and balance and need to be evenhanded in their relationships with others. While they are often critics who are prone to depression, they excel at healing and helping others improve their lives. Their actions are health conscious and focused.

People born in the fifth enneagram sign combine the qualities of Virgo and Libra. Virgo brings a keen awareness to many forms an idea can take with Libra, the sign of complete impartiality and balance. Virgo is the end of the old cycle of evolution through the zodiac or summer, and Libra is the beginning of the new cycle or autumn. The Virgo side of this sign is introverted and rather serious in outlook, while the Libra side is sociable and happy-go-lucky with an air of serenity. The Virgo-Libra combination makes for keen observers and deep thinkers who have great minds for details, planning, and teamwork. This combination is the change agent who's filled with surprise and mystery. They are idealists, unassuming, autonomous, and intuitive and have an aesthetic sense and efficient perception of reality.

Six, The Skeptic

October 14 to November 23
20° Libra to 0° Sagittarius

In the enneagram system, the sixth sign is represented by Saturn, the planet of the Skeptic, the devil's advocate, questioners, agnostics, limitations, and law and order. Individuals of this sign are more focused on one-to-one relationships, having a stable home, security, safety, and learning how to get along with others. They have an intense emotional involvement with their personal growth and are known for being charming, friendly, and loyal. Those represented by this sign can explain feelings because they have an awareness of how they feel and the feelings of others. They are passionate, natural detectives and troubleshooters and understand many mysteries. They have the spirit of a warrior but not in an openly combative way, unless it becomes necessary. They are known for being persistent, responsible, steady, and loyal. No matter how things turn out, they try to get to the bottom of things and will persist until they do so.

People born in the sixth enneagram sign have the qualities of Libra and Scorpio. The Libra-Scorpio combination is shrewd and has a flare for both drama and criticism. Their intellect tends to be highly developed, and they are often vocal about their opinions, which may rub others the wrong way. They are romantic and devoted to family, the people in their circle, and want to live near family and friends. Both Libra and Scorpio look for commitment and diligence in their plans and associations with friends and partners. Because this type combines the mental nature of Libra with the emotional nature of Scorpio, they use their great insight and inner strength to see their goals through to the end. These two signs give emotional depth to their ideas, detachment, and perspective on their feelings.

Seven, The Seeker

November 23 to January 1
0° Sagittarius to 10° Capricorn

In the enneagram system, the seventh sign is associated with Jupiter, the planet of the Seeker. The planetary symbol for this sign represents humanity's contact with transcendent intelligence and desire to comprehend the meaning of life. The people of this sign want to pursue higher education and new knowledge, discovering innovative ways of doing things, and religious or philosophical wisdom. They often have an entrepreneurial attitude toward their idealistic and educational aims, which makes them practical seekers and educators. Like many politicians, they want to know everyone and go everywhere. They like to see the big picture, pursue big plans, dreams, and visions, expand boundaries, and make the best of everything. While Initiators dwell on topics for the ordinary mind, Seekers dwell on topics for the higher mind. In addition to their love for growth, most people of this type like to feel a part of something greater than themselves. As they acquire more wisdom, they become more compassionate.

Individuals born in the seventh enneagram sign have qualities of Sagittarius and Capricorn. Because both signs are seekers of truth, they are often referred to as the scholars of the zodiac. Sagittarius represents a love for freedom, idealism, and learning about one's connection to the rest of the world. While this influence is often ungrounded, the presence of Capricorn adds determination, discipline, and focus. The combination of the fire and earth elements in this sign gives them a bold approach to moving through life. People of this sign have happy-go-lucky attitudes, realistic visions, and big dreams that can have a hand in shaping the future for humanity. The presence of Sagittarius and Capricorn in the seventh sign produces a blend of optimism and pragmatism.

Eight, The Defender

January 1 to February 9
10° Capricorn to 20° Aquarius

In the enneagram system, the eighth sign is represented by Mars, the planet of the Defender. The planetary symbol for this sign is associated with courage and the energy that both destroys old forms and manifests one's selfhood. People of this type have a blend of strong traditional and social values and work to change society's outworn ideas. They are survivors who want to be practical and move forward with big and progressive ideas in a step-by-step manner. They are independent, inventive, and focused on changing things for the better. They are sure-footed and methodical climbers who can appear lazy if they can achieve the same goals with less effort. Although the people of this type can be critical and bossy, they keep their nose to the grindstone and want to succeed. They often get away with breaking the rules to bring new things to light. They have a deep need to communicate their experience and stick with their plans.

Those born in the eighth enneagram sign have a blend of Capricorn and Aquarius. Capricorns build practical relationships to support themselves within society and the progressive views of things represented by Aquarius. Capricorn is ambitious and focused in their partnership with the unusual and far-sighted Aquarius. The Aquarian emblem of an individual pouring water describes a teacher of collective consciousness, an inventor and idealist. They are ambitious, want to rescue others from trouble, and have the will to succeed. Both Capricorn and Aquarius can be opinionated and stubborn and want to obtain the objects of their desire. While the practical, conservative Capricorn clashes with the unpredictable, unconventional Aquarian, the Aquarian presence brings originality and fun to Capricorn.

Nine, The Mediator

February 9 to March 20
20° Aquarius to 0° Aries

In the enneagram system, the ninth sign is associated with Venus, the planet of the Mediator. People of this type are known for creating harmony, understanding the forces that bind people together, and settling unresolved differences. They have a unique angle on the world that others just don't see. They are selfless in their work with others and sow seeds of transformation for the next cycle of development. Mediators introduce and promote innovative ideas to bring peace, harmony, and fairness with great sensitivity. They are pacifist by nature and want to work with others who have similar goals. They understand the feelings of others and like to resolve people-oriented problems. While they resent being told what to do, they are cooperative in the right relationship. These people react emotionally and have a thirst for knowledge and understanding. They are compassionate, vulnerable, idealistic, and fair-minded in humanitarian endeavors.

The people born in the ninth sign have the qualities of Aquarius and Pisces. The objective Aquarian concern for the whole more than for any one part increases the Piscean urge to embrace the unity of all things when serving others. Those born under the ninth sign are multitalented and feel the need to change the world. Their compassion is all-encompassing and usually rooted in spirituality. An individual of this sign often works around the rules when it comes to helping others understand one another and reach their fullest potential. The combination of the quirky Aquarius and the dreamy Pisces often produces individuals who have the greatest understanding of all signs in the zodiac. Although they see reality as an intrusion, which can make them pessimistic, they are willing to adapt and can change when necessary.

The Trinities among Soul Types

As already mentioned, enneagram signs are given by the cosmos when we enter this life at birth and represent our innermost essence or soul type. One's soul type or personality is immortal and remains the same from one lifetime to the next. For example, a certain Innovator soul might incarnate as a cook, military officer or stay at home parent and still be a creative thinker whose inventive and perceptive. Our enneagram type is an ego centered personality that is shaped by the experience we're born into and environment factors, e.g., nationality, social standing, profession, race, gender, and so forth.

One's soul type is often evident early in life but then becomes covered up by environmental factors and false personality. This superficial identity, we all develop, has little to do with who we really are. For instance, a female mediator in her mid-thirties whose been trained as an elementary school teacher and taught for years, may suddenly find that her true calling takes her back to school to become a lawyer who specializes in mediation.

The soul type or enneagram sign is composed of complementary opposite astrology signs. The complimentary pairs form two sides of a trinity that is united through the soul type. Each astrological pair that makes up the enneagram sign has a "proactive" side and a "receptive side." The proactive side is the expressive driver whose focused on the big picture. This side sets things in motion, operates in the foreground and, and plays a leading role. The receptive side is reactive, introspective and focused on details. This side follows the orders of the proactive side, operates in the background, and plays a supportive role.

The nine soul types are shown in the table in chapter 1 titled The Zodiac as Enneagram Signs and in the diagram in this chapter titled Numbered Enneagram Signs in the Zodiac. The proactive and receptive pairs are:

Soul Type	Proactive side	Receptive side
The Initiator	Aries	Taurus
The Guide	Gemini	Taurus
The Contestant	Gemini	Cancer
The Romantic	Leo	Virgo
The Innovator	Libra	Virgo
The Skeptic	Libra	Scorpio
The Seeker	Sagittarius	Capricorn
The Defender	Aquarius	Capricorn
The Mediator	Aquarius	Pisces

4

Nine Types and Planets

*And God said, "Let there be lights in the firmament of the heavens
to divide the day from the night; and let them be for
signs, and for seasons, and for days, and years."*

— Genesis 1:14, King James Version (KJV)

The enneagram system of personality types has become popular since
the 1980s. Its creator, George Ivanovich Gurdjieff or G. I. Gurdjieff,
was a Sufi mystic and pioneer in adapting Eastern spiritual teachings
for use by modern Westerners. While Gurdjieff and his students give
no source for the origin of the nine types, they are nearly identical to
the nine astrological planets or types. As with astrology, no one knows
exactly where or when or how it originated. The enneagram model
simply lays out the nine types, plus other rules, and the source remains
a mystery. Although astrology is the oldest system of psychological
types in the world, I believe that creators of the enneagram kept their
source hidden because astrology was no longer reputable as a system
of psychology.

Since the cosmos, the solar system and the universe, is reflected
within everyone, the influence of the planet types in astrology and the

enneagram are found in each person. Astrology and the enneagram have things in common and things that are different. Many components of each system are the same, and each can add to the other because they have common sources. Since there are nine planetary types, we can shift our focus from the twelve zodiac signs to the nine planets. Even though Pluto was discovered in 1930 as the tenth planet, today it is not considered a planet.

While enneagram authors don't divide the types into binary or even numbered categories, such as yang and yin or the four directions, they are divided into three categories or trinities, such as harmony, power, and ideas or beginning, middle, and end. The harmony types and planets are two, seven, and nine, which represent the moon, Jupiter, and Venus, respectively. The assertive or power types three, six, and eight represent the sun, Saturn, and Mars, respectively. The idealistic types one, four, and five represent Mercury, Neptune, and Uranus.

Those familiar with the astrology sign descriptions and enneagram types will see the direct correspondences between the two systems without chart calculations. Simply put, using the enneagram types without knowing a person's birth data yields the same result in terms of having a useful and accurate typing system. The enneagram type represents one's personal history and preferred personality and may not correspond to their enneagram sign. The enneagram sign is a map of the soul's personality, whereas the enneagram type is a map of one's personal or historical personality. Like your astrology sun sign, your enneagram sign is given at birth.

While the enneagram sign is a map of your potential, the enneagram type is determined by your history of lifetime preferences. Over a period, some people undergo a change in their enneagram type based on their external life experience and psychological development, but almost all will remain the same.

Planet Types

In this work, the enneagram types correspond to the positions of the planets in their orbits around the sun. The nine planets that can be observed from the earth include the moon, which has many characteristics of a formal planet. As observed from Earth, the sun and moon are the archetypal pair, which represents the spirit-personality or father-mother relationship and principle. They correspond to enneagram type three for the sun and type two for the moon, respectively. From there, you can count backward from type one (Mercury) to type nine (Venus), type eight (Mars), type seven (Jupiter), type six (Saturn), type five (Uranus), and type four (Neptune). The relationships among planets, enneagram types, and astrology signs are shown here. The types line up exactly with the planets as you move backward and outward from the sun or forward and inward from Neptune or type four to the sun and moon. The nine planets correspond directly with the enneagram types.

The meanings of planets are presented here as key components of the enneagram signs, along with the planets and astrology signs associated with the enneagram types. Although authors of the enneagram use different names for the types, the names used in this work are adapted from the work on the enneagram from Don Richard Riso and Russ Hudson. Most names for the enneagram signs are like the enneagram type names. They are also associated with the meaning of the astrology sun signs within the enneagram signs. Taken together, the planets in the enneagram, the four elements, and two astrology signs give us the names, themes, and meanings of the enneagram signs.

The symbols for the nine planets are made up of a combination of the circle, half circle or semicircle, and cross. These three simple symbols are organized in ways that allows us to interpret and understand all planets. At least one of these symbols is found in every planet and, in some case, two or three of these symbols. While the circle is the only symbol for the sun, it is partly used to represent the planets Mercury, Venus, Mars, and Uranus. The circle is a symbol of energy, the source of life, youthfulness, consciousness, pure yang, harmony, and the father spirit. It has no beginning and no end. It is the spark of life, seed, and movement in all. The semicircle is the only symbol for the moon. However, it is partly used to represent the planets Mercury, Jupiter, Saturn, Uranus, and Neptune. The semicircle is a symbol of the creative mind, the unconscious, the law, duality, the womb of life, pure yin, and the mother soul. It is the nonphysical part of a person that's the sum of all experience gained by the individual and the collective. The cross is a symbol of the physical body, forms, matter, manifestation, and the outer life lived on Earth. The cross is the symbol for planet Earth and is partly used to represent the planets Mercury, Venus, Mars, Jupiter, Saturn, Uranus, and Neptune.

Although the sun and moon are represented by one symbol, the other seven planets each work as an integrated unit whose goal is represented by an upper symbol—a circle, semicircle, or cross—and whose starting point is represented by a lower symbol. The planet's upper symbol or goal is also its dream outcome, aim, opportunity for growth, and potential for expansion; the planet's lower symbol is its place of origin or beginning, inherited nature, and tangible reality or limits. The planets can be interpreted or understood by contemplating the relationship between their upper and lower symbols. For instance, the circle above and cross below for Venus means that this planet represents choosing to transcend material reality and physical forms and express energy, consciousness, and harmony. The cross above and circle below for Mars means that the function of this planet is the opposite of Venus. Mars represents choosing to use one's energy, consciousness, and harmony toward the attainment of material success and to assert oneself in the reality of physical forms. Simply put, a planet's goal and ideal outcomes are supported by the foundation represented by the lowest part of its symbol.

Mercury is represented by a semicircle above, a circle in the middle, and a cross below. Since the only other planet that combines three symbols is Uranus, there is a definite relationship between these two planets.

Planets

Mercury ☿	**The Moon** ☽	**The Sun** ☉
Neptune ♆	**Uranus** ♅	**Saturn** ♄
Jupiter ♃	**Mars** ♂	**Venus** ♀

As just discussed, Venus and Mars combine the circle and cross but do so in opposite ways. The arrow, which is sometimes used with the Mars symbol, is simply a blurred cross. The remaining planets also combine two symbols. Jupiter and Saturn combine the semicircle and cross but do so in opposite ways. The meanings of Venus and Mars are opposite, and the meanings of Jupiter and Saturn are opposite. Venus and Jupiter are similar because they have identical foundations and realities represented by the cross. Mars and Saturn are similar because they have identical goals. Venus and Jupiter have different goals, and Mars and Saturn have different origins or realities. The symbols for Neptune and Jupiter are similar in that both combine the cross below with the semicircle above, but they are different. With Jupiter, the semicircle representing the unconscious or mother soul is touching the cross of matter; however, with Neptune, the semicircle is pierced by the cross of matter, resulting in a pronged fork. The pronged fork represents a greater connection between the soul and matter than the touching of the two. The definitions that follow examine the symbolic meanings of the planets and planet types in greater detail.

The table given here presents the trinity arrangements of forces and stages of development for the nine planets. These arrangements provide an additional understanding of the universal trinity principle behind the planets. In the first row of development stages, we have Mercury, the Moon, and the Sun as beginning planets; Neptune, Uranus, and Saturn in the second row are middle stage planets; and Jupiter, Mars, and Venus in the third row are the completion or ending stage planets. The beginning, middle, and ending planets also represent our individual development stage; the development stage of our close relationships; and the development stage of our relationship to society and the collective respectively.

Among the nine planets as trinity forces, the first column consists of Mercury, Neptune, and Jupiter as the affirming or active planet trinity forces. The second column consist of the Moon, Uranus, and Mars as the denying or receptive planet trinity forces; and the third column consist of the Sun, Saturn, and Venus as the reconciling or facilitating planet trinity forces.

Although Uranus and Mars are traditionally associated with revolutionary and warrior qualities, their nature is to follow orders and fight the battles for those forces that give the orders to pursue these courses of action. For instance, Mars is the foot soldier, lieutenant, or general, who works for the president or king.

Trinity Forces and Stages in the Planets

	Affirming	*Denying*	*Reconciling*
Beginning	Mercury	the Moon	the Sun
Middle	Neptune	Uranus	Saturn
Ending	Jupiter	Mars	Venus

The Reformer Type

Mercury

Reformers are associated with various aspects of originality, writing, speaking, learning, commerce, and message giving. They represent the beginning of understanding and all forms of communication. They are known for their integrity and orderliness. Those with an excessive concern for details can turn into nitpickers and perfectionists and replace actual experience with these concerns. The more advanced Reformer types are associated with the rational mind, being down-to-earth and influenced by making connections in the material world. The Reformer types are known for being logical thinkers and applying analytical discrimination to concrete reality. They often insist on accuracy to a level that can appear trivial to others. In addition to their intelligence and ability to communicate with others, they are also known for their physical dexterity.

Reformers like to confront problems head-on and are self-righteous, self-critical, and critical of others. They are never satisfied with the established order and always look for innovative ways to improve things and overcome the gap that exists between separate entities. They value goodness, integrity, and making the world a better place. Those of this type are intelligent idealists and sticklers for details. They seek precision in communications and the endeavors they support. They function to bring unseen and unconscious happenings in the universe into conscious awareness and hence manifestation. Instead of creating something out of nothing, they bring into existence those things that were already in the present but unknown. Reformers adopt new techniques, knowledge, and skills to function in an effective manner.

Mercury is the planet of the word that makes the unconscious conscious, brings heaven to earth, and serves as messenger of the gods. The Mercury archetype governs the creation of things through words. All beginnings come into manifestation through the word or Logos, and without words, nothing is created. Mercury is the transmitter of spiritual understanding to the material. This heavenly body is a symbol of the active force of intelligence that mediates between the unmanifested part of the universe and the manifested part. It represents progress through experimentation and the motivation to bring clarity to the will of the divine. This planet is also associated with the kind of divine wisdom communicated by humanity by Buddha, Christ, and enlightened individuals.

Mercury is a symbol of the trinity that brings together the father, holy spirit, and child or simply father, mother, and child. Mercury represents language and the power to make symbols, which includes all forms of data transfer. All our knowing, thinking, experiencing, sensing believing, or disbelieving is done through signs and symbols that represent facts, experiences, or entities in our mind. The chief function of this planet is to translate ideas from one level to another and to create the forms that ideas take. It is identified with creating maps of reality for thinking, speaking, imagining, dreaming, and direct experience. This planet represents the wisdom that enables people to know that concepts are no more than representations and that they are somewhat arbitrary representations at that. Even though the analytical nature of Mercury is identified with analysis, its ability to synthesize is often stronger.

The Helper

The Moon

The Helper does not understand the world by purely rational means; they understand through feelings and emotions. Helpers are known for being generous and people oriented. They are emotionally expressive, focused on human relations and empowering others, and like to give and receive love. Helpers need to feel wanted and need emotional security. They cannot be happy without a meaningful home life. They are attracted to matters that require attention and to people who require protection. Helpers place a higher value of maternal love than romantic love and demand ownership of affection to satisfy their emotional insecurity. The feelings and emotional patterns of behavior held by this type often interfere with the development of their creative self-expression. Helpers are associated with things from the past and inclined to follow tradition. They prefer to wait, follow, and learn to fit in to become a part of the established order.

The Helper type has a fondness for comfort and ease, and the home is their center of interest and activity. Individuals of this type have a sensitivity to the moods and feelings of others. Their rather extreme sensitivity to others' opinions and reactions can lead them to imagine slights when none are intended. Even though they are somewhat shy and evasive, they are often engaged in public-relations activities. By serving others, they provide the highest good that life can offer. They help others through various occupations and activities. The Helper does not understand the world by purely rational means; they understand through feelings and emotions. They are tolerant and friendly and work with those who need extra attention and acceptance. Their main lesson is to learn emotional detachment and deal with the problem of letting go of relationships that have not worked out.

The Moon is emblematic of growth, change, and our emotional nature, which shapes our outer character or personality. This planet is associated with deep feelings, the subconscious, and all that is receptive in human nature. The moon is a symbol of the emotional energy that connects and serves all life. If the sun and light are the male aspect of the universe, the moon and darkness are the female aspect. Historically, the moon has been the container or womb from which all life emerges. The moon represents the ability to attract people and shows how they relate to others. The moon is the planetary archetype of yin. Its main functions are life provider and giving form to life. While the earth gives physical structure to life, the moon nurtures and sustains this structure. Without the moon and its control over the flow of water, physical life cannot exist, nor can health be restored or maintained.

The moon or lunar influence is connected to all forms of motherhood, both literal and metaphorical. The moon is a symbol of the nurturing principle and the experience of being nurtured, protected, and supported through life. Since the moon governs oceans as well as public tides, those represented by the moon are often pulled into several types of public life. The moon often bestows psychic ability and perceives that everything is in some way connected. The moon rules hidden movement with a life all its own. The moon represents the order, principles, and laws that govern the universe. To advance in life, we must honor the flow of life created by the moon. While it appears that individuals have free will, they do not. Unless their will is aligned with the universal order and laws represented by the moon, they will not be successful. Violating this alignment is synonymous with breaking the law and facing the consequences that follow.

The Achiever

The Sun

The Achiever needs to express who they are and look for ways to make an impact in terms of their own identity. They prefer to be in the forefront of any activity where they can be recognized and dislike working behind the scenes. Self-expression is the major goal of this type, and the more they can be themselves and be accepted as such, the better off they are. These people are image conscious and want to have worth, status, and applause. They are not especially modest and can make others notice them by their demeanor. They are performers and go-getters and tend to be boastful, arrogant, and totally wrapped up in themselves. They often overestimate their own worth and do not feel it's necessary to do anything to justify their high self-opinion. They have great self-confidence and a strong need for admiration and uncompromising personal integrity. Individuals of this type enjoy being the center of attention and need to be in the spotlight, and once in it, they want to shine. These individuals are often creative in the ways of business and perhaps the arts.

Achievers cannot operate meaningfully except through their relationships with others and the environment in which they are located. They have strong attachments to family and establish themselves in society through a personalized environment. Achievers have dramatic and flamboyant personalities and express their emotions as a way of gaining social recognition. They often take huge risks because of their almost blind self-confidence. These people project themselves in the most dramatic way possible and search for pleasure and romance with others. While they have sunny, happy dispositions and attract many friends, at times they seem to be naively childish and egocentric. They want others to think well of them, and because they direct a great deal of energy toward this goal, it is frequently achieved. They are aware of the effect they have on others and study what to do to create a better effect.

The Sun is the source of energy, movement, growth, doing, or action. It is the energy within mediation and conflict but is neither mediation nor conflict. The energy represented by the sun cannot be created or destroyed, only transformed. When its energy is withdrawn, death follows; when it is present, life follows. The sun brings warmth and harmony to all things; like fire, it creates or destroys, depending on its use. The sun is a symbol of unlimited potential, eternity, and continuity of the human soul, forever expanding. The sun represents the motivating power behind all activities and the energy that enables everything to exist. Historically, the sun is the central and chief deity of all peoples. Because the sun is a symbol of boundless vitality and attraction, those represented by this planet have an aspiring nature, which results in success. They are associated with positive characteristics and the desire to express one's individuality. The sun is the archetype of the hero that sets out into the world and aims to bring order out of chaos through imposing their will.

The sun is a symbol of humanity's connection to the source of light, health, divine origins, creative abilities, and purpose. The sun is the animating force and energy in the universe that makes the world go round. Without this planet, there is no movement, no harmony, no cycles of development, and no love. Since the beginning of life on earth, the sun has produced more growth than the previous century, and this growth continues to increase at an increasing rate. The sun represents the harmony, love, knowledge, and progress of all things in the universe. This planet represents the source of all visible and invisible expansion, points of consciousness, atoms, seeds, the wheel of life, and circles. It represents the element of fire and the intuitive insights that precede thinking.

The Individualists

Neptune

The Individualist has an artistic temperament that is expressed through their ability to touch the heart and inspire emotional responses in others. This type values originality, individual uniqueness, and creating beauty. They are open to the temptations of the lower nature and to the glories of their transcendent spiritual nature more than other types. The people of this type attempt to bring together the unconscious and invisible realm of the universe with the conscious and visible realm. Because they have a lack of ego emphasis, they are often attracted to social service: taking care of the physically or mentally ill or others who need to be looked after. They love to shed light and demand no external rewards for the humanitarian services that they perform. This is often a source of difficulty in relationships with the people they serve because relationships require a clear idea of one's own personality.

The Individualists are associated with the inspirations needed to bring things into the physical world. Individuals of this type are idealistic, usually sensitive, self-aware, independent of culture and environment, naturally intuitive, and philosophical and believe that life is spiritual. Since most individuals of this type have not learned to respond to the extrasensory qualities associated with this planet, such as psychic visions and mystical inspirations, they are inclined to be unrealistic dreamers. They are often way out and weird, escapists, artists, or creative people who dislike physical work and feel constrained by established rules. Many people of this type have either not yet developed a reality system or have just transcended one. They are usually loveable, sympathetic, and comfortable to be with if you just want to relax. Because personal systems of reality, ideas of right and wrong, are often subordinate to their reality of "what is," many have a lack of confidence in themselves.

Neptune is the planet of heaven above Earth. It represents ultimate reality, the physical and nonphysical universe, and is also the most distant and mysterious planet. Neptune represents illusion and mystical illumination, depending upon one's level of spiritual development; it also represents the most beautiful and painful of human emotions. This planet represents the formless void before structure is imposed upon it and may be understood as the truth and reality beyond appearances. The presence of Neptune implies a sympathetic openness to others and the urge to serve the weak and helpless and to accept all things at once. This help is associated with the work of integrating the numerous contradictions tied to ultimate reality. Neptune represents the container and integrates the elements needed for consciousness and the reality of all forms to exist. Those represented by this planet find pleasure in life despite pain, sorrow, and disappointment.

Because Neptune is associated with aspects of the universe that are unclear, illusory, ill-defined and even imaginary, this planet is the most difficult to understand. The actions of Neptune exist in the realm of dreams and intuition, which is not easy to understand. This planet rules the unconscious and teaches without words. Those represented by Neptune have exaggerated imaginations and don't like to be specific about anything. They are aware of multisensory perceptions and psychic phenomena and look for signs. Those influenced by Neptune who have no understanding of spirituality are likely to turn to drugs or alcohol to shut out these unusual feelings. The unlimited possibilities associated with this planet are difficult for most people to deal with because to be successful in the mundane universe, they must deal effectively with concrete realities.

The Investigator

Uranus

The Investigator is idealistic and revolutionary by nature and works for the improvement of humanity. This type is creative, psychological, spontaneous, and devoted to something greater than themselves. They are driven to break out of patterns that have become too rigid, even though they may wish to stay in them. Despite being a radical and social reformer who does not need to be tied to society, they always need a group with which to identify. Many of this type are detached, rarely wedded to the status quo, and motivated to continue growing through life. While they are often ready to experience anything and give up anything, this inclination is a source of difficulty when they ignore the concerns of others. They understand that the more easily they can let go, the more easily they can move forward. Because they tend to have a lack of ego emphasis, like the Individualist, they are often attracted to social service: taking care of the physically or mentally ill or others who need to be looked after.

Investigators bring darkness into the light of day and reveal wisdom hidden in the creative mind. They are practical in the sense that their influence is always accompanied by insights into the hidden side of material forms. Those of this type are less emotional, more objective, and less likely to follow hopes, fears, or ego defenses that distract their observations. They are self-confident, have few self-conflicts, and can enjoy both work and play. Many of this type challenge society's outworn structures and bring about change. Because they can be insensitive and unfeeling in their pursuit of right, they are not especially warm or emotional. A problem for this type is that they tend to have strong social ideals about how people ought to be and do not relate easily to how people are. While they often have little concern for individuals, they have great interest in the process of revolutionary change with which they have identified.

Uranus is a symbol of the nonconformist and groups that enjoy experimentation into things that seem strange and outside the established order. Uranus points to eccentric qualities and individuals who march to the beat of a different drummer. This planet embodies the sixth sense and is associated with groundbreaking ideas, inventions, and social doctrines. It stands as a symbol of liberation from the bondage of personality and signifies the power to become a self-actualized soul. Those under its influence are extremely independent, self-willed, and reluctant to be dominated or controlled by external rules and regulations. The presence of Uranus always indicates an unexpected element and sudden burst of energy from that part of the universe that remains unexplained and hidden. This planet operates like an invisible pressure cooker that explodes with new awareness. Its nature is like the submarine that emerges from the ocean depths and a UFO that comes into view at unexpected times or places.

Uranus represents creative plans and the inspiration to move in new directions. The main flaw of this planet is that those it represents often commit themselves to society, which is no more real than the individual. Uranus has a surprising nature that presents an assertive blending of intuitive insights, practicality, the wisdom of feelings, and the rational nature of thinking to introduce new things. This planet is a symbol of the intuitive flash that leads to new discovery and the overturning of old ideas. Its socially oriented nature points to radical or innovative thinkers who are independent and self-sufficient and do not need the approval of society. Uranus personifies curiosity about everything, which leads to all sorts of discovery. No matter what those influenced by this planet do, they do it differently.

The Loyalist

Saturn

The Loyalist is associated with negative energy, complaining, and vindictiveness. This type often encounters emotional lessons that bring pain and suffering until they learn to master and control their tendency to be unforgiving when hurt. These individuals are often overly emotional because they are rigidly involved with defending their sensitive feelings from the threat of the outer world. A good match for this type is someone who can share optimistic ideas with them. As they learn when and how to let go of resentments, they gain greater emotional stability. While they learn to accept responsibilities with a serious emotional intensity, they harbor deep resentments when they feel they have been dealt with unjustly. These people are thorough, persistent, determined to achieve their goals, and almost fanatic in their adherence to principle.

Individuals of this type are careful and cautions. They are often difficult to understand because of their reserved exterior and secretive nature. They are known to be questioners, devil's advocates, and skeptics. Much more than other types, they are steady, committed, traditional, and responsible. In most cases, they go about their business without advertising themselves or their achievements. Loyalists are fiercely trustworthy and devote themselves to loved ones. They adore family and often grow more sentimental with time. The older they get, the more secure they become, and their relations with others usually become better over time. They value financial and personal security, safety, health, the established order, and approval from others. This is one of the safest types when it comes to a faithful partner. They understand that it takes time to learn the deepest and most important lessons of life. Like recurring dreams, the lessons and message for Loyalists will persist until they are learned.

Saturn is a symbol of exploring the universe of Earth's reality and learning the rules of how to make life on earth successful. The planet Saturn has historically been called the "greater malefic," the bringer of sorrows, and the planet of stumbling blocks and embodies whatever limitations exist. It exemplifies law and order and everything that contains or puts a limit to growth. The lessons of Saturn are difficult because they are about giving birth to things that cannot happen until we understand that forms take their shape from the formless. This planet is known for restrictions and reminds us of our boundaries, our responsibilities, and our commitments. Those who accept the influence of this planet find a friend upon whom they can depend to guide them safely. Saturn reminds us that before any building can be built, there must be a design and a plan for how to build it. It reminds us that everything we are is contained in the hidden pattern of our DNA.

Saturn represents those aspects of reality that come from a consensus among human beings. It does not signify truth or absolutes but a reality that is socially created. Saturn personifies the laws that must be followed for forms, structures, and the physical universe to be dealt with successfully. It is associated with difficulty when the law is not followed or well known. The way Saturn operates is analogous to how the famous iceberg model is used in depth psychology to describe the relationship between the conscious and unconscious mind. While people see the tip of the iceberg above the surface, they should understand that the major part of what is seen lies beneath the surface. The symbol for Saturn depicts the earth, above which represents appearances, and the moon below represents the hidden part of the iceberg that contains the laws that allow the tip to exist. Hence, the main lesson of this planet is to look beyond surface appearances.

The Enthusiast

Jupiter

The Enthusiast is the youth spirit, curious, and never satisfied with life as it is and wants to move on to new experiences. They are idealistic and often develop a strong spiritual sense early in life. They have an ardent desire to be free and experience life in their own way. Many want to own everything, become more important than anyone, be grander, and have an exaggerated self-opinion. Those identified with this type can also be wasteful, irresponsible, and extravagant in their generosity. While they are unconventional and self-righteous in their youth, they tend to settle down and identify with the higher consciousness in their mature years. People of this type are enthusiastic about learning and have a great need for self-exploration. They reach out to incorporate as much of the external world as possible into themselves to grow both physically and psychologically. In addition to their love for growth, many people of this type want to feel a part of something greater than themselves.

The more developed Enthusiasts want to acquire as much education as possible, make diligent students and teachers, and often associate themselves with institutions of higher learning. People of this type have a need for a system of governing their conduct and way of life. They want to make their personal conduct conform to an impersonal set of moral principles, which brings them the respect and admiration of others, including their enemies. They are known for being optimistic and energetic, and they value joy, variety, and the experience of life's possibilities. They have a deep interest in the social and philosophical ideas that have shaped history and benefit present-day society. Their breath of experience prevents them from taking narrow-minded positions based on short-term goals at the expense of long-range objectives.

Jupiter represents humanity's contact with the universal mind and the individual's tool for comprehending the meaning of life. Historically, Jupiter is a symbol of success, achievement, good luck, and every possible benefit that life can offer. Tradition regards the nature of Jupiter as the achievement of compassion gained through wisdom. This planet is associated with the gift of prophecy and the development of one's higher mental attributes. While Mercury teaches individuals how to communicate with one another, Jupiter teaches us how to communicate with the transcendent. Its presence points to individuals who believe in and promote the use of divine laws on Earth. Those influenced by this planet have the potential to expand their understanding of human life through philosophy and attain consciousness of their spiritual nature.

Those influenced by Jupiter have a strong love of religion and philosophy as both a consciousness expanding system and a system for giving humanity an understanding of its relationship to the universe. Jupiter is identified with promoting divine laws on Earth and represents various religions and religious leaders. This planet is also linked to medicine, healing, and understanding what it takes to create wholeness. The Jupiter symbol presents the message that traditional and nontraditional teachers and sources of wisdom and learning are unlimited. Jupiter is associated with openly understanding the wisdom of the creative mind. Jupiter's message is that life on earth is learning, growing, and exploring the universe of knowledge beyond the boundaries of Earth. Saturn's message, by contrast, deals with learning the established rules of how to make life on earth successful. Many of the difficulties expressed by Saturn can be lessened or eradicated by Jupiter.

The Challenger

Mars

The Challenger is constantly striving to grow in the right direction and has the energy needed to do so. While they are admired for their courage and youthfulness, they are often headstrong and act before thinking. They are power-seeking survivors who rescue others from trouble and advocate freedom of choice. They judge things by the extent of their own awareness, hence the more limited their awareness, the more limited their world. Even though they take the lead through force and push their way to the top, they should learn to cultivate the attributes of cooperation and patience. Because their passion exceeds their compassion, they often misjudge the extent of people's situations in life. As such, they should learn to examine the details of their involvements and not concentrate solely on the main idea.

Challengers want to be first and have the leadership ability to take the initiative and spark enthusiasm in others. They have the physical energy that enables them to accomplish twice as much work as the average person in the short term. While they bring out abilities in others and help them rearrange the structure of their lives to fit their need or desire, they often express themselves without consideration for other people's wishes. Many people of this type prefer someone who is very dependent on them and yet autonomous. To provide for their family, they require an occupation that involves them totally and allows them the freedom to express themselves. Their aim is high, and so is their drive to get to the top of their chosen mountain. They want to be themselves on their own terms and need less social reinforcement than other types. The Challenger type is self-directed and independent and has little tolerance for opposition or interference. They are competitive and assertive and have no desire to liken themselves to others.

Mars represents the courage, energy, and ability of individuals to meet their needs. It is associated with doing things and rather doing the wrong thing than standing and waiting. Historically, Mars has been a symbol of war, warriors, aggression, decisiveness, firmness, and destruction. This planet is associated with the energy and movement that makes short-term changes in life. Mars is the element of fire and signifies youthfulness, growth, expansion, and forward movement. The goal of Mars, like the goals of Saturn types, is to attain success in material matters, such as making things, making progress, and being competitive. The difference is that Mars approaches goals through direct and forceful means, and Saturn approaches goals through learning the laws that make material success possible. As seen in the planet's symbolism, Mars pursues goals through the energy of the sun, and Saturn pursues goals through the energy of the moon.

The purpose of Mars is to destroy old forms so that the evolved aspects of one's selfhood and the material world can take their place. Those influenced by this planet are forceful, impatient, and impulsive and can handle life courageously and cut through obstacles. Mars is associated with the motivation to hold some form of power over others and to move energy into the material world. Known as the Red Planet, Mars can reproduce the high and low aspects of a person's nature depending on their desire. Those who embody the worst of the Martian characteristics exhibit cruelty, selfishness, and pugnacity and have complete control over their sphere of influence. Those who embody the best of the Martian characteristics are good natured and warm, think before they act, and get to the heart of a matter without getting bogged down by details.

The Peacemaker

Venus

The Peacemaker has an innate ability to consider and understand the feelings of others. Close personal bonds and harmonious social relationships are of extreme importance to people of this type. They have a desire to please, which results in being well liked by others. They usually gain their status and make their living by their pleasing manners, personal relationships, and aptitude in dealing with the public, which can be applied to business, counseling, and public relations. Peacemakers can take a step back, go with the flow, listen, and seek ways to accommodate others. Because this type cannot conceive itself in a vacuum, its self-development depends upon others. They want to see justice done and work with those who have common goals.

Many Peacemakers have an active participation in social affairs because this satisfies their need to be among people. They know how to create harmony and negotiate in times of stress and unresolved differences. They will do a great deal to ensure the happiness of those around them as they feel best when others are happy. Normally, this type is warm and loving as well as socially adept. More than other types, the Peacemaker is a matchmaker. They recognize that the power of love and connection nurtures the heart and extends the life span. They excel at taking the initiative in such a way that others do not realize the initiative has been taken. Harmony is valued so much that they will compromise a great deal to keep it. They are charming, tactful, courteous, considerate, and balanced and have an ardent desire to please and not make waves. This type operates in a lighter, less serious manner than other types, but they are rarely subservient.

Venus has a big hand in any relationship that causes people to become more fully realized. Historically, this planet stands for love, and its symbol represents the use of spiritual vitality or the vitality to create harmony in relationships on the material plane. The movement of Venus is toward the spiritual part of the universe and thoughts of agreement. It reflects divine love in material form and the force that pulls things together and holds them by attraction like the sun. Wherever Venus operates, harmony is produced by something moving in accordance with nature and itself. Of all the forces that bind people together, love produces the most stable groupings. The unions produced by this planet are stable because such relationships allow people to express what they are better than they could if the union were absent. The lesson of Venus is that giving people a sense of harmony in their world is just as useful as making sure they have material resources.

Those influenced by Venus are inspired to combine their imagination and reality to create harmony in social relationships. Venus brings the qualities of the sun to all areas of life on earth—ways of thinking and acting about our values, relationships, material forms, and interactions with one another. Mars gets things started and often breaks things because of its aggressive nature, while Venus bring things to fruition and mends broken effects because of its harmonious nature. The masculine face and hardness of Mars is fulfilled by the feminine face and softness of Venus. Mars initiates, and Venus completes. Venus represents peacemaking, mediation, unification, harmony, spirituality, and love. Since Venus is an inverted Mars, the inverted peacemaker is a warrior, and inverted harmony is disharmony.

Manifesting the Types

The spiritual process of manifestation is both downward, upward, and ongoing throughout one's life. The process of downward manifestation is one of becoming an individual. In this journey, the individual separates from the transcendent or unconscious universe and takes on a physical form in the conscious universe. This movement is from the nonphysical universe to the physical universe. Downward manifestation takes the path toward personal development, individual recognition, and discovering one's uniqueness. People on this path begin with attaining self-recognition, attracting associations, friendship, and loving relationships, and creating emotional security and safety and conclude with the attainment of material forms and meeting one's material needs and wants.

Upward manifestation involves movement toward wholeness or union with the transcendent. It is the journey toward transcendence and self-actualization. Those who take this path begin by satisfying their basic need for materials, such as acquiring tangible physical possessions and material things, moving on to acquiring emotional security and safety, attracting friendship and loving relationships, and increasing their self-esteem, self-image, and importance to others and conclude with releasing everything to attain the highest level, referred to as transcendence, wholeness, or self-actualization.

Hierarchy of Human Needs Among the Types

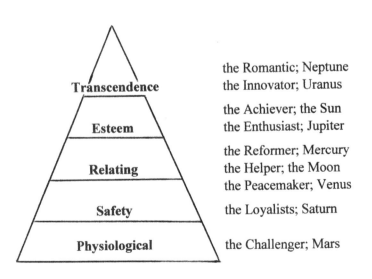

the Romantic; Neptune
the Innovator; Uranus

the Achiever; the Sun
the Enthusiast; Jupiter

the Reformer; Mercury
the Helper; the Moon
the Peacemaker; Venus

the Loyalists; Saturn

the Challenger; Mars

Transcendence

Esteem

Relating

Safety

Physiological

Psychologists Abraham Maslow's hierarchy of needs is depicted as a pyramid model. His hierarchy of needs theory is presented here along with the nine types and planets to show their associations with human needs. The model presents a clear perspective on the full range of human motivations, from physiological needs associated with Mars, the Challenger, to the highest level or transcendence and self-actualization associated with Neptune, the Individualist, and Uranus, the Investigator. His hierarchy of needs tells us that we always want something and rarely reach a state of complete satisfaction or one without any goals or desires. His theory aims to predict what kinds of desires will arise once the old ones are sufficiently satisfied and no longer dominate behavior. He developed his hierarchy as part of a general theory of motivation, not as a precise predictor of individual behavior. In his view, living at the self-actualization level means greater biological efficiency, greater longevity, less disease, better sleep, appetite, etc.

While all planets have downward and upward manifestation goals, each planet represents one of the basic levels in the hierarchy of human needs and motivations. The first level of manifestation is the physiological, which includes the need to survive, acquire material things and possessions, and meet basic financial goals, represented by Mars. The next level of manifestation is the emotional, based on needs for safety, which include stability, predictability, structure, order, and limits, represented by Saturn, the Loyalist. The next level of manifestation is the need for relationships and connections with others, which includes love and feeling part of various groups, such as family and peer groups, represented by Mercury (the Reformer), the moon (the Helper), and Venus (the Peacemaker). The next level is the need for esteem, which includes the desire for competence, individual achievement, status, fame, and recognition from others, represented by the sun (the Achiever) and Jupiter (the Enthusiast). The final level of manifestation is the need for self-actualization, which includes the need to fully use one's talents and potential to see life clearly, commit to something greater than oneself, and attain success in one's chosen tasks, represented by the Investigator and Individualist types.

Finding Your Type

There are many self-assessment surveys for determining your enneagram type. At the end of her book, titled *Emotions and the Enneagram,* Margaret Frings Keyes offers a one-hundred-item easily scored checklist to determine your enneagram personality. Don Richard Riso also presents an accurate enneagram questionnaire at the end of his book titled *Discovering Your Personality Type.* The only way to find your type without a survey is to learn about the nine types and examine each against the knowledge you have of yourself. For some people, this is done by the process of elimination, and for others, one type stands out from the group. Although the zodiac-based enneagram sign is fixed by one's birth date and time and never changes, there is a small chance that one's enneagram type can change. The formation of the enneagram type is a product of our core motivations and patterns of behaviors, which date back to early childhood.

Your enneagram type is subjective, and only you can identify it. Finding your type is a self-discovery process. A straightforward way to find your type in this work is to examine the nine types described above and identify one or ones that are most like or unlike you. Since every aspect of the nine descriptions may not apply to you, you will need to select the type or types that include the items that apply to you most. You can start by selecting the type description that seems to best describe your history. There are many online self-assessment enneagram surveys, and if you google "online enneagram self-tests," you'll gain access to free and fee-based self-testing sites.

5

Signs and Type Associations

The purpose of each soul's entrance into life is to complete a cycle, another crossroads, or another urge from one of several of its activities in the material plane.

— Edgar Cayce

Each type and sign has a unique nature or vibration that gives it certain properties. The enneagram signs and letters represent different life stage experiences and interests and express distinct aspects of the soul's personality. To the degree that we are aware of the symbolic nature of type numbers, we have an opportunity to experience them as personality types and life cycles. They reveal the structure of the nonphysical body and soul, the universe. In this book, the meanings of the types and signs help you understand the nine natural phases of life. While these stages or cycles of development have been with us since the beginning of human history as a tool for listening to the nonphysical universe, nowadays they remain in the shadow cast by the big use of objective numbers in science and mathematics. The good news is that it is well known that the psychological shadow contains our biggest source of our subjective or personal growth, healing, and fulfillment, and you can choose to embrace it.

The types, signs, cycles, and letters in one's name show the way through physical, cosmic, and emotional realities. These archetypal symbols can help you move through time and space and up and down the world axis. The study of enneagram symbols, trinities, and earth-sun cycles for nine-year and one-year periods helps to explain why you were born—your path or destiny in life and every stage of experience until you leave this planet.

Since ancient times, there have been many models and explanations to expand our understanding of the zodiac and most of the planets. With so many opinions over such a prolonged period, it is no surprise that there are some conflicting views. The table titled Enneagram Type and Sign Associations organizes the most significant associations to the enneagram types and signs and is intended to offer universal meanings for the types, signs, letters of the alphabet, stages or cycles of development, and trinity groups. The meaning of the nine planets and enneagram signs and types reveal the ego and soul personality.

Although the terms *stage* and *cycle* can be defined in the same way, I have given them different meanings. The term *cycle* applies to nine nine-year circular periods or the eighty-one-year life cycle. The term *stage* applies to one-year periods within the nine-year cycles or a nine-year period within the eighty-one-year life cycle. The enneagram sign present at the time and date of birth is fixed for life, but the stages and cycles are symbols of new growth that accumulates, expands, builds up, and reinforces itself in the process of your thinking and doing.

Enneagram Signs Through the Zodiac: By dividing the 360-degree zodiac into nine instead of twelve equal parts, we have nine forty-degree enneagram signs or stages. When the nine segments are laid over the twelve thirty-degree signs of the zodiac, the nine types can be understood as a condensed version of the zodiac. Because each numbered type is forty degrees, their meaning of it is derived from two adjacent zodiac signs in the following way. The first sign leads the way, and the second sign follows. The first sign indicates where the numbered type is coming from, and the second side points to the experience of relationships and the outside world. The first sign represents the formative version of the number, and the second sign represents the mature expression.

The first thirty degrees of the numbers one, four, and seven are aligned with the three fire signs—Aries, Leo, and Sagittarius—and the first ten degrees of the earth signs—Taurus, Virgo, and Capricorn— make up the first forty-degree segment. This tells us that the dominant expression of the first, fourth, and seventh enneagram signs are made up of the fire and earth elements. The first half or twenty degrees of enneagram signs two, five, and eight are aligned with the last twenty degrees of Taurus, Virgo, and Capricorn and the first twenty degrees of the air signs—Gemini, Libra, and Aquarius. What these signs have in common is that their dominant expression consists of the earth and air elements. Finally, the first ten degrees of enneagram signs three, six, and nine are aligned with the last ten degrees of Gemini, Libra, and Aquarius and followed by an alignment with the entire thirty degrees of the water signs—Cancer, Scorpio, and Pisces. This tells us that the dominant expression of these signs consists of the air and water elements.

Trinity Groups: The trinity is an outgrowth of reconciling the masculine and feminine faces of God. Dividing the circle into three parts or points reveals the power and meaning of three. The division of the circle or whole into three parts represents the beginning to trinities and all triangular relationships, such as father, mother, and child; conscious mind, creative mind, and manifestations; yang, yin, and the Tao; light, matter, and energy; and so forth. The division of each third of the circle by three gives us the basic meaning of three trinities—nine slices of the pie, nine points, and the nine enneagram signs and types. Among the nine points on the circle, G. I. Gurdjieff saw the first trinity as consisting of points one, four, and seven, which are associated with three affirming forces. The second trinity consists of points two, five, and eight, which are associated with three denying forces; and the third trinity consists of points three, six, and nine, which are associated with three reconciling forces.

When they are represented as stages of development, we have the beginning stage, comprised of signs one, two, and three; the middle stage, comprised of signs four, five, and six; and the ending stage, comprised of signs seven, eight, and nine. These groups represent recurring stages of the beginning, middle, and ending of the trinity forces. In addition, the beginning, middle, and ending signs can be understood as the personal, relational, and social or collective development stages respectively. The table given here presents trinities, forces, and stages of development common to all enneagram circles.

Trinity Forces and Stages

	Beginning	Middle	Ending
Affirming	1	4	7
Denying	2	5	8
Reconciling	3	6	9

Trinities are straightforward, easy to comprehend, and a central part of all enneagrams. As such, enneagrams can be understood as detailed versions of trinities because each portion of a given trinity contains a trinity within in it. For instance, a 9-year cycle contains three 3-year segments, each 3-year segment contains three 1-year segments, each 1-year segment contains three 4-month segments, etc.. In addition to the six trinity groups here, trinity arrangements of the whole are unlimited, creative, and inspiring.

For example, Russ Hudson and others describe a popular arrangement that consists of the body-centered types eight, nine, and one; the head-centered types five, six, and seven; and the heart-centered types two, three, and four. In their arrangement, the body-centered types are gut- and instinct-oriented individuals who feel life, operate in the here and now, and concern themselves with power and control. The head-centered types are intellect- and understanding-oriented individuals who seek silence and recognition of the eternal presence, and concern themselves with security and survival. The heart-centered types are identity- and passion-oriented individuals who need affection and esteem and concern themselves with the feelings and behaviors of others.

Enneagram Type and Sign Associations

Type or Stage	1	2	3	4
The Enneagram in Letters	**ajs**	**bkt**	**clu**	**dmv**
Trinity	Affirming	Denying	Reconciling	Affirming
Groups	1st Beginning	2nd Beginning	3rd Beginning	1st Middle
	Body-Centered	Heart-Centered	Heart-Centered	Heart-Centered
Enneagram Zodiac Signs	0° Aries to 10° Taurus	10° Taurus to 20° Gemini	20° Gemini through Cancer	0° Leo to 10° Virgo
Enneagram Sign Meanings	**Initiator**	**Guide**	**Contestant**	**Romantic**
	Enthusiastic	Communicators	Knowledgeable	Dramatic
	Practical	Tangible	Sensitive	Compulsive
Enneagram Sign Element Traits	**Fire**-Intuition **Earth**-Sensing	**Earth**-Sensing **Air**-Thinking	**Air**-Thinking **Water**-Feeling	**Fire**-Intuition **Earth**-Sensing
Enneagram Type Meanings	**Reformer**	**Helper**	**Achiever**	**Individualist**
	Perfectionist	Caregiver	Performer	Romantic
	Idealist	Supporter	Motivator	Artist
Enneagrams Based on Planets	**Mercury**	**Moon**	**Sun**	**Neptune**
	Association	Nurturing	Giving, Light	Inspiration
	The Word	Personality	Heart's Desire	Universal

Nine Cycles or Stages of Development

Enneagram Cycles	Reformers	Helpers	Achievers	Individualists
Initiations	Guides	Contestants	Romantics	
Nine-year Stages	Ages 0–9	Ages 9–18	Ages 18–27	Ages 27–36

Enneagram Types: In the beginning, the enneagram was not considered or taught as a type system. The creator of the enneagram, George Gurdjieff, a Sufi mystic, gives no source for the nature of its nines types; however, they are nearly identical to the symbolic meaning of the nine planets.

Enneagram Type and Sign Associations

5 enw	6 fox	7 gpy	8 hqz	9 ir
Denying	Reconciling	Affirming	Denying	Reconciling
2nd Middle	3rd Middle	1st Ending	2nd Ending	3rd Ending
Head-Centered	Head-Centered	Head-Centered	Body-Centered	Body-Centered
10° Virgo to 20° Libra	20° Libra through Scorpio	0° Sagittarius to 10° Capricorn	10° Capricorn to 20° Aquarius	20° Aquarius through Pisces
Innovator	**Skeptic**	**Seeker**	**Defender**	**Mediator**
Cerebral	Able	Hopefulness	Discipline	Knowing
Mediation	Dynamic	Regulation	Offbeat	Emotional
Earth-Sensing	**Air**-Thinking	**Fire**-Intuition	**Earth**-Sensing	**Air**-Thinking
Air-Thinking	**Water**-Feeling	**Earth**-Sensing	**Air**-Thinking	**Water**-Feeling
Investigator	**Loyalist**	**Enthusiast**	**Challenger**	**Peacemaker**
Observer	Devil's Advocate	Epicure	Protector	Mediator
Thinker	Questioner	Visionary	Boss	Pacifist
Uranus	**Saturn**	**Jupiter**	**Mars**	**Venus**
Inspiration	Teacher of Life	Wisdom	Aggression	Harmony
Revolution	Hardship	Expansion	Energy	Beauty

Nine Cycles or Stages of Development

Investigating Innovation Ages 36–45	Loyalty Skepticism Ages 45–54	Enthusiasm Seeking Ages 54–63	Challenges Defending Ages 63–72	Peacemaking Mediation Ages 72–81

The system is focused on the sacred geometry of the symbol. Over time, the enneagram morphed more and more into a psychospiritual tool.

The enneagram types are very useful for understanding oneself and others. Although all personality types represent general patterns, every individual is a unique variation within those patterns. The enneagram types are based on a person's historical preferences, which are determined by self-assessment surveys such as the one given by many online surveys and by those familiar with the enneagram types.

These types are commonly known as One, the Reformer, Perfectionist, and Idealist; Two, the Helper, Caregiver, and Supporter; Three, the Achiever, Performer, and Motivator; Four, the Individualist, Romantic, and Artist; Five, the Investigator, Observer, and Thinker; Six, the Loyalist, Devil's Advocate, and Questioner; Seven, the Enthusiast, Epicure, and Visionary; Eight, the Challenger, Protector, and Boss; and Nine, the Peacemaker, Mediator, and Pacifist. Understanding enneagram types and expanded ennead types as variations in meanings of the numbers one through nine will expand one's knowledge of the nine types and cycles or stages of development.

Type One — The Reformer is known as the perfectionist who is fixated on improvement and tends to think that nothing is ever quite good enough. They are idealistic and consistent and usually have high principles. They want to be right and to avoid being improper.

Type Two — The Helper values love, selflessness, and generosity, and they need to be needed. This type is interpersonal, compassionate, and friendly. They are caregivers, supporters, people oriented, and emotional and want to be loved and appreciated.

Type Three — The Achiever is confident and known for their focus on goals, success, and seeking validation. They are often self-starters, competitive, and role models who inspire others. They want to have worth, status, and admiration.

Type Four — The Individualist builds their identity from their view of themselves as being different or unique. They tend to be introspective, emotionally honest, and lovers of beauty. They are dreamers and want to find the meaning of mysteries.

Type Five — The Investigator is known for being detached, curious, intelligent, innovative, and able to see the world in an entirely new way. They often withdraw to contemplate and pursue understanding. They want to be knowledgeable and competent.

Type Six — The Loyalist is known for being warmhearted, likeable, trustworthy, and supported by others. They are often conflicted between trust and distrust; they don't trust others until they have proven themselves. They want security and certainty.

Type Seven — The Enthusiast is the habitual optimist, convinced that something better is just around the corner. They are seekers of knowledge, multitalented, enthusiastic, and happy-to-lucky. They want to be satisfied and pursue their plans and ideas.

Type Eight — The Challenger tends to be bossy, strong-willed, decisive, practical, and controlling. They identify with being aggressive, blunt, invincible, dominant, and confident leaders. They want power, control, and autonomy.

Type Nine — The Peacemaker is a good-natured, accepting personality who values wholeness and peace. They are easygoing and tend to avoid conflict at all costs, whether internal or interpersonal. They want harmony and stability.

The Enneagram Letters: The relationship between the letters of the alphabet and the enneagram signs is like the relationship between the earth and the sun. Just as the earth moves around the sun in nine stages, which can be represented by enneagram types, signs, and planets, so too can the letters A to Z. The enneagram-based zodiac signs and planets are at the center of all letters, words, forms of thought, measurement, explanation, analysis, growth, and existence. While planets and the numbers they represent remain in the background, they are always present as a source of power. In this work, the enneagram concept of signs and types is extended to the alphabet and one's name.

The relationship between enneagram letters as types and the three groups in which they appear (see table Enneagram Letter Groups) is like the relationships among stages within the development cycles. Just as the nine annual stages of enneagram signs are modified by each successive nine-year cycle, the enneagram letters are modified by each successive nine-year cycle. The enneagram types are modified by each successive group of nine letters.

Enneagram Letter Groups

	1	2	3	4	5	6	7	8	9
Cycle One	A	B	C	D	E	F	G	H	I
Cycle Two	J	K	L	M	N	O	P	Q	R
Cycle Three	S	T	U	V	W	X	Y	Z	

The first group or cycle of letters from A to I is followed by the second group or cycle from J to R, and the second row becomes the third group from S to Z. Instead of viewing the letters as a straight line from A to Z, they are viewed as three enneagram lettered cycles from one to nine. The trinity groups that apply to the enneagram types apply to the enneagram letters as well.

The first nine letters from A to I represent the first cycle of development in the alphabet. These letters are associated with being self-centered and geared toward the pursuit of one's personal goals. They are symbols of originality, youth, confidence, independence, expansion, and the masculine influence in the trinity that governs starting things and planning. Letters in this cycle function to create innovative ideas and thoughts that give birth to all life, which emerge from the womb letters, namely, J to R.

The second nine letters from J to R represent the second development cycle. They symbolize the growth of the individual in relation to the people personally related to them, such as significant partners, family, and extended family. The letters in this cycle are associated with relationships, cooperation, fixing things, healing, and the feminine face of the trinity whose yielding nature conquers the resistance and hardness of life. The letters in this cycle are known for being cooperative, warm, people oriented, pleasant, sympathetic, and more sociable than letters in the first group.

The letters from S to Z symbolize the third cycle of development. They are associated with the individual's integration into society. Here, the individual relates not only to the people they know but also to the social order itself, e.g., social causes, religious affiliations, political interests, and teaching others, which may not be experienced personally. The letters in this cycle are associated with the visible universe, which takes form from the formless. As the third or trinity cycle, the letters S to Z manifest the two letter cycles.

Enneagram System Features

There are two unique features in the traditional enneagram model that explain the relationships among the types. First, usually every type has characteristics of one or both types that lie adjacent to one's own that are prominent. For example, someone who is a type six might have a five wing or a seven wing. If one doesn't have a dominant wing, it is said that the wings are balanced. Although the origin of enneagram wings or subtypes remains a mystery, it makes sense that the types adjacent to one's own type have the same meaning and perhaps validity as the zodiac signs adjacent to one's own sun sign. For instance, someone who is a Leo might have a Cancer or Virgo wing. Second, every type has a type that tends to add stress and weakens its ability to be successful and a second type that tends to add security and strength to its ability to move forward.

The enneagram model seen here shows the unique connections between each numbered type and the types that represent its direction of integration and disintegration. Specifically, type one is stressed by four and strengthened by seven. Type two is stressed by eight and strengthened by four. Type three is stressed by nine and strengthened by six. Type four is stressed by two and strengthened by one. Type five is stressed by seven and strengthened by eight. Type six is stressed by three and strengthened by nine. Type seven is stressed by one and strengthened by five. Type eight is stressed by five and strengthened by two. Type nine is stressed by six and strengthened by three.

While the relationships among types is built into the enneagram model, these relationships do not apply to the enneagram signs and stages of development. Unlike the enneagram, enneagram cycles, like astrological cycles, have a fixed beginning and continue forever. The types and recurring cycles have the same basic meaning.

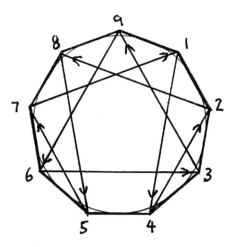

The Enneagram Typology

The enneagram types and Jung's psychological types are identified by many self-assessment tests and self-reflections that reveal a person's historical personality. These assessment tests define one's type can be found online with a simple Google search for "enneagram tests" or "psychological type tests." Even though enneagram signs and cycles, like astrology sun signs and transits, identify the potential indicated by one's birthday, these soul personalities are also connected to one's historical personality. The historical patterns that identify one's personality are based on personal preferences and experience and subject to change, but inherited potentials identified by birth date and birth names never change. The enneagram and psychological-type models measure personality based on how one has been, one's history, and an estimate of one's future personality. Astrology sun signs, like birth names, identify one's inherited personality potentials and the personality of one's authentic self.

The Signs and Cycles

Like the four natural seasons and twelve zodiac signs, the nine enneagram signs and stages represent the natural order of life on earth. They correspond to evolving psychological tendencies that are regulated by Earth's rotations around the sun. In addition, every year is a stage of life marked by the earth's return to the date of your birth. The stages, signs, and cycles are universal principles that represent natural changes of heart and have their own motivations, traits, and opportunities for growth.

As stages of growth, the sun-based enneagram signs can and do indicate elements in your life that produce the life-giving energy of advancement or the life-denying energy of giving up. They represent the unconscious manifesting into the conscious realm. The enneagram signs serve the purpose of first identifying and then completely discarding patterns that have blocked the way for your personal, social, and inner growth.

The enneagram signs and letters in one's name give meaning to the opportunities for learning and doing presented in every year of life starting from birth. The nine signs have universal meanings that are partly adopted from the twelve zodiac signs. Enneagram signs, like zodiac signs, represent and describe souls' personalities. When you ask someone, "What's your sign or type?" it's an interest in getting an insight into their inner nature. By knowing a person's birth date and name, you can get an inside look at their soul's personality and the life stage or lesson they are passing through. The enneagram sign and the letters in one's name are fixed lifetime personality symbols that move through ongoing life stages and cycles. While the enneagram sign and letters are given at birth, one's enneagram type is developed later and joins the birth sign in moving through the stages and cycles after it is established.

Throughout the span of life, every nine-year period is a life cycle, and every year within it is a one-year stage. There are nine one-year or foreground stages contained in the larger nine-year background cycles. The nine-year cycle tells where you're coming from—your foundation experience—and the annual stage tells how you should go about it— your persona or apparent experience. There are nine nine-year cycles over the eighty-one-year life span, and more can be added. The cycles and stages within them are universal and apply to everyone. They point to unexpected awakenings and will often challenge your ground of being. With every annual and nine-year period, you are a catalyst for change but not in control of the forces working through you to create them. Every birthday delivers messages from the soul on how the flow and status quo of your life should change so things don't crystallize into rigid patterns. The progression of recurring one-year stages represent signs of natural change and call us to reexamine our views as well as the views of others. You may experience what is revealed with the new stages of development as uncomfortable or the greatest thing since sliced bread.

Like a map or blueprint, the stages of development inherent in the enneagram signs offer guidelines and directions for one's life. They show where we are and where we will go. They show actions you can take to be aligned with your authentic self, soul, or cosmic order to receive the greatest opportunities and support. Over the life process from birth to death, the signs and types help us discover aspects of ourselves in the experience of living. The long- and short-term cycles, development stages, or seasons refer to your experience in life and pathway toward your destiny. They indicate the best way to seek your personal goals. In addition to showing your progress toward goals, projects, and new ideas, they bring an awareness of coming changes and experiences.

Unlimited possibilities are constantly open to every person at every age. Understanding your stages in life means to be awake and aware of what is at stake when moments of decision come in your life. The awareness and use of growth cycles leads to a fuller manifestation of your spiritual potential. The first step toward manifesting your potential is to live and work with the meaning associated with your age. One's individual development is rooted in the qualities of their birth sign and age. Understanding these qualities helps us express our authentic self—the spiritual qualities of the birthday and recurring life stages.

All life is dependent upon cycles of time, and everything has its own season. From birth to death is the cycle of life, with many smaller cycles in between. We are constantly changing with time; all is dynamic and shifting, and nothing is static. To move with the flow with life is to use the energy of time to its fullest and manifest our goals and desires accordingly.

The Ego and Soul Personality

Unlike the soul-centered enneagram sign, the enneagram type is determined by surveys that organize the historical attitudes, feelings, and behaviors that make up one's ego-centered personality. The enneagram sign, the letters in one's name, and the enneagram type are in collaboration and should be understood as a composite version of one's personality. The enneagram type represents a person's personality and their preferred and habitual ways of expressing themselves in the world as seen by others. In most cases, the enneagram type and sign are different but work in partnership with each other.

For instance, President Donald J. Trump's birthday, June 14, tells us that he was born under the third enneagram sign or the Contestant, while his enneagram type based on online opinions from experts is type eight or the Challenger. In President Trump's case, the Contestant part of his personality needs attention and achievement. This soul-centered side of the partnership is shared by his ego-centered Challenger side, which may or may not be an equal partner.

My enneagram type is five, the Investigator, and my birthday, May 25, falls in the second or Guide enneagram sign. In my case, my soul-centered Guide sign and interest in serving the emotional needs of others did not play a significant partnership role with my Investigator side until the beginning of my fourth development cycle at age twenty-seven. Over the course of this cycle, my Investigator side of teaching and working with technical subjects made lots of room for my latent interest in mysticism and psychic counseling, which has taken up most of my time until this day.

Cycles of Becoming

Cycles, phases, or stages of spiritual development point to new paths and the learning opportunities they represent. They call for sustained effort over the indicated time horizon to eliminate those elements that have become unnecessary and limiting, replacing them with superior constructs. The recurring annual stages or larger nine-year stages represent gradual and inconspicuous influences like spirit-animating living matter and causing objects to move while it itself is invisible. As already mentioned, the term cycle applies to the nine nine-year circular periods and the eighty-one-year life cycle. The term *stage* applies to one-year periods within a nine-year cycle. Stages and cycles are symbols of new growth that accumulates, expands, builds up, and reinforces itself in the process of your thinking and doing.

The table titled Life Stages and Cycles by Enneagram Sign shows the nine-year cycles and nine one-year stages in each nine-year period. The one-year stages are supported by the nine-year cycle, and they are experienced in ways that express distinct aspects of the nine-year cycle. As seen in the table, every age from zero to eighty-one is represented by a different numerical combination and describes a unique experience. The first column, titled Life Cycle, gives the first nine cycles numbered from 1-1 to 1-9 for ages zero to eighty-one. The next two recurring cycles numbered

2-1 and 2-2 represent the second eighty-one years of life from ages eighty-one and beyond. The years from eighty-one to ninety and beyond are an expanded version of the first eighty-one years in the cycle of life.

Life Stages and Cycles by Enneagram Sign

Life Cycle	Enneagram Sign & Role	Age Stage Range	One-Year Stages by Age								
			1s	2s	3s	4s	5s	6s	7s	8s	9s
1-1	*Initiation (1)*	0 to 9	0,	1,	2,	3,	4,	5,	6,	7,	8
1-2	*Guidance (1)*	9 to 18	9,	10,	11,	12,	13,	14,	15,	16,	17
1-3	*Contestant (1)*	18 to 27	18,	19,	20,	21,	22,	23,	24,	25,	26
1-4	*Romantic (1)*	27 to 36	27,	28,	29,	30,	31,	32,	33,	34,	35
1-5	*Innovation (1)*	36 to 45	36,	37,	38,	39,	40,	41,	42,	43,	44
1-6	*Skepticism (1)*	45 to 54	45,	46,	47,	48,	49,	50,	51,	52,	53
1-7	*Seeking (1)*	54 to 63	54,	55,	56,	57,	58,	59,	60,	61,	62
1-8	*Defending (1)*	63 to 72	63,	64,	65,	66,	67,	68,	69,	70,	71
1-9	*Mediation (1)*	72 to 81	72,	73,	74,	75,	76,	77,	78,	79,	80
2-1	*Initiation (2)*	81 to 90	81,	82,	83,	84,	85,	86,	87,	88,	89
2-2	*Guidance (2)*	90 to 99	90,	91,	92,	93,	94,	95,	96,	97,	98

The first cycle represents birth to the age of nine, the second cycle covers the period from age ten till age eighteen, and so forth. The meaning and experience of one's actual age is represented by the annual stage or one-year period within a nine-year cycle. For instance, the opportunities for learning and self-expression from age forty-two to forty-three are part of the fifth life cycle for innovation and specifically represented by the seventh one-year stage for seeking. This means that age forty-two is associated with universal opportunities to expand one's consciousness or education and view of life, in a significant way, in the journey through the midlife transition or investigation cycle (ages thirty-six to forty-five). This comes about because the seventh one-year stage represents an interest in expanding one's consciousness or education, collecting and analyzing information as a built-in component of all nine-year cycles. The opportunity presented by the seven-five combination of stage and cycle is to lay the groundwork for greater knowledge about the transition from the first to the second half of life.

Over the millennium, the human attributes of single-digit numbers have been of great interest. As discussed in the last two chapters, numbers are symbols that describe our inner and outer universe, the soul and personality. They bring the identity of individuals and universal laws or principles into consciousness. The life stages and enneagram signs, along with types numbered from one to nine, convey a great deal of knowledge and continue to play a significant role in all disciplines of study that seek to understand the human soul. These disciplines include new areas of science, philosophy, depth psychology, the occult, and spirituality.

6

Sign, Type, and Stage Traits

*It is impossible to study individuals without
studying the universe.*

— P. D. Ouspensky

Although the symbolic meanings for the enneagram signs, types, letters, or development stages are open-ended, the descriptions that follow tell us a great deal about the personalities and corresponding life stages they represent. As you will see, they all imply life lessons or principles to be learned. Like a sword, all types and stages of development have positive and negative attributes. It depends upon what is operating with it and whether the individual has a positive or negative attitude. While your answers to the checklist items in the last chapter will not line up exactly with the descriptions of cycle characteristics in this chapter, these descriptions will help you expand your recall, study, and organize what took place in your past nine-year periods of development and the growth that awaits you as well.

The descriptions given here represent the meanings shared by enneagram signs, types, letters, and development. These descriptions are based on the origins of personality type numbers as summarized in the table titled Enneagram Type and Sign Associations, which appears in chapter 5. The enneagram sign is based on one's date of birth and never changes. The birth date is the unchanging reference point for one's life and indicates one's potential for self-expression—the soul's personality, cosmic purpose, and destiny. The enneagram sign is permanent, and the recurrent stages of development that follow are represented by the same descriptions. The signs and cycles are intended to reveal the "big picture" of cosmos-centered divine guidance. Unlike the recurring cyclic changes, one's birth date and year is nonrecurring and never returns.

The first year of life represents the first stage, age one represents the second stage, age two represents the third stage, and so forth throughout the first nine-year cycle. The second nine-year cycle represents ages nine to eighteen and so forth. As seen in the table titled Life Stages and Cycles by Enneagram Sign, which appears in chapter 5, the nine annual stages recur every nine years.

The enneagram signs and cycles are based on the date and time of birth and reveal a person's potential or soul personality. They are indicators of one's unique slice of time, beginning, and future. Enneagram types are almost always constant, but depending on one's experience in life, they may change. While enneagram types are identified by self-assessment tests and self-reflection to find an individual's personality based on their patterns of behavior and historical preferences beyond childhood, enneagram signs are inherited at birth and never change. The enneagram sign is a symbol of the soul's personality, and the enneagram type is a diagram of the ego or human personality. One's enneagram type, enneagram sign, and cycles of development and even the letters in one's name are always in relationship. The descriptions that follow identify what the enneagram signs, types, cycles of development, and letters have in common.

The relationships among the enneagram signs, cycles, and letters of the alphabet are like the relationship between the earth and the sun. Just as the earth moves around the sun in nine stages, which can be represented by enneagram types, signs, and planets, so too can the letters from A to Z. The enneagram-based zodiac signs and planets are at the center of all letters, words, forms of thought, measurement, explanation, analysis, growth, and existence. While planets and the enneagram types they represent remain in the background, they are always present as a source of power.

As discussed in chapter 5, the enneagram concept of signs and types extends to the letters in one's name. The first cycle of letters from A to I is followed by the second cycle from J to R and the third cycle from S to Z. Instead of viewing the letters as a straight line from A to Z, they are viewed as three stages of letters from one to nine. The enneagram letter groups consisting of three cycles of letters contain stages or types one through nine—AJS, BKT, CLU, DMV, ENW, FOX, GPY, HQZ, and IR.

The first nine letters from A to I represent the first development cycle in the alphabet. These letters represent youth, confidence, independence, and function to create innovative ideas and thoughts that give birth to all life, which emerges from the womb letters, namely, J to R. The second nine letters from J to R represent the second development cycle. The letters in this cycle are more sociable than those in the first group, people oriented, and cooperative and symbolize individual growth in relation to the people personally related to them. The letters from S to Z symbolize the third cycle of development. They are associated with the individual's integration into the social order, which includes social causes, religious affiliations, political interests, and teaching others in ways that may not be experienced personally.

Sign, Type, and Stage 1

Initiator and Reformer
First Cycle Ages: 0 to 9

Traits: Enthusiasm; independence; practicality; reform-oriented; principled; idealistic; desire to explore new directions, innovative ideas, and new concepts. People in this group want to explain things and share information with others. Those represented by this group are known for being intelligent and analytical, needing to be perfect, and having exacting standards for themselves and others. They display a steamroller approach to getting things done.

Ages for Stage One: *Birth year, 9, 18, 27, 36, 45, 54, 63, 72, and 81.*

Individual development, which includes the development of one's self-concept, identity, perspective on things, and defining who one is, is central to the experience of sign and type one. The Initiator and Reformer types identify with newness, creation, and the beginning of all manifestation. They often have a difficult time acknowledging others as distinct or separate and assume that others are much the same way. Among the nine types, ones take the special place of representing new directions and innovative ways of doing things. They are driven by new energy, inspiration, new ideas, initiative, and the enthusiasm to create and produce something new. One personalities tend to be energetic, persistent, and confident. They represent the urge to keep on going until something solid gets done. They are often still going when the rest of the world has fallen by the wayside.

One is the Initiator and Reformer whose goal is to make the unconscious conscious, bring heaven to earth, and serve as messenger of the gods. They are interested in various aspects of writing, speaking, learning, commerce, and message giving and are associated with the beginning of understanding. They believe that beginnings come into manifestation through the word or Logos, and without words, nothing is created. Advanced individuals of this type are the transmitters of spiritual understanding and called enlightened individuals. They always look for new ways to improve things and overcome the gap that exists between separate entities. Ones derive their motivation from within and represent the whole. They have a difficult time acknowledging others as distinct or separate and naturally assume that others are much the same way. In this sense, Ones represent focus, single-mindedness, action, and self-projection.

Initiators and Reformers progress through experimentation, and they recognize that all knowing, thinking, experiencing, sensing, believing, or disbelieving is done through signs and symbols that represent facts, experiences, or entities in the mind. Their chief motive is to translate ideas and signs and to create maps of reality for thinking and dreaming and ways to experience things directly. They often play the role of mediators who bring together the unmanifested or invisible parts of the universe and the manifest visible parts. Since consciousness and wisdom are different from intelligence, individuals of this type, like others, may be relatively low in intelligence and still wise. They understand that all knowledge, wisdom, perception, and communication come from conscious awareness. They want to adopt techniques and use knowledge and skill to function in an effective manner.

The first type is motivated to bring clarity to the unseen and unknown happenings in the universe into conscious awareness and hence manifestation. As a personality type, they have high standards in the sense that they look for exactness in communications and the things they support. Because of their excessive concern for details, they are often called nitpickers and perfectionists and replace actual experience with these concerns. They have analytical minds and great practical reasoning abilities. They are interested in ideas that have practical application for financial success and status. Ones are down-to-earth and insist on precision and accuracy at a level that can be trivial to others.

Important lessons of this sign and type are becoming aware of others and that the experience of life does not unfold all at once. Without this awareness, their forceful convictions will become a barrier in their relationships with others. Among the positive attributes of sign one are energy, focus, youthfulness, optimism, uniqueness, creativity, quick-mindedness, ambition, enthusiasm, and intuition. Negative attributes include passivity, narrow-mindedness, arrogance, intolerance, dependence on others, and being overly dominant, aggressive, conceited, and weak-willed.

As the first complete stage of any cycle, the experience of the first sign is associated with youthfulness, independence, and mediation between the conscious and unconscious realms. Since the head is the first part of anything to move into existence or take a new course or make a new change, type one's experience is associated with new intentions, new observations, new understanding, and communicating their ideas. Moving through this stage and cycle tends to indicate openings for sharing ideas. This period often points to having creative thoughts and attracting opportunities and increased recognition from others.

In the nine-year period of early childhood, the body and basic personality structures for the future are built. The substance that will fill these structures is furnished by the physical and nonphysical conditions you were born into. Everything that happens at this organic level of development will leave its mark. In this period, children learn to feed and dress themselves, walk, talk, read, write, and do simple arithmetic. They also learn the specific dangers of their environment and the things necessary for survival, including lying, cheating, and stealing. In this period, their basic values and beliefs are instilled. This phase gives a child his or her characteristic attitude toward life.

The beginnings associated with the first sign are not immediately clear in the first two or three nine-year cycles, even though some definite events may set the stage for it. For instance, in the first third of life, the theme of one-year stages is often elusive, uncertain in character, and filled with emotional confusion. Beyond the first third, Ones are more defined by the characteristics of the Initiator and Reformer archetype. Here, the substance that fills the tangible and intangible structures for future years is furnished by what you inherited and what happened in the preceding year. New values and beliefs take root in this year.

Sign, Type, and Stage 2

Guide and Helper
Second Cycle Ages: 9 to 18

Traits: Communicators; caregivers; sensitive; tolerant; charming. Those represented by this group are relationship oriented and people pleasers who also need love and a sense of belonging. They are friendly, emotional, and understanding. Those in this group are flexible, aware of oppositions and boundaries, and need to be needed. They want intimacy, appreciation, and connections with others. They display receptiveness and wisdom.

Applicable Ages: *9 to 19, 28, 37, 44, 46, 64, 73, and 82.*

Even though they are somewhat shy and evasive, the Guides and Helpers are often pulled into diverse types of public activity. They tend to attract people, understand how to relate to others, and have the feelings and emotional energy that connects with and serves all life. Their purpose is providing service, the highest good that life can offer, and giving form to life. They express the feminine principle that brings balance to the expression of the masculine principle of the first type. Like the first sign and type, they pursue individual development, which includes the expansion of one's self-concept and identity and defining who one is. The difference is that the experience of Two is about the middle or midstage of the beginning, while one is about the beginning of the beginning. The second sign, type, and stage is about the need to form personal relationships and cooperative partnerships.

They look for ways to cooperate with others and resolve conflicts. Two individuals are inclined to be passive and patient and allow events to proceed without intervention. Although they are inclined to run away from difficult situations, they deal with them when necessary by being receptive to guidance and new ideas or insights that lead to spiritual solutions. The people of this type often experience promising new opportunities and the urge to express themselves in creative ways. They are often seen as the gifted young person who is still under the care and need of guidance from elders.

While the first sign and type is independent, the Guide and Helper seeks out others, as if to mirror their own internal struggles. Those who have not mastered the energy of oppositions become apparent victims of the conditions and people around them. They will give any amount of help if they can see the need for it. Many are organized enough to have good self-restraint and set realistic limits on how they think about things. Their understanding nature contributes to their talent for addressing obstacles, problems, and solutions to resolve them.

Twos value maternal love more than romantic love and demand ownership of affection to satisfy their emotional insecurity. They need to feel wanted and closely connected to others. They cannot be happy without a meaningful home life. They have a fondness for comfort and ease, and the home is their center of interest and activity. Because they are attached to people and things from the past and inclined to follow tradition, their feelings tend to interfere with the development of their creative self-expression. They have great sensitivity to the moods and feelings of others and often imagine slights when none are intended. They understand that letting go can be the release of destruction or a relaxed way of allowing things to be. They usually have a personal stand against the limitations imposed by others. They can assert their feelings to create situations willfully to test how their family and peers will react.

A major lesson of the second sign and type is learning to play the roles of diplomat, peacemaker, and counselor. Growth for these individuals is tied to understanding their relationship to the universe and overcoming the tendency to worry about what others may say or think. The positive traits associated with these individuals include cooperation, teamwork, balanced judgments, kindness, humility, charm, sensitivity, flexibility, and spiritual understanding. The negative side includes indifference, instability, not taking responsibility, fear of the unknown, pessimism, being weak-willed, conflict, and indecision.

The second nine-year cycle from age nine to eighteen influences not only the biological growth of the young person over the next few years but also their basic instincts and the basic psychological overtones to these instincts. These events produce either opportunities for harmonious growth or frustrating tensions. This change or phase of growth in the personality is the psychological equivalent to a new set of teeth. In this period, the "young person's" personal existence truly begins, and they reveal an increasingly individual response to life. They also learn social responsibility and pursue additional education.

The second cycle represents opportunities to make choices to step into something new, bring one's life into balance with the greater good, serve others, take a risk, or embrace an unknown. This period points to partnerships, communication, and exchanges with others that may be both harmonious and discordant. It signifies the need for social learning and to make choices between dualities, such as holding on/letting go, positive/negative, and either/or. The second period reflects the quiet power of observation and judgment about human nature, and those represented by this cycle or stage often learn to see issues in different ways. Those moving through this cycle have a broader perspective than ones because they have completed cycle one and have a more realistic ideal of what is possible.

Sign, Type, and Stage 3

Contestant and Achiever
Third Cycle Ages: 18 to 27

Traits: Sociable; warm; smooth talking; knowledgeable. These people display the qualities of achievers, performers, motivators, and go-getters. Those represented by this group are image conscious and driven, want to have worth, status, applause, and need to succeed. They seek admiration from others and to be the center and source of attention. They want to be first, create harmony, growth, and expansion and express themselves.

Applicable Ages: *2, 11, 18 to 27, 29, 38, 47, 56, 65, 74, and 83.*

The Contestant and Achiever has plans, hopes, and ideas that pave the way for things to come into existence and grow. Three is associated with a person's self-concept, identity, perspective, and understanding of who they are. Three is represented by the trinity, good luck, status, enthusiasm, psychological comfort, and the easy flow of energy into established channels of expression. Examples of the third group are apparent when individuals move in a new direction, expand their awareness, or create something new. The advanced expressions of threes are self-development, material, spiritual growth, and pursuing goals that support the greater good.

They are the most playful of all signs and types and can be entertaining and sociable. They have a built-in urge to inspire and beautify the world. They are associated with growth and expansion on all levels—physical, emotional, mental, and spiritual. Because they rely on admiration from others rather than their own beliefs about themselves, they can be their own worst enemy. They are known for their warmth, creative talent, and urge to accept others, themselves, and situations. They have an aspiring nature, which generally results in the appearance of success. The more aggressive individuals in this group employ their powers of persuasion without any qualms to get their way, even though others might be hurt in the process. These people are intelligent, humorous, and sociable and tend to control those around them. They are anxious to gain public favor and often attain success in the world without a great deal of effort on their part.

These individuals are often creative in the ways of business and the arts. They work to express who they are and seek to make an impact in terms of their own identity. They prefer to be in the forefront of any activity where they can be recognized and dislike working behind the scenes. Self-expression is the major goal of this sign and type, and the more perfectly they can be themselves and accepted as such, the better off they are. They are not especially modest and can make others notice them by their demeanor. They may even be boastful, arrogant, and totally wrapped up in themselves. They often overestimate their own worth, not feeling it necessary to do anything to justify their high self-opinion. Individuals of this type enjoy being the center of attention and must have the spotlight, and once in it, they want to shine.

Individuals of this sign and type tend to have strong attachments to their family and establish themselves in society through a personalized environment. They want people to think well of them, and because they direct a great deal of energy toward this goal, it is frequently achieved. They tend to be very aware of the effect they have on others and study what to do to create a better effect. They can give emotional depth to their ideas and, at the same time, have a degree of detachment from their feelings. They often exhibit maturity in handling human relationships and a talent for organizing facts and ideas about the depths within human nature.

Contestant and Achiever people are often identified by their personal power and leadership ability. They tend to have dramatic and flamboyant personalities and express their emotions as a way of gaining social recognition. They often take significant risks because of their almost blind self-confidence. They project themselves in the most dramatic way possible, searching for pleasure and romance with others. While they have sunny and happy dispositions and attract many friends, at times they seem to be naively childish and egocentric. They are often seen as the gifted young person who is still under the care and need of guidance from elders. On the positive side, Threes are linked to optimism, generosity, positive thinking, success, communication of all kinds, charisma, having talent, and youthfulness. On the negative side, they are known for their extravagance, hypocrisy, impatience, moodiness, disorganization, and being irresponsible, cynical, and undisciplined.

The third cycle is associated with new opportunities and the urge to express oneself in creative ways. The theme of the nine-year Contestant cycle from age eighteen to twenty-seven is the development of will and creative self-expression. Love relationships almost always become the great revealer in this cycle. When their ideal image is projected onto a real person, the experience of the difference forces them to modify their illusions. In this cycle, the young person grows out of adolescent attitudes and relationships to family or whatever may have substituted for family. At the same time, they think about organizing their life, training themselves for a job, and starting to build their own families.

In the third cycle, people make efforts to improve their life in tangible and intangible ways, such as choosing to change their direction in life, moving to a better location, and carrying most of the load to keep things upbeat and balanced. They usually learn what they can and can't do and should and shouldn't do by contrasts. In the third cycle, personal and social relationships often become the mirror image of the self and its needs. The hopes and goals from before this period should be examined in a new light and adopted to the realities of day-to-day existence.

Sign, Type, and Stage 4

Romantic and Individualist
Fourth Cycle Ages: 27 to 36

Traits: Dramatic; compulsive; popular; artistic; ideal-seekers and dreamers. Those represented by this group are independent of culture and environment and often seen as weird and way out and need to be special. They are naturally psychic, have a deep interest in the transcendent, and believe that life is spiritual. They tend to have deeper and more profound interpersonal relations. These people are philosophical and usually sensitive and self-aware.

Applicable Ages: *3, 12, 21, 27 to 36, 39, 48, 57, 66, 75, and 84.*

The Romantics and Individualists are keenly attuned to the feelings of those around them. They represent the subtle and illusive energy in the universe. They are usually dignified, benevolent, and warm-hearted and have intuitive foresight and the ability to interpret human feelings. They want to explain and give form to their dreams, visions, ideas, blueprints, and designs. This sign is associated with aspects of the universe that are unclear, illusory, ill-defined, imaginary, and often difficult to understand.

Those of this sign and type are associated with seriousness, mastery, high morals, conventional values, honesty, and ongoing education and development. They often love for the sake of shedding light and demand no external rewards for the humanitarian services that they perform. Many who have not learned to respond to multisensory qualities, such as psychic visions and mystical inspirations, are inclined to be unrealistic dreamers. They are often escapists, artists, or creative people who dislike physical work and feel constrained by physical work and established rules. More than other signs and types, they are open to both the temptations of the lower nature and the glories of their transcendent spiritual nature.

While people of this sign and type have a strong possibility of delusion and self-deception, of becoming a victim of their fantasies or a follower of a false teacher, they also have the potential for expressing a great imagination, musical, or a poetic or spiritual inspiration. They often pay attention to the subtler aspects of life, including their own inner life, ideals, and values. Because they are sensitive emotionally, they often have sudden ups and downs. They often live a life of extremes, from being bold and loud to being silent and secretive.

Romantics and Individualists often provide the inspiration needed for things to be brought into the physical world. Many of these individuals have either not yet developed a reality system or have just transcended one. They are usually loveable, sympathetic, and comfortable to be with if you just want to relax. They have exaggerated imaginations and don't like to be specific about anything. The Individualist types are often interested in psychic phenomena, see visions, and look for signs. Those who do not understand basic metaphysical principles and meditation are likely to turn to drugs or alcohol to shut out these unusual feelings. The unlimited possibilities associated with this type are difficult for most people because to be successful in the mundane universe, they must deal effectively with dualities and concrete realities.

Many people of this type are charismatic and want to bring together the unconscious, invisible realm of the universe and the conscious, visible realm. Because they have a lack of ego emphasis, they are often attracted to social service—taking care of the physically or mentally ill or others who need to be looked after. By serving others in a practical manner, these individuals gain a concrete meaning of life. Their artistic temperament is expressed through their ability to touch the heart and inspire emotional responses in others. They are sympathetic and open to others, and their emotionality is vast and extensive. They also have the urge to reach out to help and serve the weak and helpless.

Depending upon one's level of spiritual development, individuals of this type experience the most beautiful and painful of human emotions. Perhaps because personal systems of reality, personal ideas of right and wrong, are subordinate to the type-four reality of "what is," many fours have a lack of confidence in themselves. This can be a great source of difficulty in their relationships because relationships require a clear idea of one's own personality.

In the nine-year cycle from age twenty-seven to thirty-six, young adults organize and build their life the way they want, and this foundation remains in place throughout their lifetime. In this cycle, the door is opened for individuals to make gains in manifest in their unique destiny. An important part of this cycle is making choices about one's personal or social relationships. There is often a desire to establish something new and of value within one's community. In this period, people make use of their gifts to serve a consciously decided purpose instead of being simply an expression of their gifts. Despite the difficulties and perhaps inadequate means for realization, there is a deep sense that one should go on, even if motivated only by emotion or irrational enthusiasm.

In this cycle, people organize and rebuild their lives. They often experience deeper and more profound interpersonal relations with others. They are presented with the opportunity to begin asserting their true individuality and making their contribution to the world. An important part of this cycle is making a significant personal or social choice. Despite real or potential difficulties, there is a deep sense that one has to keep trying, even if their goal is not totally clear. Those in the fourth cycle usually begin to experience life as being spiritual and come to enjoy life despite pain, sorrow, and disappointment. They often demonstrate more self-sacrifice, kindness, and sympathy.

Sign, Type, and Stage 5

Innovator and Investigator
Fifth Cycle Ages: 36 to 45

Traits: Cerebral; practical; calculating; fussy; observers and thinkers; levelheaded; reclusive; studious; amiable. People in this group need to perceive, are less emotional and more objective, and have few self-conflicts. They are creative, spontaneous, and usually committed to something greater than themselves. They are intuitive and have an efficient perception of reality. They enjoy life despite pain, sorrow, and disappointment.

Applicable Ages: *4, 13, 22, 31, 36 to 45, 49, 58, 67, 76, and 85.*

Innovators and Investigators are creative, spontaneous, and committed to something greater than themselves. They are often engaged in equal-sided tugs-of-war between the past and the future and the need to integrate the two sides into something new. They often seek help in releasing the old and embracing the new by turning to well-known sources such as school, churches, and social organizations. In general, their success in making changes comes from moving beyond the tried and true, the known and established. More than other signs and types, they have opportunities to evaluate where things stand based on the past and what can be realistically achieved in the future. They are often multitalented and diverse in the depth of their understanding.

In most cases, they can guide others and combine disparate elements into a cohesive whole.

The fifth sign and type is often attracted to social service and those who need to be looked after. They are motivated to bring darkness into the light of day and expose the hidden. They have a talent for organizing facts and ideas about the depths within human nature. Most of their actions and plans are accompanied by insights into the hidden side of things. Many have an interest in learning how thing work, counseling, and teaching others about the human soul through disciplines such as religion, spirituality, science, and philosophy.

The Innovator and Investigator is often the bohemian individual and member of groups who enjoys experimenting with things that seem strange and outside the established order. They are thinkers who embody the sixth sense and are associated with innovative ideas, inventions, and social doctrines. These individuals are extremely independent, self-willed, and reluctant to be dominated or controlled by external rules and regulations. They are often idealistic, revolutionary by nature, and work for the improvement of humanity. Many are known for being self-actualizers who are driven to break out of patterns that have become too rigid, even though they may wish to stay within them.

People in this in this group are less emotional, more objective, detached, rarely wedded to the status quo, and motivated to continue growing. They like adventure and have a willingness to sacrifice security to explore transcendent and new worlds. While they are often ready to experience anything and give up anything, this inclination is a source of difficulty when they ignore individual concerns. Many of this sign and type have little concern for individuals yet great interest in the revolutionary change with which they have identified. Because they can be insensitive and unfeeling in their pursuit of right, they are not especially warm or emotional.

Fives develop creative plans on how to proceed based on a blending of intuitive insights, practicality, the wisdom of feelings, rational nature, and new things. They have an ability to find the links between the conscious and unconscious aspects of the mind. They can give emotional depth to their ideas and, at the same time, have a high degree of detachment from their feelings. While they do not follow traditional canons of logic or reason, they do operate in ways that reason can relate to. Despite being radical or social reformers who do not need to be tied to society, they always need a group with which to identify.

On the positive side, Five is focused on attaining greater stability, making commitments, and doing the right thing. Additional positives include sympathy and understanding, adaptability, curiosity, learning by doing, and imagination. The weak or negative side is associated with being immature, narrow-minded, irresponsible, inconsistent, and noncommittal, monotony, and going against the status quo. Additional negatives include being impulsive, restless, unpredictable, and erratic.

The fifth cycle from age thirty-six to forty-five is associated with self-determination and being self-sustained and aware of one's individual destiny. The midpoint of this cycle takes place from age forty to forty-one. This nine-year period brings opportunities for self-awareness in general and the symbolic midpoint in the life cycle where the past comes face-to-face with the future. Those in this cycle often experience freedom and change, but many have a tough time settling down and dealing with their fears of the unknown. Before those in this period can go on to meet their life's destiny, they must be willing to let go of external influences and consciously choose their reaction to life. If those in this cycle remain bound by another person, such as a parent or marriage partner, a group or ideology, they will have something outside themselves determining their actions and assuming responsibility for them. While this period brings new learning, it also brings struggle and conflict.

The theme of the fifth cycle is overcoming the pull of the past or a fruitless return to the past. One or more major choices—conscious or unconscious, personal or social—get made or seemingly forced upon the person by circumstances. They often adopt new and independent attitudes toward others in their personal and social life. If those in this stage remain bound by the opinions of others, they will have something outside themselves determining their actions and assuming responsibility for them.

Sign, Type, and Stage 6

Skeptic and Loyalist
Sixth Cycle Ages: 45 to 54

Traits: Able; practical; responsible; unhurried. They want safety, asylum, and stability and to live near family and friends. The people in this group tend to be pessimistic, loyal, charming, warm, seductive, and shrewd. They are known for being problem-solvers, questioners, devil's advocates, and agnostics. They are careful and steady and value tradition and predictable environments. They need structure, order, and security.

Applicable Ages: *5, 14, 23, 32, 41, 45 to 54, 59, 68, 77, and 86.*

The lessons for Skeptics and Loyalists are how to look beyond surface appearances, how to manifest things, and how to make life successful. They are associated with law and order and everything that contains or puts a limit to growth. They are known for their stability and tendency to be cautious. While they are responsible and committed to those close to them, they are difficult to understand because of their reserved exterior and secretiveness. Because the people in this group are the glue that keeps a relationship, family, or community together, they are trustworthy and have a keen sense of loyalty. The older they get, the more secure they become, and their relations with others usually become better over time. This is one of the safest types when it comes to a faithful partner.

People of this sign and type attract friends upon whom they can depend to guide them safely. They accept responsibilities with serious emotional intensity and harbor deep resentments when they feel they have been dealt with unjustly. They tend to be thorough, persistent, determined to achieve their goals, and almost fanatic in their adherence to principle. They understand that it takes time to learn the deepest, hardest, and most important wisdom of life. The lessons of Sixes are difficult because their quest to be successful in the material world cannot occur until they learn that before things can be built, there must be a design and a plan for how to build them.

Many of this sign and type are associated with negative energy, complaining, and vindictiveness. These individuals are often overly emotional because they rigidly defend their sensitive feeling from the threat of the outer world. They often encounter emotional problems that bring pain and suffering until they learn to master and control their tendency to be unforgiving when hurt. A good match for this type is someone who can share optimistic ideas with them. As they learn when and how to let go of resentments, they gain greater emotional stability in life. While they adore family and often grow more sentimental with time, they are aware that conflict and struggle are part of keeping things together.

They have a talent for troubleshooting, detective work, and criticism. Their intellect tends to be highly developed, and they often raise questions and doubts that rub others the wrong way. They look for commitment and diligence in their plans and associations with friends and partners. Because they combine their mental and emotional nature, they can give emotional depth to their ideas and can gain detachment and perspective on their feelings and deep yearnings. Despite their appearance of being cool, they can be charming, warm, practical, and mature in human relationships.

Individuals of this sign and type are devil's advocates, often agnostic, and known to be doubters or skeptics. In most cases, they go about their business without advertising themselves or their achievements. They tend to find a balance between giving comfort to and helping others when needed and getting what they need for their security. Despite being hard workers, their personal lives are usually more important than the work they do, which they often see as mainly a means to an end. Their positive attributes include trustworthiness, stability, being protective and supportive, and taking responsibility for choices. They derive joy from supporting others and often demonstrate great maturity in handling human relationships. Their less developed side includes being pessimistic, fearful of success, easily stressed, shallow, unsupportive, unaware, dishonest, and weak-willed. The weaker side is also linked to confusion and unhappiness with the conditions of their lives.

The sixth cycle from age forty-five to fifty-four are motivated to maintain an existing relationship or replace it if one needs to make a fresh start. For instance, a marriage held together for the sake of the children may dissolve when the kids grow up and leave the home. Likewise, relationships initially formed because they would advance one's career or social position can become meaningless as those career goals are replaced. Many in this cycle try to prolong youth, and some even reject association with those older than themselves as though aging were a contagious disease. As they watch their parents age and die off and their generation aging, suddenly there comes the realization that they are the elder generation. Over the course of this cycle, individuals notice that their bodies are increasingly losing energy and staying power. As they become aware of aging, many also become aware of their duty to devote serious attention to the emerging inner world.

The sixth cycle is also associated with significant new relationships or a deep relationship with someone whom you already know and are already close to. The people in this cycle are often in or headed toward a lasting relationship worth developing and committing to. They usually have an opportunity to create greater stability, harmony, and balance in their relationships and the groups in which they belong.

Sign, Type, and Stage 7

Seeker and Enthusiast
Seventh Cycle Ages: 54 to 63

Traits: Hopeful; optimistic; seekers of pleasure and excitement. Those represented by this group want fame, recognition, status, and strife to be competent. They are lifelong students and love the challenge of solving problems. They love philosophy, expanding boundaries, seeing the big picture, and creating new knowledge. Those in this group are visionary, first do something, and need to discover innovative ways of doing things.

Applicable Ages: *6, 15, 24, 33, 42, 51, 54 to 63, 69, 78, and 87.*

Most Seekers and Enthusiasts are idealists who are never satisfied with life as it is and want to move on to new experiences. They have an ardent desire to be free to experience life in their own way. Many want to accumulate things and become more important than anyone, grander, and more arrogant. This sign and type can also be wasteful, irresponsible, and extravagant in their generosity While they are unconventional, free, and self-righteous in their youth, they are likely to settle down in time and identify with the larger established order. They understand that you can't make things such as a good career, relationship, life, and so forth until you know what is required to make them.

Many sevens are introspective and have a grand vision of life and the ideas and standards that govern societies. In a word, the phrase "walk softly but carry a big stick," made popular by Teddy Roosevelt, describes the nature of this type. They are inspired to overcome opposition through polite, soft-spoken confidence and control. Personalities of the seventh sign and type rely on their intuition and sensing rather than accepting advice from others. They move through situations in life by determination, self-discipline, and hard work. An important attribute of this type is that it represents the ability to focus completely on the tasks at hand to attain goals.

Seekers and Enthusiasts are passionate about learning from teachers and other sources who have wisdom. Their goal in life is learning, growing, and exploring the universe of knowledge beyond the boundaries of their environment. They are associated with self-exploration and the development of one's higher mental attributes. While ones teach individuals how to communicate with one another, sevens teach us how to communicate with God. They believe in and promote the use of divine laws on Earth. They often expand their understanding of human life through philosophy and become conscious of their spiritual nature. They reach out to people to incorporate as much of the external world as possible into themselves to grow both physically and psychologically. This sign and type has a strong love of religion and philosophy as both a consciousness-expanding system and a system for giving them a relationship with the universe.

The more developed individuals of this sign and type seek to acquire as much education as possible, make good teachers, and often associate themselves with institutions of higher learning. Their desire to make personal conduct conform to an impersonal set of moral principles brings them the respect and admiration of others, including their enemies. They tend to have far-reaching thoughts and interests in the knowing about the nature of consciousness and how it can be applied to successfully benefit society. They have a deep interest in the social and philosophical ideas that have shaped history. They look for ways to connect with the transcendent and tend to be motivated to study the human soul through disciplines such as science, philosophy, depth psychology, and the occult. For this reason, they are often referred to as the wisdom- and truth-seeking personalities.

The positive attributes associated with this sign and type include focus, knowledge, logic, introspection, spirituality, persistence of purpose, quick-wittedness, and deep contemplation. The negative side includes being pessimistic, emotionally closed, socially awkward, distant, depressed, self-righteous, aloof, and difficult to get to know and having hidden motives and suspicions.

The nine-year cycle from age fifty-four to sixty-three is associated with acquiring wisdom, seeing oneself in innovative ways, meeting others in new people, embarking on a new kind of social participation, and adopting new spiritual activities. Since the time of ancient Greece, age sixty has been the age of philosophy in the sense of a search for essential meaning and basic values. People would not grow to be seventy years old and beyond if this longevity had no meaning for the species. In this cycle, individuals often discover the best ways to present who they are to fulfill some basic collective need of the times. Many of the people who experience this period find that their mental capacity becomes stronger. They often work at discarding what is nonessential and then record for the coming generations the harvest of their experience.

This nine-year period also marks the beginning of a person's mission to complete things by finding and communicating universal truths about the universe. Individuals in the seventh cycle are propelled into the world of unknowns, so they are constantly searching for answers. This often results in developing new philosophies or perspectives to sustain them in their pursuits. This period is also associated with opportunities for personal growth because it brings to light many beliefs, attitudes, and perceptions that are simply not true. The more those in this cycle live their lives differently from the average, routine existence imposed by modern society, the more likely this year will be positive.

Sign, Type, and Stage 8

Defender and Challenger
Eighth Cycle Age: 63 to 72

Traits: Independent; innovative; action-oriented; dreamers with reformist tendencies. These people tend to be defenders, protectors, and able to meet material needs for themselves, family, and other dependents. They pursue unusual or unorthodox courses of action. Those in this group avoid teamwork and authoritarian direction and need to be against them. They are known for their high intelligence, organizing ability, and discipline.

Applicable Ages: *7, 16, 25, 34, 43, 52, 61, 63 to 72, 79, and 88.*

Defenders and Challengers can and do pursue solutions to significant problems. More than Defenders, Challengers are like the boss with a powerful drive to succeed and rise above adversity. They are concerned with their social status and reputation, like being in control, and often lead some part of the established social order. As these individuals integrate their personal creative talents with the needs of society, they often move toward being responsible for people, things, and projects. Those in the eighth group see their mission as warriors who live to overcome new challenges and exceed their own expectations. They tend to be natural leaders who are motivated to improving the lives of thousands or millions in practical ways.

The people of this sign and type are survivors and motivated to be successful in the material universe. They are assertive and decisive and have the energy to make changes in the material circumstances of life. They personify youthfulness, growth, expansion, and forward movement. Their goal is to attain success in material matters, such as making things, making progress, and being competitive. They approach their goals through direct and forceful means. Their desire to be themselves on their own terms also means that they need far less social reinforcement than other types. Most of these individuals have little desire to compare themselves to others. They prefer to improve on their own performance, constantly becoming better and stronger. They usually act with little concern for whether their action is reasonable, prudent, timely, or even effective if self-expression is achieved.

The Defender and Challenger has the confidence and energy for constantly striving to grow in the right direction. Because they judge existence by the extent of their own consciousness, the more limited their awareness, the more limited their world. Even though they take the lead through force and push their way to the top, they should learn to cultivate the attributes of cooperation and sharing. They tend to jump on any opportunity that looks good and often do so without seeing all the consequences of their actions. They set goals for themselves and keep their nose to the grindstone until they achieve what they want. They can bring out abilities in others and help them rearrange the structure of their lives to fit their need or desire. Those of this type take the initiative and spark enthusiasm in others.

Most people find this sign and type to be good natured and warm and like the way they can get to the heart of a matter and not get bogged down in details. They are known for wanting to rescue others from trouble and taking charge during emergencies. While they are admired for their courage and youthfulness, they can be headstrong and act before thinking. The more developed people of this type and sign have learned that they get better results when they think before they act. Many of these people attract others who are very dependent on them and yet independent. To provide for their families, they require occupations that involve them totally and allow them the freedom to constantly express themselves. Defenders and Challengers look for opportunities to prove themselves before the world so that they gain recognition for the achievements that make them feel worthy. Because they are independent, they have little tolerance for opposition or interference. The most important lesson for those represented by this period is to listen to others to hear what is being said and what they are being told.

The nine-year cycle from age sixty-three to seventy-two is associated with the task of becoming an agent for a spiritual, social, or cultural purpose and to work toward changing an existing condition. The meeting of the individual and collective destiny often occurs in this cycle. Examples of this cycle may be seen in cases where people make efforts to improve their lives in tangible and intangible ways, e.g., choosing to expand their career and pursuing a defined course or significant endeavor. For many, this nine-year period points to a new pathway in their self-development. The eighth stage represents the development of an individual's life purpose and their social role or work that they identify with and by which they are identified. Since those in the eighth cycle have moved through the seventh cycle and acquired its knowledge of universal principles, they are well positioned to confront the established order.

The eighth cycle or stage is a time when you embrace who you are or want to be rather than simply follow the status quo in your life. It is often a time of inspiration, thinking big, and having hope for the future. This period points to the capacity and readiness to make important decisions or take decisive action. This cycle is also a time for reviving one's interest in bringing a far-reaching idea for change to people who prefer to keep things as they are. Individuals in this cycle often have increased physical vitality and radiate wisdom. This period is associated with the opportunity and challenge to work toward changing an existing condition in one's community. When there is disappointment instead of fulfillment, individuals in this period find new opportunities to start over.

Sign, Type, and Stage 9

Mediator and Peacemaker
Ninth Cycle Ages: 72 to 81

Traits: People- and community-oriented; need for close relationships with others; compassion and sympathy verging on spirituality. Those of this group understand the feelings of others. Having been through all eight signs, this group identifies with all types in humanity and represents the soul's complete evolutionary development. They are pacifist, desire fairness and balance in interacting with others, and need to avoid unresolved conflicts.

Applicable Ages: *8, 17, 26, 35, 44, 53, 62, 71 to 81, and 89.*

Mediators and Peacemakers are motivated to find harmony and agreement, reach conclusions, take care of unfinished business, and serve humanity. They are associated with spiritual awareness and understanding life. They accept social responsibilities and often make humanitarian contributions to enhance the quality of life for others. They are seekers of spiritual awareness and share this knowledge with others. Those of this sign and type tend to evaluate people based on what they can do for the larger community or cause. They are often natural leaders, generous, and flexible and know that the world is part of a larger spiritual universe.

Nines have a deep understanding of life, strength of character, wisdom, intuition, and high idealism. A major spiritual motto among Nines is that "the more you give, the bigger will be your reward."

They grow and learn through tolerance, compassion, selflessness, and generosity. The positive traits of Mediator-Peacemakers include creativity, influence, and accomplishment and being honorable, trustworthy, romantic, self-sufficient, compassionate, and humanitarian. Their negative traits include the inability to concentrate, worry, deception, and disappointment with life's realities, and being withdrawn, careless with finances, distracted, and possessive.

Individuals of this type make use of their passion for fairness and balance to create harmony in human relationships. Of all the forces that bind people together, this type understands that love produces the most stable groupings. They have a big hand in any relationship that causes people to become more fully realized. They believe that giving people a sense of harmony is just as useful as giving material resources. While eights get things started and often break things because of their assertive nature, the harmonious nines bring things to fruition and mend broken things. The masculine hardness of the eighth type is fulfilled by the feminine softness of the ninth type.

Individuals represented by the Mediator and Peacemaker archetypes are often popular and well liked and often have many friends. They want mental stimulation, companionship, and social interactions. Their pleasing manners and aptitude in dealing with the public can be applied in counseling and public relations. They understand the feeling of others and believe that harmonious social relationships are of great importance. Along with their consideration for others, they have a desire to please, which results in being well liked by others. They manifest deep compassion and sympathy and understand the unity of all life. People in this group are romantic and sensitive. They know what it is like to be in another person's shoes. They are often inspired by intuition and have an innate ability to inspire artistic creativity in others.

Many nines have an active participation in social affairs because this satisfies their need to be among people. They know how to keep the peace and negotiate in times of stress and unresolved differences. They are called Peacemakers because they know how to get along and can often get what they want from others by apparently giving in. They will do a great deal to ensure happiness for those around them as they feel best when others are happy. Normally, this sign and type is warm and loving as well as socially adept. More than any other planetary type, they recognize the power of love and connection to nurture a healthy heart and extend the life span. They excel at taking the initiative in such a way that others do not realize the initiative has been taken.

This nine-year cycle from ages seventy-two to eighty-one represents the gradual working out of spiritual and ancestral karma. This period is associated with endings and the need for new values and a new phase in the development of one's destiny or character. It teaches that every death is followed by birth and that the fulfillment of the old creates the new. The ninth period contains the seed or blueprint for the next nine-year cycle and suggests confident preparation for the coming new beginning. This nine-year cycle also represents the positive and progressive ascent of the fulfillment of one's collective and social responsibilities.

The ninth cycle often brings to light the spiritual debts carried over from the previous eight phases, which may be worked on or settled or remain a mystery. As the last of the nine-year cycles, this cycle contains the knowledge of all previous cycles, bringing things to fruition and a glimpse of the new beginning to come. Unlike the previous eight cycles, this cycle represents the greatest opportunity to manifest completion. This period indicates the ending or closure of something in your life, such as a significant material possession, relationship, or situation that you are attached to. Those in this period reduce their attention on the materialistic aspects of outer life and focus on their inner world. In this cycle, people broaden their outlook on life and focus on the big picture rather than details. Those in the ninth cycle often express feelings of warmth and love of home, family, and friends. The current ninth cycle contains the seed or blueprint for the next nine years and suggests confident preparation for the coming new beginning, which is the second time to experience the first nine-year cycle.

7

Sign and Type Pair Meanings

*How people treat you is their karma;
how you react is yours.*

— Wayne Dyer

This chapter explains the basic nature and relationships created in all possible pairs formed by the enneagram types and signs. The descriptions of numbered pairs in this chapter can be used in several ways. They are a guide to how numbered pairs will interact when they are brought together by two different individuals or stage-cycle combinations for one individual. They can help you understand three factors in combination. For instance, if you are a type two and in an eight/nine cycle, you can investigate eight/nine, eight/two, and two/nine. These descriptions will give you an idea of how you may experience each combination. While you can use this process to explain combinations of more than three factors at the same time, e.g., your personality type and cycles of development in relation to another's personality type and cycles, the combination of factors can become unwieldy.

The meanings that follow expand upon the relationship compatibility between types and signs given in the table. The meanings for the pairs are the same regardless of how the pair is ordered. For instance, the meaning of four/eight is the same as the meaning of eight/ four. While the meanings are the same, how they are applied with individual numbers may vary. For example, the individual numbers may refer to one's enneagram type, sign, or stages of development or the compatibility between two individuals in a relationship.

Compatibilities Among Types, Signs, and Cycles

All relationships among the types, signs, stages, and cycles are shown in the Sign and Type Compatibility table and explained in the following section. These explanations address the motives, interests, and choices habitually made by the types in relation to one another. The nine signs and types are type one, the Initiator-Reformer; type two, the Guide-Helper; type three, the Contestant-Achiever; type four, the Romantic-Individualist; type five, the Innovator-Investigator; type six, the Skeptic-Loyalist; type seven, the Seeker-Enthusiast; type eight, the Defender-Challenger; and type nine, the Mediator-Peacemaker.

Type compatibilities can be understood from the perspective of similarities among them, such as trinity groups. The first trinity group includes the aggressive types (ones, threes, and eights), the retreating types (fours, fives, and nines), and the compliant types (twos, sixes, and sevens). The second trinity group includes the harmonious types (threes, sixes, and nines), the neutral types (ones, fives, and sevens), and the challenging types (twos, fours, and eights). The third trinity group includes the body and feeling types (eights, nines, and ones), the soul and intuitive types (twos, threes, and fives), and the mind or thinking types (fives, sixes, and sevens).

Most type compatibilities are viewed from the perspective of relationships among individuals. These relationships consist of individual-to-individual enneagram signs, individual-to-individual enneagram types, and an individual's enneagram sign and type. For instance, the table given here tells us that the relationship between individuals of enneagram types five and six falls in the neutral category, while the relationship between a type one and type five falls in the easy and harmonious category. The relationship between individuals born on June 15 and January 20, for instance, or the enneagram signs three and eight, falls in the difficulty category. An additional example is the case of an individual born under enneagram sign two, whose enneagram type is five. The enneagram sign defines one's potential expression and soul personality, and the enneagram type defines one's motivations, historical preferences, and ego-centered personality.

Let me say a few words about this last combination as it belongs to me. While the union between my enneagram sign and type was unsettling for the first thirty years or so of my life, it has since worked out well for me. Prior to this time, my professional life was defined as the Investigator or the fifth enneagram type. Since then, my professional life shifted to include a balance between type five and the Guide or the second enneagram sign. The type-five side of my work was being a university professor of management science and a statistician, and my combined sign two–type five work has been and remains as an intuitive counselor and spiritual teacher. My birthday-based second enneagram sign contributes a great deal to my emotional depth, and my enneagram type five defines my detached, intuitive, observant, and cerebral side. Together, I see them as the source of my ability to read, understand, and explain deep emotions.

Sign and Type Compatibilities

		1								
Sign-Type	1	E	2							
Sign-Type	2	N	N	3						
Sign-Type	3	E	N	N	4					
Sign-Type	4	D	N	N	N	5				
Sign-Type	5	E	D	E	N	E	6			
Sign-Type	6	N	D	D	D	N	N	7		
Sign-Type	7	E	E	E	N	E	N	N	8	
Sign-Type	8	N	D	D	D	D	D	E	N	9
Sign-Type	9	E	E	E	N	N	D	E	E	E

E = usually balanced and harmonious

N + usually unbiased and neutral

D – usually oppositions and difficulty

The enneagram typology model shown here reveals its wisdom for the relationships among the types in a uniquely different way. While this feature of the enneagram model is not used in this work, it will serve as a reminder for those familiar with the enneagram. In the enneagram system, every numbered type has a positive companion number that builds up, adds strength, and works to further its goals. The arrow pointing at the number comes from the strengthening type number, and the outward pointing arrow strengthens the number it's pointed at. For example, five is strengthened by eight and weakened by seven. Some enneagram numbers suggest a different compatibility letter (E for easy, N for neutral, and D for difficult) than those shown in the chart, which are based on the relationships among planets as enneagram types. The suggestion is that while five is strengthened by eight, it is also weakened and diminished by eight. As seen throughout the typology, the arrow leading into a number indicates a strengthening influence, and the arrow leading away points to a weakening influence.

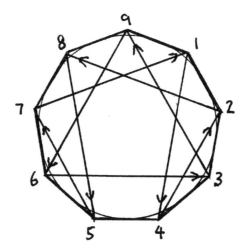

The Enneagram Typology

The discussion of the type compatibilities that follow mainly apply to relationships between signs and types, such as between two enneagram types or two enneagram signs or between an enneagram sign and type. The full meaning of how these pairs interact with one another can be understood when they are applied to one's relationship with others and with oneself. Even though the descriptions of pairs given here deal with enneagram signs and types, there is great value in applying their meaning to understand the relationships between an individual's life cycle and stage combination and between their sign or type and any life cycle or stage. The summaries given in the table titled Sign and Type Compatibilities apply to cycles and stages as well, and they are all explained here as numbered pairs. Because each enneagram type is aligned with a planet, the planet combinations are included in the description of pair compatibilities. This addition will be useful for those familiar with planetary meanings.

Pairs with One, Initiators or Reformers

One-One

One-one unions are about learning. In this case, learning tends to come easy because both sides are curious. Relationships represented by the one-one combination understand what the other side is saying with great clarity and have few miscommunications. This combination tends to increase each party's discovery and understanding of new information. They often take the time to think over important issues and work out a solution, and their thinking is more aligned with current trends.

One-one planetary pair: Mercury joined with itself

One-Two

Those represented by the one-two union tend to alternate between concentrating all their focus in only one area of expression—masculine or feminine, aggressive action or passive action. With this combination, the self-centered and independent energy of one often overpowers two's cooperative nature. People with this union are active, adaptive, aware, and sensitive to others. The main goal with this combination is attaining peace of mind or psychological balance.

The one-two combination is often plagued with misunderstanding between thinking and feeling. In this union, the objective and subjective sides don't see things the same way. The one side sees and talks about objective things, while the feeling side represented by two feels and talks about subjective things. In most disagreements, they are both right but expressing different sides of the coin. These differences are growth producing and rather difficult to deal with and stretch one's thoughts and feelings. On the positive side, each side is aware of the other's feelings and plans. On the negative side, each side has the tendency to overthink the past and their feelings about the other.

One-two planetary pair: Mercury joined with the moon

One-Three

The one-three combination is filled with mental energy. The three side speeds up the one side, and one focuses on three's energy in the direction of communications. Three's enthusiasm and confidence shines a big light and makes for confident and optimistic communications. This combination points to expressing good feelings, a quick wit, and the tendency to have a sharp tongue. Individuals, couples, or stage-cycles with this combination usually both display increased intelligence and decreased listening as they absorb little new information. With this pair, the one side is too busy thinking about what to say next, and the three side is too busy speaking to think things through.

The one-three combination points to creativity and the ability to act with focused mental energy in things associated with the Competitor's aims—being sociable, clever, and playful. While this union tends to hinder one's objectivity, its presence gives the mental energy to get beyond this shortcoming. In addition, these people have a solid desire to communicate, to know, and to understand things.

One-three planetary pair: Mercury joined with the sun

One-Four

The one-four connection brings together the intellect and psychic impressions. The Four side of the partnership has an interest in art and design and attempts to understand and explain the beauties and mysteries of the nonphysical universe, but these efforts are only partly visible to the Initiator side. Communications between these signs, types, or stages often come with misunderstandings because neither side fully hears and understands the other. This pair is like squeezing the proverbial square peg into a round hole.

Individuals with this combination tend to focus on overcoming many material obstacles to achieving full self-expression. They talk about their dreams as if they were real and do what they can to manifest them. In addition to this otherworldly interest, they express their will through home and family and the urge to build security and fulfillment. Those represented by the one-four union often have a need to establish themselves in society through a highly personalized environment. Many have a talent for understanding intuitions and multisensory perceptions.

One-four planetary pair: Mercury joined with Neptune

One-Five

The union between ones and fives is decidedly masculine. In this partnership, both sides are ambitious, need to be on top, and express themselves through actions that require strength and courage. The one side or partner is easily bored by routine tasks and often disrupts the thoughts and speech of the two side. The parties represented by this combination give a good relationship to one another and tend to be aggressive and self-assertive in their approach to life. Many of the people in this union are inclined to be fighters and daredevils who seek challenge or feel challenged.

These signs and types are both communicators, but the one side is more focused on objective topics, whereas the five side is focused on progressive change and unexpected happening. The parties in this union have thoughts about progressive ideas. Because their thinking and planning is often ahead of their time, they experience difficulties in situations that require them to be conventional or follow the established order.

One-five planetary pair: Mercury joined with Uranus

One-Six

This combination puts an added burden on learning how and what to communicate. The six side tends to depress one's confidence by playing the devil's advocate and insisting on doing things "the right way," whereas one does not need to question itself. The one-six pair can be difficult because the goals of the two parties in this relationship are very different. The six side needs to understand the often-hidden knowledge of how to do things and the feelings involved before attaining success, whereas one's success depends on communicating with others so that understanding can take place. Six needs to think things through and understand to avoid making mistakes, whereas one simply tries to create an understanding.

The people with this combination don't always pick and choose their words carefully or speak slowly enough to be understood. Thus, they tend to have difficulty communicating their emotions with each other. They often doubt themselves, which shows up as being worried that they could have said or done things better. The one side of this combination can indicate a serious outlook on life and good powers of concentration, while the six side tends to be socially awkward and lack self-confidence.

One-six planetary pair: Mercury joined with Saturn

One-Seven

The one-seven union represents ventures into new and unexplored realms of knowledge and experience. This combination is associated with a new understanding and work with what is generally called the nonphysical universe or occult. In addition to introducing an intuitive quality full of surprised and sudden flashes of insight, those represented by this numerical pair can be genius despite being erratic and unpredictable.

The planets behind one and seven are communicators and have a lot in common. The difference is that ones use the objective mind and like to explain ordinary and immediate life realities, whereas sevens like to use intuition and the higher mind to explain the universal and big-picture life realities. One communicates the letter of the law, whereas seven communicates the spirit of the law. Ones are detail oriented and focus on personal matters, whereas sevens are broadminded and focus on the impersonal matters.

One-seven planetary pair: Mercury joined with Jupiter

One-Eight

Individuals with the one-eight combination often become verbal warriors with sharp tongues. They want to express their desires and observations and become impatient with those who don't get their point right away. On the positive side of this relationship, eights make ones quicker on the uptake and able to understand things at a faster pace. On the negative side, the aggressive and impatient nature of eights pushes the communications expressed by ones to become more aggressive, impatient, and off-putting to those who don't think as fast.

Of all the combinations, one-eight presents the greatest challenge. Individuals with this union advance in life with the assistance of their quick wit, enthusiasm, and productive nature. This comes about because eights energize and accelerate the self-expression and ambitions of ones. Much of what they achieve is gained by being assertive in direct and indirect ways. While this combination implies a self-confident approach to life, it can also inspire individuals to express themselves.

One-eight planetary pair: Mercury joined with Mars

One-Nine

Like the unions between one and three and one and seven, the union between one and nine is harmonious. Those represented by this combination are often generous with their time and accomplish things through their pleasing personalities and optimistic natures. Their positive outlook enables them to better help others and take advantage of their environments. This combination often brings opportunities for self-expression and spiritual education.

The relationship between ones and nines favors pleasant and harmonious communications. They are liked by most people and can be completely present to the people they are speaking with. This combination promotes greater sociability, lightheartedness, human kindness, and greater cooperation than either the one or nine side can provide alone. This is a good partnership for business and personal communications. When together, these two partners tend to excel at and feel good about receiving and giving information and knowledge.

One-nine planetary pair: Mercury joined with Venus

Pairs with Two, Guides or Helpers

Two-Two

The partnership between twos is one of emotional comfort and warm feelings about home, security, and family. On the positive side, those in this union tend to live in harmony and feel comfortable with each other, and there is little friction between them. On the negative side, they are prone to more mood swings than usual and often find it difficult to move beyond the past or accept the new. The saying "no pain, no gain" often applies to this pair. There is often little growth with this pair because the two partners are more into themselves and less interested in growth opportunities from outside.

Two-two planetary pair: The moon joined with itself

Two-Three

The two-three union is neither difficult nor easy. On the bright side, twos want to help threes to be more of themselves. By nature, twos remain emotionally centered and support others to get into the flow of life. The fiery nature of threes often pushes the twos out of their comfort zone. In such cases, the three side influences the two side to become so hurried that it turns away from three's expanding energy.

The union between two and three brings together the unconscious and conscious realms of experience. For instance, the conscious thoughts and communications between partners are influenced by unconscious feelings and emotions. This union points to individuals being aware of their emotional nature and responses as well as the effect of their intentions. The people in this partnership are sensitive to what others think of them and often understand the public mood.

Two-three planetary pair: The moon joined with the sun

Two-Four

Those with this union are strongly influenced by the emotional attitudes of other people. This partnership is often difficult because the balance between personal and transcendent needs is hard to maintain. The two-four combination brings together the need for personal safety, security, and understanding with an interest in idealism and connecting with the transcendent.

On the positive side, the two partner of this union wants to nurture and help the four partner expand and grow into their potential. On the difficult and perhaps negative side, the four side wants to bring together their elusive and transcendent reality to the relationship-oriented two side. Feelings run deep in this union, and those in it often experience their interests as going through phases, from personal emotional to transcendent spiritual concerns.

Two-four planetary pair: The moon joined with Neptune

Two-Five

The partnership between twos and fives is unsettling because the natures of these signs and types are so different. Two is personal and emotional, and five is intuitive, detached, and cerebral. Twos want safety, security, and emotional peace, and fives want to change things that have become too settled. Twos want to produce comfort and serve those who need help, whereas fives want to change things that need changing.

The union between two and five generates strong feelings that can lead to outbreaks of anger and depression. This partnership can be a difficult union because the natures of twos and fives are so different. This combination tends to bring opportunities to learn about the virtues of being cautious and pursue good causes when they are guided by knowledge.

Two-five planetary pair: The moon joined with Uranus

Two-Six

Even though the two-six union tends to be practical and responsible, it is also known for being pessimistic and detached. The disciplined emotional nature of this pair is often mistaken for coldness. The often cool exterior between these numbers can lead one partner to believe that the other does not need love and support. Because they are reticent to express their personal needs, they may keep each other at arm's length. This combination often exhibits a lack of affection and interaction and may appear to be overly cautious and defensive.

In this union, one partner tends to see the other as a wet blanket. The two partner wants to demonstrate his or her maternal instincts by helping and protecting others. Six wants to create material success, but this goal is delayed until they understand how to attain the success they want.

Two-six planetary pair: The moon joined with Saturn

Two-Seven

The two-seven relationship is beneficial to both sides. Seven lifts the spirit of two, and two provides stability and service to seven. The helpful twos want to serve and nurture growth, and the growth-oriented sevens want to pursue new ideas and expand their knowledge of the universe. The two side supports the goals of the seven side, and seven's optimism and energy inspires two.

Individuals in this partnership tend to look for emotional freedom, excitement, and novelty. This combination suggests the presence of intuitiveness, imagination, and an inner understanding of themselves and others. The two-seven union has an uplifting and optimistic influence on both partners and gives the urge to find meaning in everything that happens. It also indicates disruptions of old patterns of living and breaks with the past and disruptions in their development or support.

Two-seven planetary pair: The moon joined with Jupiter

Two-Eight

In this partnership, twos tend to follow eight's leadership, and two's influence softens eight's aggressive nature. The union between twos and eights makes for a blunt, straightforward, and passionate approach to each other and to life. Eights bring enthusiasm, independence, and confidence to the partnership, and twos bring their receptive, maternal, and caregiving nature. The parties in this union are likely to be impatient and want to grow up quickly.

Although those with this union are devoted to attaining success, their need for flexibility, pleasing others, and moderation are always present. Twos want to give and receive help, support, and understanding, and eights want to assert themselves with confidence. While eights will defend two's "weaker" approach, its approach can be rough and unsympathetic. Those in this partnership learn to have self-restraint and conservative views and adopt a practical and common-sense approach to life.

Two-eight planetary pair: The moon joined with Mars

Two-Nine

This partnership is beneficial to both members. The parties in this union have a strong interest in beauty and harmony, which often takes the form of artistic or design interests and creating beautiful environments. Two supports nine's need for balance, harmony, and peace; nine's humanitarian goals are nurtured by two's helping nature. Both the two and nine sides of this union learn to have greater sensitivity and tact and use charm in dealing with others.

Individuals with the two-nine partnership tend to develop sympathy, generosity, and the desire to bring good to others. Many in this union tend to have an interest in social welfare and political action. While they identify with religious and educational causes, their emotional attachments to home, family, and material possessions can inhibit these social urges.

Two-nine planetary pair: The moon joined with Venus

Pairs with Three, Contestants or Achievers

Three-Three

The three-three union brings increased energy and a stronger identity with the qualities of this sign, type, stage, or cycle than we see with an individual three. This combination greater brings to light the strong and weak qualities of the threes. Each partner brings out or supports the qualities of the other partner. This union is likely to be neutral because the qualities expressed cannot be judged as simply easy or difficult. However, the more each party accepts himself or herself, the more beneficial will be their relationship with themselves, their partner, and others.

Three-three planetary pair: The sun joined with itself

Three-Four

The three-four combination unites the largest source of energy, growth, and harmony in the universe with the largest source of transcendent wisdom in the universe. The enthusiasm and power of three helps to bring four's world of visions and multisensory perceptions into the light of day. The three side of this union expands and clarifies the meaning and purpose of four's unconscious realm. This combination can bring about a new understanding about messages from the deeper mind, which often come through an avenue such as clairvoyance, dreams, and mystical experiences.

This combination points to learning about spirituality, intuition, and communicating with the transcendent. Its presence is a sign that the messages and wisdom from the deeper mind, unconscious or transcendent, is the major source of information received, communicated, or manifested. Those represented by the union of three and four usually builds upon or expands their knowledge and understanding of their connection to the unseen universe.

Three-four planetary pair: The sun joined with Neptune

Three-Five

Individuals represented by this numerical pair are inclined to be competitive and show that they possess more knowledge or intellectual superiority than others. The three side of this union tends to inspire the five side to express himself or herself with greater confidence and directness. The five side inspires the three side to rebel against the established order and change what needs changing. Because this combination is observant, of quick learners, and mentally assertive, those it represents make for excellent investigators and rebels who want to report their findings.

All things concerned, this partnership is beneficial to both parties in the union. The connection between the ever-expanding and optimistic energy of three and the intuitive, detached and upending nature of five produces many innovative plans. The changes linked to this combination are usually sudden, unexpected, and dramatic.

Three-five planetary pair: The sun joined with Uranus

Three-Six

Because the parties are so different, the three-six union is challenging. The three-six combination is like driving a race car with the brakes on. The upbeat energetic and growth-oriented three is held back by six's questioning and wet-blanket approach to doing things. The six of this union needs to learn the rules of the game or society before they can be successful.

More than in most combinations, threes learn from sixes that life has its limitations. The progressive side of this partnership is often frustrated by the stubborn and cautious side. The individuals and couples with this union tend to be hard on themselves because they set higher goals than most. While they can be rigid and demanding and expect others to live up to their high standards, they are usually willing to take on more than their share of responsibilities.

Three-six planetary pair: The sun joined with Saturn

Three-Seven

The three-seven connection is beneficial to both sides of this union. The energetic, warm, and ever-expanding nature of three helps advance seven's need to explore new ideas and learn new things about the spiritual universe. Both three and six are enthusiastic, optimistic, and eager to grow in beneficial ways. Both have a cheerful outlook of life and see goodness in the world. While this union can be generous with its time and money, the parties tend to promise more than they can deliver.

People with the three-seven partnership tend to become more independent in their thinkers and will not accept ideas simply based on tradition. This pair is associated with opportunities for expansion in the areas of philosophy, religion, and higher education. This union promotes originality, mental genius, and lightning-quick minds. These individuals often gain many insights through intuitive flashes and have an interest in expanding their knowledge.

Three-seven planetary pair: The sun joined with Jupiter

Three-Eight

Those represented by the three-eight union tend to be confrontational and can rub people the wrong way. Although these partners are ambitious and impatient, they often encounter difficulties in gaining positive recognition. Unlike the three-seven union, which seeks to explore new ideas and learning things about the spiritual universe, the three-eight union is eager to pursue their goals and get things done. While this pair may not be socially popular, both parties become energized and can push people to make things happen.

The three-eight connection expands the competitive spirit of the eight and often produces individuals who look for a fight. The difficulty in this partnership comes about when both sides are eager to get things done, can't sit still, and don't think things through before acting. While the parties in this combination are aggressive and confident and do everything they can to prove themselves, many remain insecure.

Three-eight planetary pair: The sun joined with Mars

Three-Nine

The three-nine combination is beneficial to both sides. The expansive, harmonious, and optimistic energy of three is very compatible with nine's need to promote peace, harmony, and goodness. Those represented by this union are charming toward and enjoy each other. They prefer to make peace and bring people together, but they are inclined to walk away from those who are indifferent or overly aggressive.

Partnerships and individuals united by the three-nine combination want to use their verbal ability to heal or guide others in activities such as teaching, counseling, ministering, or leading others. Three brings out the energy and enthusiasm behind nine's urge to have diplomacy in communicating with others. The actions of this union are based on a consideration of what will produce the most beauty, balance, and harmony. These individuals tend to exhibit grace of expression in speech and writing. Nine brings out three's soft-spoken and charming manner to magnify its sense of beauty and harmony.

Three-nine planetary pair: The sun joined with Venus

Pairs with Four, Romantics or Individualists

Four-Four

The four-four union in partnerships, individuals, or stages is associated with great imagination, dreaming, artistic expression, and communicating with the creative and transcendent mind. This combination expands the expression of the qualities represented by four. Those represented by this combination tend to romanticize, idealize, and exaggerate their interests. While this union is enthusiastic about communicating with the nonphysical universe, it is difficult for the parties to communicate or manifest their otherworldly ideas. Individuals with this union love a good time, make enjoyable companions, and often learn to express their artistic creativity and psychic interest.

Four-four planetary pair: Neptune joined with itself

Four-Five

The experience of four and five combined produces a kind of hidden revolution. The four-five union can be beneficial and challenging for both parties. This combination brings a new understanding of messages from the deeper mind, which often come through psychic methods or experiences. Those in this union tend to be independent of culture and environment and experience many unexpected and sudden changes, which are often connected to them through their spiritual and intuitive nature.

Although the intuitive, feeling four and the intuitive, thinking five have a shared intuitive connection to the transcendent, they have their misunderstandings. The creative emotional nature of four and the creative intellectual nature of five help them succeed but often at the expense of each other. The mystically oriented four brings an otherworldly view to five, and five brings observation and greater clarity to four's ideas.

Four-five planetary pair: Neptune joined with Uranus

Four-Six

The goals of the four-six union are often difficult to attain because their concerns and ways of operating are hard to reconcile. This combination has the potential to create new relationships because the six side of the relationship brings form and structure, while the four side brings intangibility and formlessness. Six wants to create material success based on the laws of reality, while four expresses its reality based on imagination and inspiring dreams.

In this partnership, fours want to express their formless and idealistic reality, even though it may not be understood, whereas six insists on knowing the meaning of four's reality before they can express it. Individuals represented by the four-six union have an inner need to express themselves through intangible, artistic, and harmonious endeavors. They tend to surround themselves by comfortable circumstances and perhaps a family, even though this may take years to achieve.

Four-six planetary pair: Neptune joined with Saturn

Four-Seven

The four-seven combination is beneficial to both parties in this union. Both parties want to experience and express the mysteries of the unseen spiritual universe. The difference is that the seven side of the partnership wants to learn about direct contact with the soul, whereas the four side wants direct contact or experience with the soul. This partnership is about growth, creative imagination, intuitive ability, compassion, and learning. With this pair, the path to success involves understanding the soul's message and pursuing their vision.

This union represents an unusual, changing, and ever-expanding personal growth situation. Those with this combination tend to experience the dissolution of old patterns of living, breaks with the past, and disruptions in their development or level of support. Many four-seven unions produce situations where the partnership is at odds with their social, economic, or ethnic backgrounds yet still need to assert their individuality.

Four-seven planetary pair: Neptune joined with Jupiter

Four-Eight

This partnership is difficult for both parties because their natures are so different. The four-eight combination tends to experience conflict between spiritual and material interests. While eights will defend the spiritual approach of Romantics, their defense is often rough and unsympathetic. Those with this pair often feel alienated from being helped or not helping those who accept their intuitive and spiritual nature.

Eight brings confidence, enthusiasm, and independence to four's need to experience and express the formless universe. In this union, eight inspires four to pursue a more practical and commercial expression of its spiritual nature. The intangible nature of four tends to make eight feel uninspired and directionless. Eight wants to assert itself in the concrete material world, whereas four wants to experience the union between material reality and the transcendent.

Four-eight planetary pair: Neptune joined with Mars

Four-Nine

Nines want harmony, fairness, and cooperation, and fours want to experience heaven on earth. Nine is a charming and smooth communicator who can help spread four's message of mystical experience. This union helps explain and integrate the intuitive and spiritual aspects of relationships that are often overlooked or never seen.

This union is like having good live music to accompany a spiritual or religious service to create better reception.

This partnership is beneficial to both sides and tends to be warm and supportive to all. The four-nine pair brings a compassionate understanding of other people's feelings and relationships. In addition to increased sensitivity to the transcendent, this pair brings an openness to other ideas. The connection between four and nine is associated with openness to others and the desire to examine hidden mysteries regarding one's place in the universe.

Four-nine planetary pair: Neptune joined with Venus

Pairs with Five, Innovators or Investors

Five-Five

The five-five union is the most progressive and change-producing partnership arrangement. The five-five union represents the midpoint expressions of two worlds. Five-five individuals and partners bring together the intuitive, transcendent, and thinking perspectives. The five-five couple brings together the need for change that is often sudden and unexpected with a concrete understanding of how and when the change is taking place. This union between or within individuals demystifies and promotes the mystery of transformation by presenting the bridge between past and future, known and unknown, conscious and unconscious.

Five-five planetary pair: Uranus joined with itself

Five-Six

This pair inclines the parties toward passionate involvements of all types. The major lesson for the five-six union is to find the balance between the need for significant relationships and individual self-expression. Five's interest in innovation and often revolutionary change is joined with six's desire to proceed with caution and follow the established order to attain success. In this union, the parties learn that life has limitations on what can and cannot be done.

This partnership can be challenging for both parties because they are so different. The five-six union is like driving a race car with the brakes on. The upbeat, energetic, and revolutionary five is held back by the questioning and wet-blanket style or approach to six. The progressive five in this partnership is often frustrated by the stubborn and cautious six. The Innovator wants the Skeptic to learn the rules of the game and how things work.

Five-six planetary pair: Uranus joined with Saturn

Five-Seven

This combination is usually beneficial to both partners. The revolutionary and disruptive five brings sudden and unanticipated changes, while the optimistic seven brings enthusiasm to pursue innovative ideas and learn new things. Along with the appearance of good luck, the five side brings a more inclusive and far-reaching philosophy to seven. Even though the styles of five and seven are different, the unexpected events and changes of five are often beneficial to seven's broader understanding.

Individuals represented by this union tend to fight for their freedom and have an absolute desire for independence and nonconformity. They have a natural revolutionary spirit and may lead an organized endeavor or movement to bring about changes. These individuals avoid having a dull life by constantly pursuing advanced knowledge and new ideas. Seven inspires five to expand and grow, and five inspires seven to check out new and unexpected opportunities that seem to come out of the blue.

Five-seven planetary pair: Uranus joined with Jupiter

Five-Eight

Although individuals in this partnership are not known for sitting still to think things through before acting, they are eager to pursue their goals and get things done. Those represented by the five-eight union tend to be confrontational and often rub people the wrong way. While this pair may not be socially popular, they are a bundle of energy that can push people to make things happen. With this union, the revolutionary way of five produces needed changes that the warrior eight will promote.

This combination points to the capacity for demanding work, enduring strength, and courage in resolve dangerous or difficult situations. Because they are ambitious and impatient, they often encounter difficulties in gaining positive recognition. As the individuals in this partnership learn to be cautious and prudent, they tend to resent those who will not learn to change.

Five-eight planetary pair: Uranus joined with Mars

Five-Nine

The people with this partnership of types learn to expect the unexpected in their dealings with others. This type combination is associated with attracting exciting people into the lives of those who have it. The harmony-oriented nine points to opportunities to change the way to relate to other people. The nine side of the union tends to soften the unexpected and disruptive experience brought on by the five side. While this union prefers to make and keep the peace, they are inclined to walk away from those who refuse to accept changes to the established order.

The union between five and nine produces an abundance of energy and enthusiasm. Individuals in this union tend to be zealous in the pursuit of changes to the status quo, which they consider to be necessary on behalf of those less fortunate. Partners and individuals with the five-nine connection will likely have opportunities to use their verbal ability to heal or guide others.

Five-nine planetary pair: Uranus joined with Venus

Pairs with Six, Skeptics or Loyalists

Six-Six

This union presents an opportunity to do things the right way or redo the things that were not done correctly. Although the six-six combination is considered difficult by most, the union between the two produces great results for individuals and partners who follow the established order. Even though everything is slowed down when these two types are together and delay seems commonplace, this couple usually leads to achievement and maturity. Here, the six-six pair learns that their success is directly related to understanding the rules governing their endeavors. When the rules are ignored or not followed, things crash and burn or undergo a course correction.

Six-six planetary pair: Saturn joined with itself

Six-Seven

The six-seven combination tends to experience the range of emotions from depression to optimism and from a lack joy in life to great joy. The six-seven union can lead both sides to believe that they don't have a passion to pursue their ideals and advanced education. This union has the appearance of being somber and a wet blanket in the eyes of many. Six brings seven a disciplined, organized, and responsible approach to life, and seven tends to awaken six to the freedom to pursue knowledge and explore their dreams.

The six-seven partnership is usually more inharmonious than harmonious. However, even though the parties are very different, this union can be beneficial when seven helps six become more optimistic and when six helps seven become more practical and realistic. Although the midpoint or place of balance between six and seven may not be ideal for either partner, it is the most reliable path to success.

Six-seven planetary pair: Saturn joined with Jupiter

Six-Eight

Although both parties want to manifest success, the six approach is parent-like and conventional, while the eight approach is childlike and independent. Six tends to follow eight's leadership, and six's cautious nature tends to slow down eight's aggressive nature. Eight brings confidence and independence to six's cautious and traditional approach.

In this union, the cautious "play by the rules" approach of six is united with the steamrolling and often brash approach of eight. The result is that eight is slowed down by the established order from six, and six is taxed by the constant eagerness of eight to push forward hurriedly. This union presents challenges and opportunities for success to both partners. Six's urge to play by the rules opposes eight's urge to get around the rules and follow the beat of its own drummer.

Six-eight planetary pair: Saturn joined with Mars

Six-Nine

In this union, the six side wants to create material success by following an established plan, while the nine side wants to create fairness and harmony. On the positive side, the warm and cooperative approach of nine eases the cautious and pessimistic approach of six. On the negative side, the "play by the rules" traditional approach of six can be a drag on nine's charming nature. The six goal of creating material success and the nine goal of creating harmony often work well together.

The six-nine combination unites the artistic, creative, and peacemaking ability of six with nine's desire for material success. The people in this union tend to be friendly, sociable, and helpful to those who are less fortunate. Nine adds understanding, warmth and charm to six's loyal and steady nature. Nine is a charming and smooth communicator who can help six's interest in attaining concrete material success.

Six-nine planetary pair: Saturn joined with Venus

Pairs with Seven, Seekers or Enthusiasts

Seven-Seven

The seven-seven union increases the urge to explore new ideas and pursue advanced knowledge for individuals and partners. Because those with this combination are more optimistic and enthusiastic about all that they do, they often meet with success. While the union of two sevens is beneficial to both parties, too much growth and expansion can lead to greed and waste. The appearance of good luck is often present in this union. This pair is also associated with easy improvements and little resistance to the gains that come with its growth. More than in other situations or relationships, this combination seems to bring opportunities for progress in one's development and self-understanding.

Seven-seven planetary pair: Jupiter joined with itself

Seven-Eight

The seven-eight combination is usually beneficial to both sides. Seven's thirst for advanced knowledge and exploring new ideas is moved in the direction of eight's unexpected and often revolutionary ways. Eights want to change things for the better and are supported by optimistic, growth-oriented sevens. This union in partnerships and individuals brings opportunities to expand one's life in independent and unanticipated ways.

This union is confident, aggressive, and original and suggests lightning-quick minds. People represented by the seven-eight combination tend to be independent thinkers and will not accept ideas simply based on tradition. This pair represents the competitive spirit of eight and seven's interest in growth, philosophy, and higher education. Even though they are eager to explore unusual ideas, they want to understand things for themselves.

Seven-eight planetary pair: Jupiter joined with Mars

Seven-Nine

Those represented by the seven-nine combination dislike discomfort to such an extent that they facilitate peace through acts of generosity and creating harmony. Their dislike of aggression and threatening situations implies that they prefer to live around agreeable people and live in beautiful surroundings. The seven-nine combination favors teachers, ministers, counselors, and leaders whose careers require the verbal ability to heal or guide others.

This union represents increased harmony and ease in getting things done. Sevens add enthusiasm and growth opportunities to the peacemaking works that motivate nines. This is an excellent combination for stepping outside the normal boundaries of cooperation and fairness and expanding them by venturing into new territory. Those who stand up to assert themselves with this union will likely do so with greater charm and confidence and be rewarded for their good work.

Seven-nine planetary pair: Jupiter joined with Venus

Pairs with Eight, Defenders or Challengers

Eight-Eight

The eight-eight partnership and individual tends to be direct, blunt, and aggressive. These individuals tend to be confrontational and often rub people the wrong way. The eight-eight union is eager to pursue their goals and get things done. Those represented by this pair tend to focus their energy on narrow objectives and can perform painstaking work. They learn to accept the unexpected in their dealings with others. Their difficulty comes about because they are impatient and don't think things through before acting. While this pair is not socially popular, they are a bundle of energy that can steamroll their way to make things happen.

Eight-eight planetary pair: Mars joined with itself

Eight-Nine

Because the vitality and warm energy of the eight-nine union is just below the surface, it can be felt by others. The union between eights and nines represents an abundance of creativity, energy, and enthusiasm. Their passion is apparent when it comes to going after what they want. The actions in this union are based on a consideration of what will produce the most beauty, balance, and freedom of expression.

The union between eight and nine represents an abundance of energy and enthusiasm. The people with this combination possess great creativity and personal magnetism and attract people into their lives on impulse. This union brings together a pleasing blend of self-assertion and cooperation. They know how to assert themselves without stepping on each other's toes.

Eight-nine planetary pair: Mars joined with Venus

Nine-Nine, The Mediators or Peacemakers

The nine-nine combination for partnerships, individuals, stages, and cycles greatly expands the expression of nine's qualities. Since nine is all about relationships, cooperation, harmony, and peacemaking, adding another nine qualifies this partnership as having magic. People with this pairing have big hearts and hefty appetites for the finer things in life. This pair gives the ability to get what you want when you want it and is often called "the match made in heaven." They hear and know what the other person is saying and have no miscommunications. They are usually attractive to others, love a good time, make enjoyable companions, and often attempt to express their artistic creativity in practical or commercial ways. While eights start things and often break things because of their aggressive nature, nines create harmony, bring things together, mend what is broken, and bring things to fruition.

Nine-nine planetary pair: Venus joined with itself

8

The First Third of the Life Cycle

The only person you are destined to become
is the person you decide to be.

— Ralph Waldo Emerson

Since ancient times, stages of life, cycles of development, and seasons have been considered the "soul of nature," which gives form and order to life. Since the universe is one entire process, we can say that phases of the universe mean the turning of the one. The stages represent many overlapping fields of energy. The energy field of every individual is related intimately to the larger energy field of his or her cosmic environment. Through an understanding of the enneagram signs and the trinities within them, we can know the meaning of our stages and cycles of development.

Many people have come to believe that there is an invisible organizing pattern within living things, a sort of psychological pattern that guides and determines the form that energy will assume. The essence of everything is the ground of the thing's being, that which makes the thing what it is. This tendency toward patterns in nature can be seen in everything, from evolutionary theory to the predictable patterns of human physical and psychological development.

No matter what label might be used to name these universal laws, whether archetypes or essences, the fact remains that such forces exist in and represent the patterns of traits that influence each of us. The nine stages and cycles are the language of universal principles, the natural order in individual lives, and a way of seeing forms changing with time. They are forms of intuition that can be identified and read to understand the soul. Whereas the intellect can reveal the secrets of outer life and the workings of matter, it is intuition that reveals the secrets of inner life and the field of personal experience. The fact that enneagram stages and cycles provide us with unique combinations of archetypes gives them a cherished place as spiritual, psychological, or occult tools.

Life Stage and Cycle Awareness

The enneagram stages and cycles of development refer to living realities that are inexpressible in any other way. While we can never express in words the transcendent realities of the cosmos, we can still make use of the stages and cycles when we let them represent universal patterns, principles, and forces. Some of the values embracing life phases that can contribute to your understanding of human development and the steps you can take to align yourself with the soul's universality patterns are given here. The nine stages and cycles reveal cosmic patterns in a straightforward way that enables us to deal more effectively with our habits and with ourselves. Recurrent phases help us see that the lifetime experience of our existence is subject to an already established order and cyclic rhythm. This clarity helps us develop patience with the opportunities and timing of universal order. The stages and cycles can provide us with faith in something greater than our ego consciousness and therefore faith in our authentic self.

The first cycle of development covers the first nine years or stages of life, from birth to age nine. This nine-year period is called a life cycle and represents where you are coming from. It points to the main themes or qualities you will experience as part of this nine-year period. Individual years within a cycle tell us how the cosmos and nonphysical universe will express the nine-year periods from birthday to birthday. As symbols, these cycles express both the personal and universal at the same time. The nine one-year stages within each cycle are enneagram signs or archetypes that represent the characteristics of a person's experience and the opportunities presented to them. Every year of life is associated with a unique set of traits and lessons. Every annual stage of development in the nine-year cycle has a role for individuals to play. And those who align themselves with the role indicated by each stage will be able to better understand their unfolding development, opportunities, and life lessons and express the soul's personality—their authentic self. Those aware of their stages and cycles of development are aware of more opportunities for learning, growing, and going with the flow. This universal life cycle and cosmic order can help individuals better organize the activities in their lives, understand others, and take advantage of opportunities presented.

Every age starting with birth is represented by the annual solar year, which expresses itself through nine enneagram signs viewed as one-year stages and nine-year cycles. The descriptions that follow lay out the themes, meanings, and relationship between the stages and cycles. For most ages, an example is included on how the age may be experienced. The second eighty-one-year life cycle, beginning at age eight-one, is a recurring and advanced version of the first eighty-one years of life.

Every birthday points to a new part of oneself coming into being and represents an opening to a new direction and new opportunities. A person's success in any stage of development depends in part on embracing the growth potential of that stage or enneagram sign. The people and situations in one's life will present the opportunities to learn the lessons of this stage. The environment and the people in it will indicate areas where you are leading and following others in the development of a better understanding of the year. The organizing principle of every birth year represents the governing themes and traits of that year's experience.

Living from Birth to Age Twenty-Seven

The beginning or first third of life is represented by the active and affirming forces of the trinity and the desire to initiate action. The focus of these early years in the life cycle is a fondness for starting things, often with little regard in sustaining them in the future or planning for future growth. Those in this stage of the life cycle tend to look for their own style and area of focus. Those in the early years of this cycle, before age nine, often start projects and walk away without finishing them. As soon as the activity or project can continue on its own, they lose interest. Those in the middle part of these early years, ages nine to eighteen, are associated with unlimited possibilities but often experience difficulties in dealing effectively with concrete reality. They have exaggerated imaginations and often unique, unusual, or otherworldly ideas. Those in the last part of these early years, ages eighteen to twenty-seven, develop an interest in seeing the big picture, begin to understand what is going on in the larger external world, and work to make the best of everything.

Individuals in the first third of life have the temperament to meet immediate situations and issues, solve them, and move on to something else. They tend to shoot first and argue afterward. They lend energy, ambition, and a go-getter spirit to their relationship with life. The difficulties faced by those in these early years are faults and unlearned lessons of the previous life. But like any difficulty, inherited or inherent, they can be changed by constructive action. These young people tend to be impatient with more sensitive people, such as those in touch with feelings and subtleties that others don't notice. Although this dimension is present in most situations, it is usually overlooked because they are too attached to seeing things through the judgments of "either/or" thinking.

The entire range of our attitudes toward life itself and toward the experience of being alive is associated with the qualities inherent in the first third of life. They represent an outer-directed energy into the world and the aspirations and inspirations that motivate us to do so. As personality types, they represent the universal radiant energy that flows spontaneously in an inspired and self-motivated way. They are all associated with experience centered in personal identity. They personify those who have great faith in themselves, enthusiasm, and unending strength. While not always consistent, their rather black-and-white view of life allows them to direct their willpower consciously better than those in the middle and last thirds of life. They may come across as rather willful, even overpowering at times, rushing into things with such haste that they unintentionally cause destruction or hurt feelings in others. They are represented by the term "steamrollers."

Individuals in this age group are often the most creative and productive of the three groups. They represent impulse more than deliberation and the desire for direct action in solving problems. They bring initiative and creativity together with practicality and the desire to produce things in tangible form. These affirming stage individuals have the potential and ability to conserve and direct their rather formidable vitality and channel their enthusiasm toward specific ambitions. They are generally happiest when they go off on their own to meet the challenges of the outer world rather than relying on established social roles or educational routes to attain success. "Steamrollers" tend to be insensitive and gross, and they are neither reflective about themselves nor careful about whom they may crush in their efforts to get where they're going. They rarely display behavior that could be termed tactful.

The Initiator Cycle

Initiator Traits Common to Ages 0 to 9: Enthusiastic; independent; practical; perfectionists; associated with beginnings and beginners; exploring new directions, ideas, and concepts; idealists; principled; crusading; energy center; communicates messages; explains things; unifies parts; brings things together; agreement; coming together; potential; self-expression; steamroller approach.

Related Planet and Zodiac Signs: *Mercury, 0° Aries to 10° Taurus*

Good habits formed at youth make all the difference.

— Aristotle

The first nine years of life are represented by the first enneagram sign or the Initiator archetype. The nine-year Initiator cycle deals with individual development, which includes one's self-concept, identity, and perspective and defining who one is. This entire period is about learning new ways of doing things, moving in new directions, and giving birth to everything anew. Young children in this phase of life grow through awareness of themselves. Their ability to obtain that awareness is achieved through their experience of all the latent forces of their existence before the Initiator period.

The Initiator sign or stage represents the first year of life from birth to age one and may be understood as the resurrection and beginning of new life. It marks the greatest early childhood experience and the greatest expression of innovative thinking. The first year gives the newcomer his or her characteristic attitude toward life, along with new values and beliefs.

The Guide sign or stage represents the second year of life from age one to two and deals with learning about relationship differences and new ways to serve and cooperate with others, such as parents and siblings. This year is about exploring one's environment and beginning to understanding boundaries, such as what they can and cannot do or get away with.

The Contestant sign or stage represents the third year of life from age two to three and is associated with new growth and the urge to express oneself in creative ways. This year is also about asserting oneself with greater energy and presence.

The Romantic stage or sign represents the fourth year of life from age three to four and brings opportunities to learn and express one's unique views and opinions. In this year, children become more independent and begin to discover how different they are from others. They also tend to exaggerate, tell lies, and romanticize things.

The Innovator stage or sign represents the fifth year of life from age four to five and brings unexpected and often sudden opportunities to help the young child to make changes. These changes help them assimilate their development and gain greater independence. This year also brings an interest in overcoming the pull of the past and adjusting to a new future.

The Skeptic sign or stage is associated with the sixth year of life from age five to six and represents the need for family-oriented stability. It represents the desire to conform to an established order and questioning things that may or may not agree with that order. While this year moves the young person to pursue friendships with others, they tend to be cautious and skeptical about new connections.

The Seeker sign or stage is associated with the seventh year of life from age six to seven and is associated with growth. It brings opportunities for new learning and for pursuing new ventures. This year also brings out one's inventive side and interest in being free to experience things on their own.

The Defender sign or stage represents the eighth year of life from age seven to eight and is about being assertive and independent and accomplishing things that they want. This year brings increased independence, vitality, and an interest in self-development, being first, and achieving tangible success.

The Mediator stage or sign represents the ninth year of life from age eight to nine and brings the urge to clean up loose ends and prepare for the next year and cycle of development. This year brings an interest in understanding the needs of others, learning the value of teamwork, cooperation, and participating in social activities.

The Guide Cycle

Guide Traits Common to Ages 9 to 18: Warm communicators; tangible, tolerant; charming; caregivers; servants, relationship-oriented;

friendly; people pleasers; tactful; feeling-type personality; prefers to follow rather than lead; aware of oppositions; flexible; cooperative; consciousness; dividing lines; interest in understanding oneself and others; receptiveness, motherhood; wisdom.

Related Planet and Zodiac Signs: *The Moon, 10° Taurus to 20° Gemini*

> *Youth is easily deceived because it is quick to hope.*
>
> — Aristotle

Age nine—those represented by the Initiator stage of the Guidance cycle tend to alternate between putting their attention on only one area of interest, such as pursuing an independent project or joining a group endeavor that requires cooperation with others, taking the lead or following another's lead, or being aggressive or passive. Here, one's interest in relationships is influenced by their need for independence and thinking about things in their own way. This one-two combination points to a difficult year because both sides are like opposite sides of the same coin.

The one side sees and talks about things from an objective perspective, while the two side sees and talks about things from the subjective perspective. Both sides are right but express different views. The differences between the Initiator and Guide expressions are growth producing and stretch one's thoughts and feelings. The main lesson of this year is learning to find the balance between opposing interests and between how one thinks and feels about things.

Recall your main experience(s):

_____

Age ten is represented by the second enneagram sign or the Guide for both the stage and cycle. The second sign is usually a time of emotional comfort and warm feeling about helping others, security, and family. The purpose of this year is learning to fit in and cooperate with others. On the positive side, those of this age tend to be in harmony with others.

On the negative side, they often find it difficult to move beyond the past or accept the new. The saying "no pain, no gain" often applies to this cycle-stage pair. In this year, there is often little or no growth because the two sides are more into themselves and less interested in outside growth opportunities. Examples of the age ten experience include participation in teamwork activities and following the lead of friends or authority figures.

Recall your main experience(s):

Age eleven is associated with the third sign of the Contestant, which deals with expressing one's self-image, promotion, growth and achievement. The main experience of this year is expressed through the expansion and increased energy of one's youthful involvements and approach to life. The presence of a three-two union is also associated with expanding one's friendships and social connections. Examples of this stage include significant growth in an existing endeavor or friendship or the start of new learning.

This year is represented by the Contestant and Guide combination, which brings together one's sunlike, fiery, go-getter side with their very different moonlike side, represented by their need to cooperate, follow, and assist others. The lesson of this year is learning to communicate one's feelings and interests with greater enthusiasm. Those who move through this year experience more sensitivity to what others think of them and often understand the temperament of those in their circle.

Recall your main experience(s):

Age twelve is associated with the foreground fourth sign of the Romantic, which deals with idealistic, visionary, and individualistic interests. The background theme of this year is represented by the longer Guide archetype, which deals with following, serving, and cooperating with others. Examples of this year include the experience of being a nonconformist or idealist or simply pursuing rather strange interests in a significant way.

The four-two combination is about expanding and nurturing one's independent and often way-out interests. This combination is often difficult because the relationship between one's conventional needs for personal security and unconventional interests is not easy to maintain. Those who move through this year are often strongly influenced by the emotional attitudes that other people have toward their interests. In this year, many individuals will experience their home life and other interests going through significant changes.

Recall your main experience(s):

Age thirteen is represented by the fifth enneagram sign or the Innovator, which includes interests in objective thinking, change, and making adjustments in one's behaviors. This new kind of interest is experienced in ways that personify this aspect of the longer Guide cycle for supporting one's relationships with others. The five-two combination tells us that this year is about moving away from past ways of relating to oneself and others and toward more conscious ways of connecting with those we are close to, e.g., making the transition from preteen to teenager.

In this year, the new stage-five influence of this wants to upend and change things that have become too settled, while the long-term second cycle wants safety, security, and emotional peace. The Guide influence wants to help those who need help, whereas the Innovator stage wants to change things that need changing. The opposing natures of the fifth stage and second cycle tend to both blind people to common sense and caution and motivate them to pursue good causes.

Recall your main experience(s):

Age fourteen is defined by the sixth sign or Skeptic archetype, which includes being dependable and practical in ways that are helpful, flexible, and relationship oriented. The main lesson of this period is understanding and making choices about one's close relationships with others. Examples of this age include learning and discerning the nature of one's relationships with others and making improvements in one's close relationships.

Although this stage-cycle combination suggests a shared interest in relationship security, it is otherwise inharmonious. The six-two period tends to bring the experience of notable depression and a lack of joy in life. Even though this year points to being practical and responsible in one's relationships, it can be experienced as a period of being overly cautious and pessimistic. Those moving through this year want to create tangible success, but this goal is delayed until they help others attain success for themselves as well.

Recall your main experience(s):

Age fifteen is associated with the seventh enneagram sign or Seeker stage, which brings enthusiastic interests in learning new things, seeking new experiences, and the acquisition of knowledge. This year brings an urge to experience new pleasures and excitement and help others. Examples of this combination include acquiring an interest in higher education, a training program, and learning about significant current events.

The seven-two stage and cycle combination is beneficial to both sides. In this year, the security-oriented two or Guide sign wants to serve and nurture growth, and the growth-oriented seventh sign wants to pursue new ideas and expand their knowledge of what's available. Two supports the goals of seven, and seven's optimism and energy inspire two. This age is also associated with an increase in one's development, excitement about one's goals, and positive changes in mood.

Recall your main experience(s):

Age sixteen is associated with the eighth sign or Defender archetype, which deals with thinking big, self-determination, aggression, and ambition. Those who move through this year are confident and hopeful about the future and take control of things regarding their next step in life and in relationships with others. In this year, the longer Guide cycle is often undercut by the rough, unsympathetic, and high-powered energy of stage eight. Examples of this age include making plans and pursuing a significant new goal.

The eight-two combination points to an intense, straightforward, and passionate approach to being number one. The eight side of this union brings confidence, enthusiasm, and independence to the maternal and caregiving nature of the two side. The new presence of eight in this partnership may move two to advocate for fast food, impatience, and the need to grow up quickly. This year is often challenging because two wants to help support and understand, while eight want to asserts itself with intensity and power.

Recall your main experience(s):

Age seventeen is associated with the ninth sign of the Mediator, which deals with humanitarian interests, harmony, connecting people, and competing or resolving things. These traits are expressed in ways that advance one's desire to pursue and serve an organization or cause larger than they are. Examples of this year include ending or beginning a personal relationship, leaving or starting school, and supporting humanitarian endeavors.

This year is associated with emotional responses to beauty and harmony, which often take the form of artistic or design interests and creating beautiful environments. The nine-two union makes for a beneficial year of being sociable, compassionate, and diplomatic. Two supports nine's need for fairness, harmony, and peace, and nine's humanitarian goals are nurtured by two's helping nature. This year also points to a time when people tend to be happy-go-lucky, warm, and supportive and want to bring good to others.

Recall your main experience(s):

The Contestant Cycle

Contestant Traits Common to Ages 18 to 27: Sociable; talkers; warm; influential people; doers; cheerful; knowledgeable; achievers; performers; motivators; upbeat; optimistic; energetic; go-getters; image-conscious; creators of innovative ideas; growth; heart's desire; identifies with being the source and center of attention; success; harmony; creative; easygoing; kindness; interest in growth and expansion; self-expression.

Related Planet and Zodiac Signs: *The Sun, 20° Gemini to 0° Leo*

> *Everything happens to everybody sooner or*
> *later if there is enough time.*
>
> — George Bernard Shaw

Age eighteen represents the first enneagram sign or Initiator stage, which deals with being independent, communicating messages, and introducing innovative ideas. This year is also influenced by the new Contestant cycle, which deals with expressing one's image, self-promotion, and going after one's goals with a great deal of energy. This year is associated with new growth, optimism about the future, and pursuing many new ventures.

The one-three combination is a beneficial year. It is filled with the kind of mental energy that energizes one's interest in learning and communication. Those who move through this year tend to do so with enthusiasm, confidence, and a willingness to take risks. This combination points to expressing good feelings, a quick wit, and the tendency to have a sharp tongue. This year also points to interests in being sociable, communicating with others, and learning new things.

Recall your main experience(s):

Age nineteen is associated with the second sign of the Guide, which deals with personal relationships, cooperation, and assisting others in ways that support the nine-year Contestant cycle for performance and achieving success. The themes of this year deal with self-reflection, self-discovery, and growth in one's personal relationships. Examples of this year include a meaningful relationship experience and growth in one's self-understanding.

The two-three union brings together the subjective, helpful, and private side of life with the energetic, objective, and public side. The lesson for this year is learning to express one's feelings and presence in their communications with others. Those who move through this year tend to be sensitive to what others think of them and usually understand the temperament of people around them. In this year, the receptive Guide energy is pushed out of its comfort zone by the fiery Contestant energy.

Recall your main experience(s):

Age twenty represents the union between the third stage and cycle, which brings increased energy and a stronger focus on the sunlike Contestant qualities of achievement, growth, harmony, and pursuing success. This once-in-a-lifetime combination brings greater awareness of the light to the strong and weak qualities of the three-three union. The message of this year is that the more you accept yourself, the more beneficial your relationship with yourself and others will be.

The experience of this year personifies the optimism, growth, harmony, and qualities of enthusiasm associated with three. It is a year for expressing one's unique identity that is beyond being a teen yet not an official adult. This three-three union represents patterns of action that expand the harmonious Contestant energy of one's experience. This year is a source of strength and perhaps difficulty for those who are out of step with the urge to express and promote their identity.

Recall your main experience(s):

Age twenty-one is represented by the enneagram sign of the Romantic, which deals with becoming aware of multisensory perceptions, ideals, and the odd or eccentric. The larger Contestant cycle represents self-expression, creativity, growth, performance, and promotion. The activities of this year often deal with support one's individual uniqueness. Examples of this union of stages include acting on the urge to express one's dreams and artistic interests.

The four-three combination brings together the largest source of transcendence wisdom with the largest source of energy, growth, and harmony in the universe. Thus, many aspects of the very different unconscious realm and multisensory perceptions are brought into the light of day. For many, this year presents an opportunity to unite intuition and spirituality with one's individual uniqueness. Those in this year may learn things about themselves that were completely unknown.

Recall your main experience(s):

_____

Age twenty-two is associated with the detached and investigative influence of the fifth enneagram sign or Innovator stage. Here, the fifth sign is personified in ways that support and express the Contestant cycle. This stage-cycle combination points to opportunities to change things that need changing. Illustrations of this year include the experience of unexpected new growth that expands one's view of the world.

Individuals represented by the five-three year are inclined to be competitive and want to prove that they possess more knowledge or intellectual superiority than others. They tend to rebel against the established order, accept unanticipated changes, and express themselves with great enthusiasm. In this year, unexpected and dramatic changes are experienced with increased energy and harmony. Those who experience this year are usually motivated to investigate things and communicate their findings.

Recall your main experience(s):

_____

Age twenty-three is represented by the sixth enneagram sign or the Skeptic archetype, which includes taking on new responsibilities and making commitments to solidify one's place in life. These interests are personified in ways supported by the Contestant cycle for expanding one's personal and social image. This year is about the experience of growing up and becoming like a parent. Illustrations of this year include taking responsibility for one's development and achieving one's goals.

The sixth-three union is challenging because the cautious and secretive nature of the Saturn-like Skeptic is very different from the fiery, optimistic, and harmonious sunlike Contestant. The reticent and devil's-advocate approach of those who move through this year are eager to achieve success but must first know what is required to be successful. The upbeat, energetic, and growth-oriented three is often held back by the questioning and wet-blanket approach to doing things by six.

Recall your main experience(s):

Age twenty-four is defined by the seventh enneagram sign or the Seeker archetype, which represents pursuing big plans, advanced education, and opportunities to experience new things. This year is beneficial because both the stage and cycle represent positive expansion and growth. The main experience of this age is increased energy and a new awareness of one's self-image, self-development, and relationships.

People who move through the seven-three year learn to think for themselves and not accept ideas simply based on tradition. This year is associated with expansion and an interest in philosophy, religion, and often higher education. In this year, people want to understand and prove things for themselves and constantly seek the new or unusual. They often gain insights through intuitive flashes and have an interest in learning about and perhaps communicating directly with the nonphysical universe.

Recall your main experience(s):

Age twenty-five is associated with the sign of the Defender, which includes the qualities of independence, self-determination, and aggressiveness. These qualities are expressed in ways that advance the nine-year Contestant cycle for growth, social image, promotion, and achievement. The focus in the eight-three year is thinking big and acting upon our hopes and plans. Examples of this age include attaining a significant goal or recognition.

The Defender-Contestant combination inspires confidence and aggression. This union often motivates people to be confrontational and may rub others the wrong way. In this year, people tend to be ambitious and impatient, and their blunt style often encounters difficulties in gaining positive recognition. Unlike the seven-three combination of the previous year, which seeks to explore new ideas and learn things about the universe, this year's eight-three combination tends to bring an eagerness to pursue one's goals and get things done. In this year, people tend to act before thinking things through.

Recall your main experience(s):

Age twenty-six is represented by the ninth sign or the Mediator, which deals with humanitarian activities aimed at peacemaking and bringing things to completion. These themes are personified in ways that support and express the final year of the larger Contestant period for growth, creative expression, promotion, and achievements. Many activities of this year deal with the completion of development that was started with this nine-year cycle or age eighteen. Examples of this completion year include supporting a humanitarian goal and pursuing a significant spiritual or educational development activity.

This combination makes for a beneficial year because the expansive, harmonious, and optimistic energy of the Contestant is compatible with the Mediator sign. The Venus-like urge to promote peace, unity, and goodness is compatible with the sunlike urge to be expansive, harmonious, and optimistic. Those who move through this year tend to be easygoing and want to be nice to others. This union often represents an interest in diplomacy, bringing people together, and pursuing actions that will produce the most beauty, balance, and cooperation.

Recall your main experience(s):

9

The Middle Third of the Life Cycle

There is nothing permanent except change.

— Heraclitus

The middle third of life from ages twenty-seven to fifty-four represents the denying and receptive forces of the trinity and the desire to preserve and sustain. The focus of these middle years in the life cycle is on activities carried out daily in a predictable and reliable manner. The most obvious characteristic of this stage of life is stubbornness and persistence. In these middle years, one's experience of life is motivated by the desire for practical and useful results. In this stage, people learn to reason things out before acting. They instinctively know that understanding is a condition for complete and correct utilization.

The middle years are the most consistent and persistent of the three life stages. The denying force produces a movement through life that is a quiet, organizing, and motivated by principles. Those in this stage of life tend to be reservoirs of energy and power. They are known for being stubborn and rarely deviate from a set path. They have a definite pattern and resist all outer interference that will alter it. The experience of this stage of life is the most difficult to describe as the basic motivations are seldom obvious and do not reveal themselves willingly. However, those in this stage tend have the self-discipline to change ingrained negative or less useful patterns of behavior into constructive ones.

The middle years are associated with the level of experience wherein we try to satisfy our basic needs in the practical world: possessions, money, job, reputation, health, etc. They point to individuals in touch with their physical senses and the here-and-now reality of the physical world. Those in these years are linked to the world of forms and usually have a great deal of patience. They rarely must be told how to fit into the world of making a living, supplying basic needs, and persisting till a goal is reached. Those in this group tend to be passive or receptive and only speak out and assert themselves when their "thing" is endangered or their security is threatened. They tend to be cautious, conventional, and dependable. Unlike those in the first third of the life cycle, those in the middle third are involved with the practical world in ways that often limit their imagination. These limits increase when they rely too much on things as they are or as they appear to be. The denying forces of the middle years are associated with a narrowness of outlook and a limited ability to deal with the abstract and theoretical realms of activity.

Individuals in this group have an alternating pull between the thinking and feeling approach to life and the intuitive and sensing approach. While these approaches are incompatible, there is not so much conflict as there might seem. When those in this stage learn to focus within themselves, they can combine intellectual and conceptual awareness with a practical awareness of concrete objectives. The most positive trait of this individual is that they have practical grounding upon which their ideas are based, and many have an innovative perspective on getting things done in the outer world. As a group, the years from twenty-seven to fifty-four are associated with forethought, detachment, practical intelligence, and analysis. While the people in this stage of life can be sensitive to others, impulse and displays of emotions are not their way of operating, and they often distrust those who personify such qualities. The middle years are also associated with organizing and working with established situations and concrete details without getting overwhelmed.

The Romantic Cycle

Romantic Traits Common to Ages 27 to 36: Dramatic; compulsive; popular; artistic; dreamers; ideal-seekers; visionary; rebels; free agents; escapists; interest in manifesting dreams and mothering; way out and weird; often unrealistic; brings the unconscious into consciousness; limitations; expressive; concretizing; self-restraint; decision; psychic awareness; karma.

Related Planet and Zodiac Signs: *Neptune, 0° Leo to 10° Virgo*

> *One person can make a difference,*
> *and everyone should try.*
>
> — John F. Kennedy

Age twenty-seven represents the sign of the Initiator, which deals with new directions, new opportunities, independence, and learning and communicating practical information. Since this year also marks the beginning of the nine-year Romantic cycle, the one-four combination points to a new and youthful interest in pursuing rather eccentric hopes and dreams. Examples of this year include the pursuit of a significant ideal or individualistic endeavor.

The one-four combination brings together the intellect and intuition in a way that creates something unique. In this year, communications with others may contain misunderstandings because the objective and subjective parties don't understand the other with sufficient clarity. For many, the experience of this year is like squeezing the proverbial square peg into a round hole. Many of those represented by the one-four union begin to establish themselves in a highly personalized and unusual way.

Recall your main experience(s):

_____

Age twenty-eight is represented by the second sign or the Guide, which deals with cooperation, being of service, and fostering the development of others. In this year, individuals have an interest in being flexible and helpful in their effort to personify the larger cycle for embracing one's individualistic and unusual interests. This year is represented by the experience of receiving guidance or insights that deepen self-understanding and eccentric interests.

The two-four combination is often beneficial because the two side wants to nurture and help the eccentric side expand and grow into its rather mysterious, otherworldly potential. This combination is often difficult because the relationship between personal and transcendent needs is not easy to know or maintain. Those who move through this year will likely be influenced by the emotional attitudes of other people. In addition, many will find fulfillment through domestic interests and emotional ties to family.

Recall your main experience(s):

Age twenty-nine is represented by the third or Contestant sign, which points to self-expression, growth, and promotion. Here, people have an interest in their public image, performing, and communicating as their way to advance the larger Romantic cycle. Many of this year's activities will deal with seeking new areas of growth and giving birth to new opportunities. Examples of this age include creating and nurturing the growth of new endeavors.

The three-four combination unites the largest source of energy, growth, and harmony in the universe with the largest source of transcendence wisdom in the universe. In this year, the very different world of multisensory perceptions and far-out interests are often brought into the light of day. This year may bring a new understanding of messages from the creative mind, which often comes through new feelings, dreams, and intuitions and gives us the urge to learn about spirituality, intuition, and psychic realities that have not yet been defined.

Recall your main experience(s):

Age thirty marks the fourth stage and fourth cycle combination, which points to an increase in imagination, artistic expression, and inspiration from the nonphysical universe. This union greatly expands one's understanding and expression of the Romantic archetype. Those represented by the four-four year tend to romanticize, idealize, and exaggerate. While this year tends to bring an excitement about communicating with the nonphysical universe, it is difficult to explain or manifest these otherworldly ideas.

Those moving through this year are often attractive to others, love a good time, make enjoyable companions, and often attempt to express their rather weird and individualistic interests in practical ways. Examples of this year include building a new or stronger relationship with one's intuition and spirituality in a way that enhances their life.

Recall your main experience(s):

Age thirty-one marks the beginning of the Innovator phase in the Romantic cycle. The qualities of one's experience in this year are associated with change, correction, and beginning to integrate a new way of being in ways that incorporate the Romantic cycle, which brings new interests in spirituality and the unconscious into their life. This five-four year brings a desire to experience the transcendent in a significant way. Examples of this age include starting or ending a career or relationship or making significant life changes.

The fifth or Innovator stage of the Romantic cycle is likely to be experienced as a kind of hidden revolution. This combination of energy can bring a new understanding of messages from the unconscious, which often come through feelings and intuitions. This union is characterized by unexpected and sudden changes. In the foreground, those moving through this transition year experience changes in their awareness and thinking, which increases their understanding of the deeper mind.

Recall your main experience(s):

Age thirty-two is represented by the sixth enneagram sign or Skeptic stage of the nine-year Romantic cycle. As such, this year often points to an interest in psychic or multisensory awareness and understanding of the inner world in ways that help us give meaning and established order. The experience of this year often helps people accept greater responsibility in the organized world while continuing to understand their intuitive nature. Examples of this year include accepting an important new responsibility or commitment based on a Neptune-like foundation, such as new psychic awareness and understanding of the transcendent and self-actualization.

In this six-four year, people want to express their Saturn-like need for skepticism, even though their interests in the transcendent may not be deeply understood or accepted. Those who move through this year have an interest in expressing themselves through intangible endeavors. While this year is about success based on the laws of established reality, the nine-year Romantic cycle inspires people to express their interest in getting insights through imagination and the subjective mind.

Recall your main experience(s):

Age thirty-three represents the seventh sign or Seeker stage, which points to optimism, excitement, and the pursuit of visionary interests. The Romantic cycle brings opportunities to expand one's imagination, intuition, and connection with the nonphysical universe in ways that support the current consciousness-raising year. Examples of this year include efforts to increase one's spiritual development and self-knowledge.

The seven-four combination is beneficial to both the stage and cycle of this union. Both sides want to experience and express the mysteries of the unseen spiritual universe. The difference is that the Seeker side wants to learn about direct contact with the soul, whereas the Romantic side wants to experience direct contact. In this year, people often experience a dissolution of old patterns, breaks with the past, and disruptions in their level of support.

Recall your main experience(s):

Age thirty-four is associated with the eighth sign or Defender archetype, which represents a confident, enthusiastic, and aggressive approach to life. The eight-four combination is difficult because the natures of the Mars-like eight and the Neptune-like four are very different. The main lesson of this year is finding the balance between asserting one's ideas and listening to the creative mind's subjective message. Examples of this year include taking the lead to assert one's subjective interests and offbeat plans.

The union between the Defender stage and the Romantic cycle makes for a blunt and passionate approach, expressing the formless universe and communicating with the deeper mind. The presence of eight in this combination moves four toward a more practical and down-to-earth expression of its spiritual and mystical nature. The intangible nature of four can make the eight side of this union feel uninspired, lazy, and directionless.

Recall your main experience(s):

Age thirty-five marks the last or Mediator stage of the nine-year Romantic cycle. In this year, people often bring things to fruition or completion, make peace with the past nine-year period, and plant seeds for the next nine-year cycle. This is a beneficial stage-cycle year that inspires those in it to be warm and supportive to all. In addition to an increased awareness of the spiritual universe, this year brings an interest and openness to ideas from others.

This year is associated with openness to others and the desire to examine hidden mysteries regarding one's place in the universe. In addition to increased sensitivity to the spiritual universe, this pair brings an interest in new and unusual ventures. The union between four and nine makes for a sociable and spiritual nature. Nine adds understanding, warmth, and charm to four's connection with the transcendent. This union will help those who move through it to explain many unknown aspects of relationships that are often never seen.

Recall your main experience(s):

The Innovator Cycle

Innovator Traits Common to Ages 36 to 45: Cerebral; mediation; practical; fussy; observers; thinkers; researchers; reasonable; calculating; levelheaded; recluse; personal drive; freedom; focus; inventiveness; change; correction; integration; studious; intelligent; psychological; wise; amiable; versatile; midlife transitions; identity; centered; equilibrium; harmony.

Associated Planet and Zodiac Signs: *Uranus, 10° Virgo to 20° Libra*

You can't help getting older, but you don't have to get old.

— George Burns

Age thirty-six marks the first year or Initiator stage, which represents beginnings, exploring new directions, and communicating innovative ideas. This stage is expressed in ways that support the Innovation cycle, which represents observation, thinking, and a psychological approach to making changes. The first stage in this new cycle brings an openness to opportunities for new knowledge and beginning to recognize that we are approaching life's midpoint. Examples of the five-one period include reviewing or reviving a significant goal from the past that has not been fulfilled.

The union between the first or beginning stage of this cycle makes for energy expressing itself through the confident communication of ideas. Individuals represented by this combination learn to become more independent in their approach to life. This year is about image-consciousness, progressive ideas, and new plans for one's life. Individuals moving through this year may experience difficulties in situations that require them to follow the established order.

Recall your main experience(s):

Age thirty-seven is associated with the second enneagram sign or the Guide stage, which represents helping others, teamwork, and cooperation experienced in a way that supports the nine-year Innovation cycle. Those in this year tend to be friendly and service oriented and want to express this dimension of the larger Innovator cycle. The main qualities of the two-five union are represented by flexibility and allowing events to proceed without one's intervention. Examples of this year include pursuing a new relationship and ending or changing a relationship.

The opposing natures of the moon-based second stage and the Uranus-based fifth cycle can both blind people to common sense and caution and motivate them to pursue noble causes. While the new second-stage influence wants safety, security, and emotional peace, the fifth cycle wants to upend and change things that have become too settled. Since the background or Innovator cycle brings the urge to change things that need changing and the current stage wants to help those who need it, the goal for this year is to work toward a smooth change.

Recall your main experience(s):

_____

Age thirty-eight is beneficial to the ever-expanding and optimistic energy of the Contestant and the detached and investigative energy of the Innovator. This year's three-five union is associated with expressing the qualities of one's image, growth, and independent thoughts. The union of stage and cycle here points to embracing the natural expansion of one's existence and changing things that need changing. Illustrations of this year include expanding a new or existing relationship and significant, new personal or career growth.

Individuals represented by this stage-cycle pair are inclined to be competitive and show that they possess more knowledge or intellectual superiority than others. They are more inclined to rebel against the established order and express themselves with greater confidence. In this stage, the often unexpected and dramatic changes associated with the Innovator cycle are experienced with increased energy and harmony.

Those who experience this year are often motivated to study things and communicate their findings with great enthusiasm.

Recall your main experience(s):

_____

Age thirty-nine marks the fourth enneagram sign or the Romantic stage. The qualities of one's experience in this year are associated with getting insights from the unconscious, owning their individualistic nature, and manifesting their dreams. This fourth stage is expressed in ways that personify the larger Innovation cycle, which deals with making changes and adjusting one's course in life. An example of this year's four-five combination is learning to express the transcendent in a significant way.

The fourth or Romantic stage of the Innovator cycle is likely to be experienced as a kind of hidden revolution. This combination of energies often brings a new understanding of messages from the unconscious, which often come through feelings and intuitions. Those moving through this year will have an active intuitive nature, which helps them understand the unexpected changes that seem to come out of nowhere and explain their connection with the deeper mind—their own self-realization.

Recall your main experience(s):

_____

Age forty marks the greatest expression of the Innovator themes, such as investigation, objective awareness, the unexpected, change, and correction. This happens because the fifth stage and cycle are united toward the same goals. This five-five union is a source of strength and perhaps difficulty for those who are out of step with the Innovator energy. This year brings together the need for change that is often sudden and unexpected with a concrete understanding of what changes are taking place.

The five-five Innovator stage and cycle union is potentially the most progressive, startling, and change-producing combination in one's lifetime. This union represents the midpoint expression or bridge between two worlds, such as the first and second half of life or starting or ending a sincere relationship or career. It links the intuitive side of the transcendent and the thinking side of reality. The experience of this year helps people contemplate the mystery of transformations in their life.

Recall your main experience(s):

Age forty-one is represented by the qualities of the sixth enneagram sign or the Skeptic stage of the Innovator. This year is challenging because the energies of the Saturn-like six and the Uranus-like five are so different. In this year, the experience of the six-year stage of the Skeptic stage, which points to being pessimistic and doubtful, is expressed in the larger Innovation cycle that deals with moving forward to make needed changes despite limitation.

In this year, six's desire to proceed with caution is jointly expressed with five's desire to make revolutionary changes. This makes the current year feel like driving a race car with the brakes on. The upbeat, energetic, and revolutionary five is held back by the questioning and wet-blanket approach to doing things of six. In this year, the progressive and change-oriented Innovator energy is frustrated by the stubborn and cautious Skeptic energy

Recall your main experience(s):

Age forty-two marks the beginning of the seventh enneagram sign or the Seeker archetype, which points to the pursuit of big ideas, plans, growth, and self-discovery opportunities. The current year is expressed in ways supported by the larger cycle for innovation, change, and correcting one's situation in life. In some cases, the cerebral influence of this Innovation year is undercut by the seventh cycle's need or pleasure and excitement.

While the revolutionary and disruptive Innovator influence brings sudden and unexpected changes, the optimistic Seeker brings enthusiasm to pursue innovative ideas and learn new things. Even though the styles of five and seven are different, the unexpected events and changes of fives can be beneficial to seven's broader understanding. As a result, this age brings an interest in expansion and growth that comes with the experience of sudden opportunities that seem to come out of the blue.

Recall your main experience(s):

Age forty-three is represented by the eighth sign or the Defender stage, which brings about an aggressive approach to change and thinking about one's hopes and plans. Those represented by the Defender-Innovator year tend to be confrontational and rub people the wrong way. In this eight-five year, people often focus their energy on well-defined, progressive, and narrow objectives to get things done. Examples of this year include pursuing a big goal aimed at moving an individual group or perhaps society in a new direction.

This year is not easy too because it gives a tremendous drive to attain individualistic goals, which is frustrating when they are not reached. This combination points to the capacity for demanding work and the courage to pursue difficult situations. Problems come about because people moving through this year don't sit still long enough to think things through before acting.

Recall your main experience(s):

Age forty-four is represented by the ninth sign or the Mediator archetype, expressing itself at the end of the progressive Innovator cycle. Because the year coincides with the ninth stage and the end of the fifth cycle, it points to gaining an understanding of the current year and past nine years, bringing things to fruition, and planting the seeds for learning the coming one-six year. An example of this year includes working to making a thoughtful and meaningful change in or to one's group or movement.

Many people who move through this stage and cycle experience the unexpected and want to create peace and harmony in their dealings with others. The harmony-oriented nine and independent-thinking, change-oriented five attract exciting people into one's life and opportunities to change the way they relate to other people. The Venus-based Mediator influence tends to soften the unexpected and often disruptive experience brought on by the Uranus-based Innovator. Those who move through this year want to both keep the peace and make needed changes.

Recall your main experience(s):

The Skeptic Cycle

Skeptic Traits Common to Ages 45 to 54: Able; dynamic; practical; attractive; intelligent; pessimistic; secretive; seductive; troopers; shrewd; humanitarian; responsible; devil's advocates; supporters of family; close association; questioner; doubting Thomas; unbelievers; agnostics; charming; warm; family-oriented; harmony; detective; manager; troubleshooter.

Related Planet and Zodiac Signs: *Saturn, 20° Libra to 0° Sagittarius*

> *A man who views the world the same at fifty*
> *as he did at twenty has wasted thirty years of his life.*
>
> — Muhammad Ali

Age forty-five marks the first year of the nine-year Skeptic cycle. Here, the Initiator's interest in beginnings and exploring new directions is experienced in ways that aim to enhanced the longer cycle. This year can be difficult because the Initiator and Skeptic goals are very different. Individuals who experience this stage often have episodes of depression because the environment insists on things being done the right way and fitting into the established order.

The influence of the Skeptic cycle wants us to understand the hidden universe of laws and feelings before attaining success, whereas the success of the Initiator depends on communicating with others so that understanding can take place. The six side needs to think things through to avoid making mistakes, whereas the independent and expressive one side wants to understand and act without being held back and simply tries to create an understanding. This new way of being becomes the next year's interest in helping and supporting others.

Recall your main experience(s):

___

Age forty-six is defined by the second enneagram sign or the Guide archetype, which includes helping and assisting others and attaining emotional security. In this year, individuals tend to be flexible and care for others in ways that support the Skeptic's need for loyalty, commitment, and family. The main lesson in this period is understanding our close relationships with others. An illustration of this year includes the experience of making improvements in one's close relationships.

Although this stage and cycle union suggests a shared interest in relationship security, it is otherwise inharmonious. When the Guide stage is joined with the Skeptic cycle, it is often accompanied by emotional coolness, some depression, and a lack of joy in life. Even though this year points to being practical and responsible in one's relationships, it may also be a year of increased pessimism.

Recall your main experience(s):

___

Age forty-seven is defined by the Contestant archetype, which includes growth, optimism, being sociable, harmony, and self-expression. Here, people are upbeat, energetic, and image conscious in ways that bring out the best of the Skeptic's need for commitment, loyalty, and family relationships. The main goal of this year is growth and expansion in one's emotional life and social security. Examples of this year include the growth of a notable new endeavor and receiving support from close associates or family.

The third stage of the Skeptic cycle is challenging because the cautious, established order nature of the Saturn-like six is very different from the fiery, optimistic, and harmonious sunlike three. The reticent and conventional Skeptic cycle energy is opposed by the Contestant's restless and expansive nature. Generally, the upbeat, energetic, and growth-oriented Contestant is held back by the questioning and wet-blanket approach to doing things by the Skeptic.

Recall your main experience(s):

Age forty-eight is represented by the fourth enneagram sign or the Romantic stage, which is associated with dreamers, ideal-seekers, and the appearance of unusual interests. This year often points to an interest in psychic or multisensory awareness and understanding the inner world in ways that help us give meaning to the established order. The main goal of this year is about deepening one's understanding of their individuality.

In this four-six year, people want to express their individualistic view of reality, even though it may not be understood or accepted by the down-to-earth need for skepticism. Those who move through this year have an interest in expressing themselves through intangible and often weird endeavors. In this year, the Romantic stage inspires individuals to express their interest in getting insights through imagination and the subjective mind, while the Skeptic cycle wants to attain success based on the laws of established reality.

Recall your main experience(s):

Age forty-nine is associated with the fifth sign or the Innovation stage, which deals with transitions through sudden and often startling midlife changes. The main goal of this midpoint in the Skeptic cycle is making thoughtful and needed changes to create stability for yourself and those close to you. Examples of this five-six year include being off-balance and in a place of uncertainty yet grounded in the faith that things will work out.

The current five-six year is challenging for both parties because they are so different. Here, the Innovator's transpersonal and progressive interests in change are joined with the Skeptic's need for security, desire to proceed with caution, question things, and play by the rules, and approach to attain success. In this year, the energetic and revolutionary five is held back by the devil's-advocate, skeptical, and conventional six.

Recall your main experience(s):

Age fifty represents the greatest expression of the Skeptic archetype because the sixth stage and cycle are the same. This year represents an emphasis on the values of loyalty, commitment, family, and stability. The focus of this period is taking actions that help discover answers by questioning things, troubleshooting, and finding emotional security. Examples of this year include learning or pursuing an established activity, idea, or endeavor.

This year presents an opportunity to do things the right way, redo the things that were not none correctly, or make a course correction. Although the Skeptic's energy is considered difficult for people at most, it can produce remarkable results for those who proceed with caution and follow the established order. In this year, people often learn that their success or failure is directly related to understanding the rules governing their endeavors.

Recall your main experience(s):

Age fifty-one is associated with the seventh sign or the Seeker stage, which includes the pursuit of new ideas, big plans, a quest for pleasure, excitement, and often higher education. However, this growth-oriented stage is limited by the unhurried and deep-rooted approach of the background Skeptic cycle. Examples of this year include learning and teaching spiritual wisdom in one's organized circle or community.

Those in this Seeker-Skeptic year tend to experience a range of emotions, from depression to optimism and a lack of joy to great joy. The goal of this union is for people to pursue a disciplined, organized, and responsible approach to life with the freedom to explore new projects and acquire knowledge of the universe. This year's goal is for seven to expand its interests and for six to understand and support seven's attainment of success.

Recall your main experience(s):

Age fifty-two is defined by the eighth enneagram sign or the Defender stage, which points to an aggressive urge to assert one's ideas and power in ways that are advanced or supported by the well-established Skeptic cycle. This year is about expanding one's reputation, self-determination, and actions to create security for those who depend on their leadership. Examples of this age include pursuing goals that expand one's innovative ideas in ways that are supported and an established position or community.

Because the energies in the eight-six combination are incompatible, this year presents both problems and opportunities for success. The brash and often steamrolling approach of the Defender and the cautious "play by the rules" approach of Skeptics are tied together. The result is that eight is slowed by established order and that six is taxed by the constant eagerness of eight to push forward hurriedly. The Skeptic's urge to play by the rules opposes the Defender's urge to get around the rules and follow the beat of its own drummer.

Recall your main experience(s):

Age fifty-three is defined by the ninth sign or Mediator archetype, which includes interests in creating harmony, serving community, uniting people, and completing things. Mediators are charming and smooth communicators who can help spread the Skeptic's urge to maintain strong relationships and attain concrete material success.

Examples of this year include ending a long-term relationship and releasing outdated ways of relating to others.

In the current year, the Mediator's energy wants to share its positive attitude toward creating fairness and harmony, while the Skeptic's energy wants to create material success by following an established plan. On the positive side, the warm and cooperative Mediator eases the cautious and pessimistic influence of the Skeptic. On the negative side, the "play by the rules" traditional approach can be a drag on nine's charming nature.

Recall your main experience(s):

10

The Last third of Life and Beyond

*We are made wise not by the recollection of our past
but by the responsibility for our future.*

— George Bernard Shaw

The last third of life from ages fifty-four and beyond is represented by the mediating and reconciling forces of the trinity and the desire for self-discovery, change, transformation, and adaptation. These life-completing years deal with the need to allow things to survive and run their course as realities continue to change. The people in this group are adaptable and less resistant to change than the other two groups. While they do not always initiate change, they coexist with it well. They are far more open to suggestions than the other two groups. They can take whatever has been created and sustained by the other two groups and transform it into something better. They tend to preserve life by entering the feelings of others. They feel the need for regular relationships with other people of like mind for social involvement that allows them an outlet for expressing their ideas. The first nine years of this period, from ages fifty-four to sixty-three, are associated with the expansion of thought and creative expression. The second nine years from ages sixty-three to seventy-two are associated with the experience of feelings and emotional peace, and the third nine years from ages seventy-two to eighty-one are associated with knowledge that comes when the intellect is suspended to listen to the soul.

As a group, those in the reconciling years are pliable and adapt to circumstances. It is this quality that makes them easygoing, tolerant, and free-flowing. Their interests are centered in direct and highly personal relationships with people. They are great joiners and are interested in the minute details of personal living. They are good imitators and give things a new slant and a new angle. Because the versatile quality of self-learning can lead those in this group into too many different avenues, they need to watch this tendency to scatter their energy. Those who are less mature will experience more changes and tend to lack persistence and strength of will. In addition, they are prone to negativity and worry and apt to exaggerate anything of a negative nature.

The entire range of personal relationships is experienced in the last third of life, which comprises not only the way we approach various kinds of relationships but also the social urges and intellectual needs that motivate these behaviors. People in this part of life tend to have an increase in their imagination, creative abilities, and interest in counseling and the healing arts. They seek out other people of like mind and experience on the emotional and soul level. While neither the thinking nor the feeling world is alien to those in this self-learning stage of life, they often feel pulled between the intellectual and emotional approaches to life represented by these numbers. They tend to give greater depth to their ideas and often gain detachment and perspective on their feelings and deeper interests. People in this stage of life are more sensitive than those in the first two stages and often tempted to be impractical and unrealistic.

Individuals in this part of the life cycle represent forces that function through the mind to shape patterns of things to come. While they are in touch with their feelings and in tune with the nuances and subtleties that many others don't notice, they also can detach themselves from the immediate experience of daily life. Because they don't feel the need to get heavily involved with the other person's worries or emotions, this detachment enables them to work with all sorts of people. These people play the roles of actualizing creation in the broadest social level and potentially touching the lives of millions. Since feelings, by their very nature, are partly unconscious, self-learners are aware of the unconscious mind and are themselves unconscious of much of what really motivates them. The reconciliation theme of this group suggests that its members are associated with the process of gaining consciousness through a slow but sure realization of the soul's deepest yearnings.

The Seeker Cycle

Seeker Traits Common to Ages 54 to 63: Hopeful; optimistic; pursues grandiose ideas, plans, and growth opportunities; inventive; excitement; curious and astute observers; pleasure and excitement seekers; epicure; visionary; generalists; idealistic; inventors; awakeners; psychic; able and usually willing to change; wise; brilliance; gratitude; devotees; students of philosophy and higher education.

Related Planet and Zodiac Signs: *Jupiter, 0° Sagittarius to 10° Capricorn*

*I've learned that people will forget what you said,
people will forget what you did, but people will
never forget how you made them feel.*

— Maya Angelou

Age fifty-four is represented by the first enneagram sign or the Initiator stage, which includes interests in exploring new directions and concepts, bringing parts together, and explaining things to others. This stage supports the Seeker cycle, which represents growth opportunities and consciousness-related themes. Examples of this year include the pursuit of opportunities to acquire and communicate new knowledge.

The Initiator-Seeker union represents ventures into new and unexplored realms of knowledge, experience, and higher education. This combination points to a year of new understanding of the nonphysical universe, the occult, and the transcendent. Both the first stage and seventh cycle deal with communication and have a lot in common. The lesson of this year is to integrate the letter of the law and details with the spirit of the law and broadmindedness.

Recall your main experience(s):

Age fifty-five is associated with the second sign or the Guide stage, which deals with helping or caring for others, cooperation, and understanding relationships. Those in this year tend to be friendly and have an interest in understanding relationships and collaboration efforts that are enhanced by the optimistic and curious Seeker cycle. Examples of this year include a new understanding of relationships and pursuing a course in spiritual education or practices.

The second stage and seventh cycle make for a beneficial year because the receptive, emotional, and service-oriented Guide sign provides stability for the growth-oriented Seeker's interest in pursuing new opportunities and knowledge. The Guide supports the goals of the Seeker, and the Seeker's optimism and energy inspires the Guide. In this year, one's interest in relationships and service is greatly helped by the enthusiastic energy and growth opportunities provided by the Seeker cycle.

Recall your main experience(s):

Age fifty-six is represented by the Contestant stage within the nine-year Seeker cycle. This year is beneficial because both the stage and cycle represent positive expansion and growth. The main experience of this age is increased confidence and awareness in one's self-expression, self-development, status, and relationships with others. Examples of the year include the significant growth of an existing relationship, business, or learning experience that expands one's consciousness.

Those who move through the three-seven combination tend to think for themselves and do not accept ideas simply based on tradition. As indicated by the Seeker cycle, this year is also associated with pursuing big plans and an interest in philosophy, religion, and advanced or higher education. In this year, people want to prove things for themselves and constantly seek new opportunities. They often gain insights through intuitive flashes and have an interest in learning about and perhaps communicating directly with the nonphysical universe.

Recall your main experience(s):

_____

Age fifty-seven is associated with the fourth enneagram sign or Romantic stage, which points to opportunities to expand one's imagination, intuition, and connection with the nonphysical universe. This stage supports and helps expand the longer period of consciousness raising represented by the Seeker cycle. This year is about opportunities to plan or build upon a significant and established consciousness-raising endeavor. Examples of this year include efforts to increase one's spiritual growth and self-knowledge.

The four-seven combination is usually beneficial to both the stage and cycle because both sides want to experience and express the mysteries of the unseen spiritual universe. The difference is that the Seeker influence wants to learn about direct contact with the soul, whereas the Romantic influence wants direct contact and experience. Those moving through this year often experience the dissolution of old patterns of living, breaks with the past, and disruptions in their development or level of support.

Recall your main experience(s):

_____

Age fifty-eight is represented by the fifth sign or the Innovator archetype, which is associated with an interest in changing and correcting one's situation in life in unexpected and often sudden ways. The interests of this year greatly assist the larger Seeker cycle for pursuing innovative ideas, big plans, and opportunities to increase one's education. However, the cerebral approach of stage five is somewhat weakened by the subjective approach of the Seeker.

While the current revolutionary and disruptive Innovator year brings sudden and unanticipated changes, the optimistic Seeker influence brings an enthusiasm to pursue new ideas and learn new things. Even though the styles of five and seven are different, the unexpected events and changes of five are usually beneficial to seven's broader understanding. As such, this year brings an interest in expansion and growth that comes with the experience of sudden opportunities that often seem to come from out of the blue.

Recall your main experience(s):

Age fifty-nine is associated with the sixth enneagram sign or the Skeptic archetype, which includes being responsible, committed, warm, and shrewd in one's approach to life. When combined with the Seeker cycle, this year is about the need to bring comfort and order to activities that support growth and improvement. Examples of how this year is experienced include improving one's home or relationships and pursuing new opportunities for growth.

Those with the Skeptic-Seeker combination tend to experience a range of emotions from depression to optimism and a lack of joy to great joy. Their rather cool exterior can lead others to believe that they don't have a passion to pursue their ideals or greater education. The goal of this year is the pursuit of a disciplined, organized, and responsible approach to life and doing so with the freedom to explore one's dreams and knowledge of the universe.

Recall your main experience(s):

Age sixty is associated with the once-in-a-lifetime seventh Seeker stage and cycle, which introduces the urge to explore new ideas and opportunities for growth and the pursuit of advanced education or spiritual knowledge. Because those with this combination will usually feel greater optimism and enthusiasm in all that they do, they often meet with greater success. While the seven-seven combination is beneficial in most cases, too much growth and expansion can lead to waste and greed. The appearance of good luck is present in this year. This age, universally known as the age of wisdom, is also associated with easy improvements and little resistance to the gains that come with one's growth. Examples of the year include pursuing significant new projects, self-discovery, or spiritual education that helps us understand our relationship to the universe.

Recall your main experience(s):

Age sixty-one is defined by the eighth enneagram sign or the Defender, which points to being self-determined and aggressive and having the urge to assert one's ideas and power. The Defender stage tends to expand the growth-oriented and adventurous Seeker. The most important activity of this age is to fully embrace who one is and wants to be. Examples of this age include the attainment of an important goal or notable status.

The eighth stage and seventh cycle is beneficial to both sides. The Defender's sudden, unexpected, and often revolutionary ways are energized by the Seeker's thirst for advanced knowledge and interest in moving in and exploring new directions. Eight's urge to change things for the better is often well supported by the optimistic, growth-oriented seven. This energetic year brings opportunities to expand one's life in independent and unanticipated ways. In this year, many people gain insights through intuitive flashes and pursue their interests in the spiritual universe.

Recall your main experience(s):

Age sixty-two is represented by the ninth enneagram sign or Mediation archetype, which points to growth, resolving conflicts, keeping the peace, and pursuing community interests. This nine-seven year is associated with creating harmony and finding new solutions to significant problems, mysteries, and situations that are nearly complete or have just been completed. Examples of this year include resolving a notable problem or completing a significant business endeavor or relationship.

The nine-seven union is easygoing, and each side benefits the other. This Mediator-Seeker combination points to a year of harmony in bringing things to fruition or getting things done. The Mediator brings new opportunities to create harmony and peace to the Seeker's enthusiasm. Those who move through this year will likely do so with greater charm, confidence, and rewards for their good work.

Recall your main experience(s):

The Defender Cycle

Defender Traits Common to Ages 63 to 72: Offbeat; innovative; leaders; fighters; advocates; dreamers; champions; disciplined; protectors; vigilantes; conquerors; being first; bossy; intense; independent; aggressive; defense attorneys; awareness of karma and limits; self-determining; individualistic; uniting force; foundation; feeling powerful and centered; action-oriented.

Related Planet and Zodiac Signs: *Mars, 10° Capricorn to 20° Aquarius*

> *At age twenty, we worry about what others think of us. At age forty,*
> *we don't care what they think of us. At age sixty, we discover*
> *they haven't been thinking of us at all.*

> — Ann Landers

Age sixty-three is represented by the Initiator archetype, which points to youthful vitality, beginnings, and communicating new ideas. Because these ideas support the Defender cycle, they will likely come across with greater self-determination and independence when asserting themselves. This Initiator-Defender combination brings an opportunity to create and promote something new. Examples of this year include being more assertive in direct and indirect ways when communicating one's ideas.

Many people who experience this stage and cycle become verbal warriors with sharp tongues. They are inclined to express their desires and observations with gusto. Those in the one-eight union can be impatient with others who don't get their point right away. On the positive side, people in this year understand things at a faster pace. On the negative side, they can be too aggressive, impatient, and off-putting to those who think too slow.

Recall your main experience(s):

_____

Age sixty-four is represented by the second enneagram sign or the Guide, which includes cooperation, understanding, and caring for others in the foreground, and the sign of the Defender in the background. The focus of this year is assisting or serving others in ways that can enhance their desire to be assertive and direct in advancing their causes. Examples of this year include the deepening of existing relationships and using teamwork to achieve a specialized goal.

The union between the Guide stage and Defender cycle makes for a blunt, straightforward, and passionate approach to caregiving and relationships. The two-eight combination is difficult because the maternal Guide stage is incompatible with the independent and aggressive approach of the Defender cycle. While the practical and assertive Defender side of this combination will advocate for the subordinate and weaker Guide, their approach is usually rough and unsympathetic.

Recall your main experience(s):

_____

Age sixty-five is associated with the third enneagram sign or the Contestant, which brings energy to one's image, growth, self-promotion, and achievement. These qualities expressed get an added boost from the Defender cycle, which represents independence, self-determination, and aggressiveness. The focus of the Contestant-Defender year is thinking big and acting upon one's hopes and plans. An example of this age includes attaining a significant goal.

Age sixty-five is represented by the union of the upbeat and optimistic Contestant and the Defendant, which makes for an aggressive, action-oriented year. This union includes the urge to act with a sense of urgency that may become confrontational and rub others the wrong way. Throughout this year, people tend to be ambitious and impatient and encounter difficulties in gaining positive recognition. The people moving through this year are often bundles of energy who can push others to make things happen.

Recall your main experience(s):

Age sixty-six is associated with the fourth sign or Romantic stage, which deals with expanding one's awareness and experience of the transcendent. When combined with the Defender cycle, this combination tends to be difficult because four and eight are so different. The goal of this year's stage and cycle is finding the balance between listening to its subjective message of the creative mind and asserting one's ideas and plans in an aggressive way.

The union between the Romantic and the Challenger makes for a blunt and passionate approach to expressing the formless universe and communicating with the deeper mind. The presence of eight in this combination moves four toward a more practical and down-to-earth expression of its spiritual and mystical nature. The intangible nature of fours tends to make eights feel uninspired or lazy and directionless. Examples of this period include taking the lead to assert one's subjective interests and offbeat plans in a direct manner.

Recall your main experience(s):

Age sixty-seven is associated with the fifth sign or the Innovator stage, which represents levelheadedness, objective thinking, and often unanticipated change. This stage is expressed in creative ways that support the assertive intensity and power of the Defender. This midpoint year represents learning by doing new things to advance one's work and affairs. Examples of this year include finding a way to move forward despite being at a significant crossroads between two important worlds or directions.

Those represented by the five-eight combination often experience the unexpected, impatience in getting things done, and unsolved conflicts. The difficulty in this year comes about because the people moving through it don't sit still long enough to think things through before acting. For many, this year seems to be frustrating because the goals they are pursuing may not be reached. The problem for those moving through this year is often the result of focusing their energy on narrow objectives and instant gratification.

Recall your main experience(s):

Age sixty-eight is defined by the sixth enneagram sign or the Skeptic archetype, which includes an interest in loyalty, being overly cautious, and family-oriented stability. This staged is opposed by the sign of the Defender cycle, which gives the urge to be independent, assertive, and direct and to protect the things they are responsible for. The Skeptic is the glue that gives a relationship, family, or community its stability, while the Defender is the action-oriented urge to be self-determined. Examples of this year are represented by the metaphor of driving a car that's pulling an oversized trailer.

Although the Skeptic-and-Defender combination is incompatible because their energies are so different, the year presents both problems and opportunities for success. In this year, the brash steamrolling approach of the Defender and the cautious "play by the rules" approach of the Skeptic are tied together yet opposed to one another. The result is that eight is slowed down by the established order and that six is taxed by the constant eagerness of eight to push forward hurriedly. The Skeptic's urge to play by the rules opposes the Defender's urge to get around the rules.

Recall your main experience(s):

Age sixty-nine is defined by the seventh sign or the Seeker stage, which resides in the longer Defender cycle. Those moving through this this stage have an interest in the rather aggressive pursuit of new ideas or experiences or expanding their education. In this year, the Seeker lends added energy and power to the Defender cycle. The most important activity of this age is learning to fully embrace who we are and what we want to be.

The seven-eight stage and cycle combination is usually beneficial to both parties. The Seeker's thirst for advanced knowledge and interest in moving in exploring new directions is energized by the Defender's independent, unexpected, and often revolutionary ways. And eight's urge to change things for the better is often well supported by the optimistic, growth-oriented seven. This energetic year brings opportunities to expand one's life in independent and unanticipated ways. Even though those in this year are enthusiastic about exploring new and often unusual ideas, they need to understand and prove things for themselves.

Recall your main experience(s):

Age seventy represents the Defender stage and cycle, which points to the urge to be self-determining, direct, aggressive, and an advocate for freedom. Those represented by this pair tend to focus their energy on narrow or well-defined objectives and can perform painstaking work. Many people in this period have difficulty because they are impatient and don't think before acting.

The increased double-eight energy brings an interest in pursuing one's goals and getting things done. While this pair may not be socially popular, they are a bundle of energy who can throw their weight around to make things happen. This year's theme represents activities that build upon one's reputation in the established order and on a material level. Examples of this year include increases in one's opportunities to organize and lead others.

Recall your main experience(s):

Age seventy-one is represented by the Mediator archetype, which is associated with the urge toward peacemaking, unification, harmony, spirituality, and love. This year is supported by the larger Defender cycle, which is associated with aggressiveness, firmness, self-determination, and the need to take charge and rescue others. Examples of this year include asserting oneself to create fairness and balance in their endeavors.

The nine-eight stage-and-cycle combination points to an abundance of positive creative energy, passion, and enthusiasm. The vitality and warm energy of the Mediator-Defender union is just below the surface and is often felt by others. In this year, one's passion is apparent when it comes to going after what they want. The actions inspired by this union are usually based on a consideration of what will produce the most beauty, balance, and freedom of expression. This union brings together a pleasing blend of self-assertion, cooperation, and personal magnetism.

Recall your main experience(s):

The Mediator Ages

Mediator Traits Common to Ages 72 to 81: Knowing; emotional; self-knowledge; middle person; settling or solving problems between people; pacifist; relationship counseling; humanitarian; referees; legal advisors; bringing things to fruition; matchmakers; accommodating; selfless; growth-oriented; helpers; consciousness; teachers; community interests; completion-oriented.

Related Planet and Zodiac Signs: *Venus, 20° Aquarius to 0° Aries*

> *Nobody grows old merely by living a number of years.*
> *We grow old by deserting our ideals. Years may wrinkle*
> *the skin, but to give up enthusiasm wrinkles the soul.*
>
> — Samuel Ullman

Age seventy-two is represented by the sign of the Initiator, which points to enthusiasm, beginnings, and sharing information with others. These themes are expressed in ways that support the nine-year cycle for mediation, self-understanding, making connections, and creating peace. This year is the start of a new nine-year phase associated with enthusiasm about opportunities, humanitarian causes, and expanding one's self-awareness. Examples of this year include significant beginnings and completions.

Those moving through the Initiator-Mediator combination are often philosophical and generous and have exacting standards. They are inspired to accomplish things through their pleasing personalities and optimism. Their positive outlook enables them to better help others and take advantage of their environments. This is a good year for giving and receiving information and knowledge and for business and personal communications. This combination promotes greater sociability, lightheartedness, kindness, and cooperation than either the Initiator or Mediator forces can provide alone.

Recall your main experience(s):

Age seventy-three is associated with the sign of the Guide, which includes individuals motivated to help, understand, and cooperate with others. These traits are expressed in ways that highlight this dimension of the nine-year cycle for mediation and bringing things to fruition. The main activity in the year is giving and receiving guidance and positive connections with others. Examples of this year include significant acts of allowing situations to develop and resolve themselves rather than intervening.

This year is associated with highly emotional responses to beauty and harmony, which often takes the form of artistic or design interests and creating beautiful environments. The Guide-Mediator combination is beneficial to both sides and brings out one's social interests, compassionate nature, and natural diplomacy. Those moving through this year have a desire to pursue fairness, harmony, peace, and humanitarian goals. This age confers sensitivity, tact, and great charm in dealing with others.

Recall your main experience(s):

Age seventy-four is represented by the by the sign of the Contestant, which deals with growth, optimism, self-image, performance, and achievement. This sign advances the nine-year mediation period and represents humanitarian interests, peacemaking, and working with others who have a common goal. Overall, this year is associated with social interests, creating harmony, and communicating positive thoughts. Illustrations of this year include inspiring people to create something new that has the potential to benefit society.

The Contestant-Mediator combination is a beneficial year for optimism, expansion, and goodness. Those who move through this year usually adopt an easygoing manner and want to be nice to others. They have an interest in diplomacy and bringing people together. They prefer to make and keep the peace and usually walk away from those who are indifferent and overly aggressive. The actions taken by those influenced by this period are based on a consideration of what will produce the most beauty, balance, and cooperation.

Recall your main experience(s):

Age seventy-five represents the fourth enneagram sign or the Romantic archetype, which includes an interest in paying attention to the creative mind or unconscious and psychic perceptions. These interests are expressed in ways that highlight this part of the nine-year cycle for mediation, conflict resolutions, and cooperation. The fourth stage of the ninth cycle also points to the urge to produce something ideal and significant that serves humanity.

The four-nine year is a beneficial to both sides because the Mediator and the Romantic tend to be compatible. In addition to increased sensitivity to the spiritual universe, this pair brings an interest in openness to other ideas. The fourth stage of the last cycle is associated with compassion and an understanding of other people's feelings, especially in relation to oneself. The union between four and nine makes for a sociable, compassionate, and spiritual nature. The Mediator adds understanding, warmth, and charm to the Romantic's connection with the transcendent.

Recall your main experience(s):

Age seventy-six is represented by the fifth enneagram sign or the Initiator, which points to being committed to something greater than oneself, objective thinking, investigation, and making both needed and often unexpected changes. These qualities are expressed in ways that are enhanced and supported by the Mediator cycle, which stands for harmony, cooperation, and bringing people together. This age is also associated with the awareness of going back and forth between two worlds, such as one's past and future, as we contemplate embracing them. An example of this year includes settling one or more significant unresolved conflicts.

The people in this stage-cycle combination learn to expect the unexpected in their dealings with others. The harmony-oriented nine points to opportunities to change the way they relate to other people. The Mediator side of the union tends to soften the unpredicted and often disruptive experience brought on by the Innovator side. The five-nine union inspires individuals to make and keep the peace. Here, people pursue changes to the status quo, which they consider to be necessary for the less fortunate.

Recall your main experience(s):

Age seventy-seven is defined by the sixth sign or the Skeptic stage, which includes family commitments, community relationships, and problem solving. The practical, stable, security-oriented, and loyal Skeptic's energy is softened by the Mediator's smooth communication, charm, and peacemaker qualities. This year is about keeping the peace and completing unfinished business. Examples include ending a long-term relationship and improving the status of one's group.

In the six-nine union, the six side wants to create material success by following an established plan, and the nine side wants to share its positive attitude to create fairness, harmony, and unity. On the positive side, the warm and cooperative approach of the Mediator eases the cautious and pessimistic influence of the Skeptic. On the negative side, the traditional "play by the rules" approach of the Skeptic can be a drag on the Mediator's charming nature.

Recall your main experience(s):

Age seventy-eight is represented by the seventh sign or the Seeker, which represents expansion, enthusiasm, and pursuing advanced knowledge or higher education in ways that support the Mediator's interests in creating balance and unity and bringing things to fruition. This year is associated with pursuing new ideas and big plans. Examples of this year include learning new subjects and helping others resolve significant problems.

The seven-nine union is beneficial because the Seeker brings positive energy and optimism to the goals represented by the Mediator. This year brings increased peace of mind, good luck, and ease in getting things done. Those who move through this year tend to experience opportunities to venture into new territory and increased cooperation in their relationships. They usually stand up to assert themselves with charm and confidence.

Recall your main experience(s):

Age seventy-nine is associated with the eighth enneagram sign of the Defender, which represents the Mars-like urge to act with an aggressive, independent, and often innovative or progressive approach in their doing things. This urge is supported by the Mediator cycle and helps the Mediator's influence be more direct in dealing with others. Much of this year deals with completing the unfinished parts of one's legacy or the previous years in this cycle. Examples of this year include acting to finish unfinished business and working to bringing peace and cooperation among others.

The eight-nine union points to a beneficial year for both sides and represents an abundance of creative energy and enthusiasm. The vitality and warm energy of the Defender-Mediator union is just below the surface and is often felt by others as one's passion. In this year, an individual's passion is apparent when it comes to going after what they want. The actions inspired by this union are usually based on a consideration of what will produce the most beauty, balance, and freedom of expression.

Recall your main experience(s):

Age eighty—the nine-nine combination amplifies the expression of the Mediator archetype. Since nine is all about relationships, cooperation, and completion, adding another nine qualifies this year as having magic. Those who move through this year usually have big hearts and hefty appetites for the finer things in life. They tend to be good listeners who hear what others are saying and have little miscommunication. They are usually attractive to others, love a good time, and often attempt to express their creativity in practical or commercial ways. Central to this year is an awareness of the stirrings of new life within and the settling of spiritual debts carried over from how you lived the previous nine years. Examples of this year include giving one's time and treasure to serve humanity and working with others to produce contracts or agreements.

Recall your main experience(s):

The New Life After Eighty

The first nine-year cycle after age eighty begins with age eighty-one. Like the Initiator cycle from birth to age nine, the second time the first or Initiator cycle is experienced from eighty-one to ninety represents the conscious mind and new beginnings. However, the second experience of the Initiator cycle is much more connected to the subjective mind or unconscious. Unlike the first Initiator cycle from birth to age nine, the second Initiator cycle includes the great relief of having gotten "past it" and feeling entitled to sit on the sidelines. All nine-year cycles beyond age eighty also include the attainment of happiness and contentment. Because the entire second life cycle from ages eighty-one to one hundred sixty-two has the second sign or Guide archetype as its foundation, those beyond age eighty-one have already learned that loving others is more important than being loved. By eighty-one, death and new life have become familiar. Friends, colleagues, exes, and former lovers die, and they have learned that dying isn't so bad.

The themes for ages eighty-one to ninety and beyond are an advanced version of the themes from birth to age nine and beyond. For instance, the experience of moving from early childhood to preschool and elementary school before age nine does not apply to those in the eighty-one-to-ninety age group. While the first Initiator cycle deals with learning to take care of oneself and becoming independent of others, the second Initiator cycle deals with learning about one's relationship with others and one's dependence upon them. The meanings given for the stages and cycles from birth to eighty-one are greatly influenced by the first enneagram sign of the Initiator archetype. These meanings are included in the second life years, starting with age eighty-one, but they are greatly influenced by the second enneagram sign or the Guide archetype.

The themes for the old ages of eighty-one to ninety-nine and beyond represent the Initiator and Guide cycles. They are advanced versions of the childhood themes from birth to age eighteen and beyond. While the first nine years of life are associated with youthful inexperience, energy, impatience, and physical appearances, life from eighty-one to ninety is associated with new self-knowledge, one's relationships with others, and interests in listening to the soul.

The Second Initiator Ages

Instead of the union between stage and cycle, such as one-one, one-two, one-three, etc., in the first eighty-one years of life, ages beyond eighty are represented by a third or full life cycle number. For example, age eighty-one is represented by one-one-two, age eighty-two is represented by two-one-two, age eighty-three is represented by three-one-two, and so forth. While the experience for ages ninety and beyond are not given in this work, they can be understood by reading over the descriptions for the Guide sign from ages nine to eighteen. The meaning for these ages only needs to be adjusted by including the Guide sign or two to the given one-year stages and nine-year cycles. For instance, age ninety is represented by one-two-two, age ninety-one is represented by two-two-two, age ninety-two is represented by three-two-two, and so forth. The meanings of Initiator ages from eighty-one to ninety follow.

Age eighty-one is represented by the first stage and cycle of the Initiator. This message is that this year is about learning, communicating information to others, beginnings, and having high standards for oneself and others. Those in the one-one year understand and express themselves with great clarity of meaning and precision. They hear what others say and tend to have few misunderstandings. The one-one year includes more thinking than the influence of one combined with another number and is more aligned with current trends. In addition, individuals in this year often take the time to think over important issues and work out a solution.

Because the foundation for the entire second life is ruled by the Guide archetype, the objective influence from the Initiator and the subjective influence from the Guide tend to be expressed together.

In this year, the more cerebral one side has the greater influence, and individual communications are slanted more toward thinking than feeling one's relationships to other people.

Recall your main experience(s):

Age eighty-two is associated with the second sign or the Guide archetype, which includes caregiving, cooperation, relationships, and understanding. Those represented by the one-two union tend to alternate between the masculine and feminine sides of their nature. With this combination, the self-centered and independent energy of one can be over powered by two's friendly and helping nature. People with this union are active, creative, aware, and sensitive to others. The main lesson or goal of this combination is attaining peace of mind and psychological balance. This combination points to a somewhat difficult year because both sides want to be expressed but find themselves in the position of representing different sides of the same coin. The main lesson of this year is learning to find the balance between opposing interests and between how one thinks and feels.

The independent, thinking influence of the one and the feeling-oriented influence of two are in partnership throughout this year. In this union, the objective and subjective sides of one's nature are expressed together. However, the feeling-oriented two side has the greater influence. In this year, an individual's communications are slanted more toward feelings and relationships to others than toward thinking and being independent. These differences are growth producing and stretch the relationship between a person's thoughts and feelings. Those who move through this year tend to overthink the past and their feelings about others.

Recall your main experience(s):

Age 83 is represented by the third sign of the Contestant, which points to enthusiasm, expansion, and achievement. Here, the one-year Contestant stage supports the nine-year Initiator cycle, and this three-one combination adds energy and support to the eighty-one-year Guide cycle. The three-one union points to expressing good feelings and a quick wit, which rests on a foundation of serving others. While those who move through this year tend to experience increased intelligence, the three-one-two combination tends to reduce one's ability to absorb new information. This happens because the three-one side tends to crowd out two's ability to listen and absorb.

The three-one-two combination represents the urge to create and the ability to act with focused mental energy in things associated with the Guide's aims—serving others and being helpful and understanding. While this union tends to hinder one's ability to be receptive, its presence gives the mental energy to get beyond this shortcoming. In addition, those who move through this year have a solid desire to understand and communicate their knowledge of the emotional and subjective side of relationships. This year also points to interests in being sociable, communicating with others, and learning new things.

Recall your main experience(s):

Age eighty-four represents the fourth sign of the Romantic, which points to psychic awareness and bringing the unconscious into conscious awareness. This sign has an outward influence on how the nine-year Initiator cycle and the eighty-one-year Guide cycle are expressed. Those represented by the four-one-two union tend to alternate between putting their attention on bringing together their thoughts and feelings and otherworldly and often psychic impressions. In this year, their rather eccentric hopes and dreams tend to influence their thinking-feeling judgments. Examples of this year include the pursuit of a significant ideal or individualistic endeavor.

The four-one-two combination brings together intuition, the intellect, and feelings in a way that creates something unique. In this year, communication with others often contains misunderstandings because the objective and subjective parties don't understand the other with sufficient clarity. For many, the experience of this year is like the squeezing the proverbial square peg into a round hole. Those represented by the one-four union often want to establish themselves in a highly personalized way.

Recall your main experience(s):

Age eighty-five marks the fifth enneagram sign of the Innovator archetype, which represents an observant, thoughtful, and psychological approach to making changes. In this year, the fifth sign has an influence on how the nine-year Initiator cycle and eighty-one-year Guide cycle are expressed. Individuals represented by this five-one-two union need to find an acceptable balance between pursuing their independent projects and helping others. Since the five-one part of the union gets greater attention than the two part, the balance leans toward placing more emphasis on thinking and objective aspects than on feeling and subjective aspects. Examples of the five-one period include reviewing or reviving a significant unfulfilled goal from the past.

The union with the fifth Innovator stage of this cycle makes for an energy that expresses itself through the confident communication of new and often sudden ideas. Individuals represented by this combination learn to become more independent in their approach to life. This year is about image-consciousness, progressive ideas, and plans for one's life. Those moving through this year often experience difficulties in situations that require them to follow the established order.

Recall your main experience(s):

Age eighty-six marks the sixth or Skeptic sign, which points to being cautious, pessimistic, and questioning. In this year, one's loyalty and motivation to play the role of devil's advocate has an influence on how the longer Initiator and Guide cycles are expressed. Here, the relationship and feeling-oriented influence of two and the independent, thinking influence of the current one year need to be balanced with the pessimistic and Saturn-like energy of six.

This year can be difficult because the Skeptic and Initiator-Guide goals are very different. Individuals who experience this year often have episodes of depression because the environment insists on things being done the right way and fitting the established order.

The influence of six needs to understand the often hidden universe of laws and feelings before attaining success, whereas the success of the one-two union depends on communicating with others so that understanding can take place. The six side needs to think things through to avoid making mistakes, whereas the independent, expressive, and caregiving one-two side simply tries to create an understanding. These new interests and directions represented by six become the next year's interest in helping others.

Recall your main experience(s):

Age eighty-seven is represented **by** the seventh enneagram sign of the Seeker, which points to optimism and pursuing advanced education, big ideas, and growth opportunities. This year begins a blend of interests in exploring new directions and concepts, bringing parts together, and explaining things to others. Here, the service and feeling-oriented influence of two and the independent, thinking influence of one are influenced by the enthusiastic Jupiter-like seven. This year is beneficial because the elements of seven, one, and two are mostly compatible with one another. Examples of this year include the pursuit of opportunities to acquire and communicate new knowledge to serve and help others.

The seven-one-two union represents ventures into new and unexplored realms of knowledge, experience, and ways of serving others. This combination points to a year of new understanding and explaining the nonphysical universe, the occult, or the transcendent. The seventh stage and first nine-year and eighty-one-year cycle deal with communications and have a lot in common. The lesson of this year is to integrate the letter of the law and its details with the spirit of the law or broadmindedness.

Recall your main experience(s):

Age eighty-eight is represented by the eighth sign or Defender archetype, which is associated with taking the lead, aggressiveness, and independence. The Mars-ruled eighth sign has a reputation for impatience and being a verbal warrior. When combined with the longer one-two combination, eight makes them quicker on the uptake and able to understand things as a faster pace. It points to youthful vitality, beginnings, and communicating new ideas. Because these ideas are supported by the Defender cycle, they will likely come across with greater self-determination and independence when asserting oneself. The eight-one-two combination brings an opportunity to create, promote, communicate, and serve others in new ways. Examples of this year include being more assertive in direct and indirect ways when communicating one's ideas.

Many people who experience this year become innovators and action-oriented and advocate for the underdog. They are inclined to express their desires and observations with gusto. The one-eight assertive side of this needs to make peace with the receptive two side. The main lesson of this year is learning to find the balance between opposing interests and between how one thinks and feels about things. Without this balance, they are too aggressive, impatient, and off-putting to those who don't get their point right away.

Recall your main experience(s):

_____

Age eighty-nine is represented by the ninth enneagram sign or the Mediator archetype, which points to self-understanding and making connections and peace. When the Venus-like nine is combined with the ideals and enthusiasm of one and the warm, friendly, helping nature of two, good things usually happen. Those represented by the nine-one-two union are generous with their time and accomplish things through their pleasing personalities and optimistic natures. This year brings opportunities for self-awareness, self-expression, and helping others in humanitarian causes. Examples of this year include significant beginnings and completions in one's service or interactions with others.

Those who move through this year are often cooperative, philosophical, and generous in their relationships. Many are inspired to accomplish peacemaking tasks and bring people together through their optimism and pleasing personalities. Their positive outlook enables them to better help others and take advantage of their environments. This is a good year for receiving and giving information and knowledge and for communicating with others. This combination promotes greater sociability, lightheartedness, human kindness, and cooperation than the influence only nine, one, or two can provide.

Recall your main experience(s):

11

Name and Letter Types

To know yourself, you must spend time with yourself.
You must not be afraid to be alone. Knowing
yourself is the beginning of wisdom.

— Aristotle

The birth name is a tremendous symbol of consciousness. The importance of one's original name is identical to that of the exact date and time of birth in astrology: both are given at and tied to the moment of birth. While there are few personality maps that reveal as much information as the birth name, this may be a burden as well as a blessing. Birth names point to areas of personality growth, spiritual growth, and one's style of expression. They function to help spell out one's unique mission in life. In this sense, they represent undeveloped territory that will be explored and further defined in terms of what can be built or produced by the individual. The inherited or adopted data in one's name gives you an accurate portrait of your personality and the personality of your soul. While we enter life with a birth date and name, name changes can affect our projected ego-centered personality. Because name changes are chosen by the individual, given by others, or adopted, they are like the enneagram type. Name changes do not replace the birth name, but they can modify the way you are seen by others and how you go about reaching your goals.

As the earth moves around the sun in stages represented as enneagram signs, the nine stages can also be represented as the letters A to Z. These ongoing Earth rotations are the basis for identifying seasons of the year, the enneagram signs and the stages and cycles of development for both the life span and letters of the alphabet. Enneagram signs and planets are at the center of all letters, words, forms of thought, measurement, explanation, analysis, growth, and existence. While planets and the numbers they represent remain in the background, they are always present and a source of power. When the enneagram concept of signs and types is extended to the alphabet, the meaning of letters in one's name or names can greatly expand how they understand themselves.

The Alphabet and Enneagram

The relationship between enneagram letters as types and the three groups in which they appear is like the relationship between stages in the nine-year development cycles. Just as the nine annual stages of enneagram signs are modified by each successive nine-year cycle, the enneagram letters are modified by each successive group of nine letters. The first group or cycle of letters from A to I is followed by the second group or cycle from J to R, and the second row becomes the third group from S to Z. Instead of viewing the letters as a straight line from A to Z, they are viewed as three enneagram-lettered cycles or groups from one to nine. The trinity groups that apply to the enneagram types apply to the enneagram letters as well.

All numbers are rooted in single digits from one to nine. While there are different systems and ways to interpret the symbolic meaning of each letter of the alphabet, in this work, the twenty-six letters are defined as enneagram letters, patterned after the nine planets, enneagram types, and enneagram signs and cycles as presented in this work. We can always add the numbers represented by two or more digits together until we come to one single-digit number. For instance, the root of 26 is 2+6=8, the root of 11 is 1+1=2, and the root of 22 is 2+2=4. The number values of the alphabet letters are summed up in the universal chart given here.

Enneagram Letters by Group

	1	2	3	4	5	6	7	8	9
Cycle One	A	B	C	D	E	F	G	H	I
Cycle Two	J	K	L	M	N	O	P	Q	R
Cycle Three	S	T	U	V	W	X	Y		

Letters and numbers

1-A	2-B	3-C	4-D	5-E	6-F	7-G	8-H	9-I
10-J	11-K	12-L	13-M	14-N	15-O	16-P	17-Q	18-R
19-S	20-T	21-U	22-V	23-W	24-X	25-Y	26-Z	

The nine planets, enneagram types, letter groups, and, by extension, signs, stages, and cycles are the same distinct nine universal laws that never deviate from the principle behind the law by which they are governed. In addition, letters are universal formative principles that define and communicate everything that has existence, and numbers contain their own characteristics and measure everything that has existence. Like every manifestation, each of the nine numbers has their own nature and wavelength, which is measurable. Each enneagram number represents three letters (except nine, which represents two letters) and indicates specific areas or fields of experience in which the letters operate.

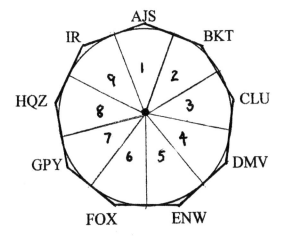

Letter Stages and Cycles around the Zodiac

The first nine letters from A to I represent the first cycle of development for the alphabet. These letters are associated with being self-centered and geared toward the pursuit of one's personal goals. They represent originality, youth, confidence, independence, and expansion. As a cycle, these letters are assertive, adventurous, outgoing, youthful, energetic, optimistic, and intense. They symbolize the beginnings of awareness, increased understanding, and communicating through words. They represent the innovative ideas and thoughts that gives birth to all life, which emerges from the womb letters, namely, J to R. The letters A to I are associated with the father principle that sets things in motion through new areas of consciousness. They express the masculine face of the trinity that is associated with starting things, planning, and losing interest as soon as the new beginning can continue without their help.

The second nine letters from J to R represent the second cycle of development. They symbolize the development of the individual in relation to the people personally related to them, such as significant partners, family, and extended family. They are relationship centered and pursue partnership goals instead of personal goals as represented by the first nine letters. The letters in this cycle are associated with relationships, cooperation, fixing, and healing things. The letters in this second cycle are known for being cooperative, warm, people oriented, pleasant, sympathetic, and more sociable than letters in the first group. The letters J to R magnify the beginnings of awareness and understanding that were communicated through the first nine letters. They are associated with the feelings and emotional energy that connect and serve all life. They are associated with the mother principle that nurtures the growth and expansion of the seeds planted by the letters A to I. They express the feminine face of the trinity whose yielding nature conquers the resistance and hardness of life. These letters also exemplify the order and principles of law that govern life.

The letters from S to Z symbolize the third cycle of development. They are associated with the individual's integration into society. Here, the individual relates not only to the people they know but also to the social order itself, e.g., social causes, religious affiliations, political interests, and teaching others, which may not be experienced personally. Compared to the first two letter cycles, the letters in this cycle are more self-conscious, serious, moderate, tactful, reflective, and focused on the established order. As the third or trinity cycle, the letters S to Z manifest the first two letter cycles. These letters bring a concrete presence and form to the intentions, feelings, and emotional energy of the ideas put forward by the first two letter cycles. They teach us to look beyond appearances and first impressions, such as the tip of the iceberg. This part of the trinity of letters is born out of the womb represented by the second cycle from J to R. They stand as symbols of the physical manifestation principle of the trinity, which includes forms, things, results, bodies, and results. The letters in this cycle are associated with the visible universe, which takes form from the formless.

The presence of the first letter of a name, letters in the same group, missing letter groups, and the number of letters in the trinity groups for the full birth name are all meaningful components of an individual's soul personality and ego-centered personality for non–birth names.

While other arrangements for the study of letters and trinity groups can be created, the scope of meanings for the enneagram letter types and individual name topics in this closing chapter are given here.

- First letters in names
- Missing letters in groups, e.g., the eighth or HQZ group
- The sum of letter numbers in a birth name or adopted name
- The sum of letters in each part or the body, mind, and soul trinity group

All letters, names, and numbers have meanings that represent distinct universal principles and characteristics and measure all things in existence, but the first or leading letter of a name, missing letter groups, and the sum of letters in a name are the most significant components. The first letter indicates specific, goals and the sum of letters indicates dimensions of experience. The lead letter is like the engine of a train; it is the major active principle that signifies the name's motivation. Missing letter groups in one's full birth name indicate the person's greatest shortcomings and opportunities for growth. They represent one's shadow or unconscious aspect of personality, which the conscious mind does not identify. The enneagram letter groups that follow are applied to the topics given above.

The Initiator and Reform Type Letters—AJS

The first enneagram letters are represented by Mercury, the planet of the word that makes the unconscious conscious, brings heaven to earth, and serves as messenger of the soul. The first letters are associated with all aspects of writing, speaking, learning, commerce, message giving and receiving, and the beginning of understanding. All beginnings come into manifestation through the power of the word represented by the first letters, and without this power, nothing is created. Because the first letters rarely accept the established order, they look for new ways to improve things through and to bridge the gap that exists between separate entities. They are mediators between the unmanifested nonphysical part of the universe and the manifest physical part; they represent the motivation to bring clarity to the will of the transcendent.

Among the enneagram letters, the first letters AJS as name leaders or in groups of letters take the special place of representing new directions and innovative ways of doing things. Their approach to life is usually creative and independent. The main function of the three letters represented by Mercury is to translate ideas and signs from one level to another, creating different maps of reality for thinking, speaking, imagining, dreaming, and sampling observations to experience reality directly. They are associated with the ability to shift quickly from one level of signs to another, like physical dexterity and communicating with others and calls for intelligence. Individuals whose first or last names begin with these letters want to adopt techniques and the use of knowledge and skill to function in an effective manner.

Because the letters AJS indicate a concern with details and are associated with youthful recklessness, those influenced by this symbol often run the danger of being superficial learners. The main lesson for type-one letters is becoming aware of others and learning that life does not unfold all at once. Many individuals with these letters have an excessive concern for details and can turn into nitpickers and perfectionists and replace actual experience with these concerns. They represent focus, single-mindedness, action, and self-projection. Mercury's influence behind these Innovator- and Reformer-type letters motivates them to apply their logical thinking toward analytical discrimination. Those of this type often insist on minute precision and accuracy to a level that can appear trivial to others.

Names with no letters in the first or ASJ group are very rare. Missing letters in this group are an indication that the person has difficulty in understanding and communicating ideas and thoughts in words and in moving concepts from the unconscious into consciousness.

The Guide and Helper Type Letters—BKT

The second enneagram letters are represented by the moon, the planet of inner growth, change, and the emotional nature that shapes one's outer character or personality. The second letters symbolize feeling and the emotional energy that connects and nurtures all life. They are connected to all forms of literal and metaphorical motherhood, give form to life, and provide for the life they give. These letters are receptive by nature and act as the container or womb from which all life emerges. They point to the ability to attract and relate to people. Unlike the independent- and creative-approach first letters, the emotion patterns of behavior held by second-letter individuals often interfere with the development of their creative self-expression.

Among the enneagram letters, individuals with letter type two want to help others through various occupations and activities. The main goal of the three letters represented by the moon's influence is to serve others and provide the highest good that life can offer. They are attracted to people who require protection and to matters that require attention. The letters BKT are associated with understanding the world through feelings and emotions more than by purely rational means represented by the letters AJS. The second letters often indicate psychic ability and perceive that everything is in some way connected. Because those represented by these letters are tied to things from the past and traditions, they prefer to wait, follow, and learn to fit into the established order. They need to feel wanted and emotionally secure and cannot be happy without a meaningful home life. They want maternal love more than romantic love and demand ownership of affection to satisfy their emotional insecurity.

The main message of these letters is that success only comes about when an individual's will and universal order and laws are aligned. Violating this alignment is synonymous with breaking the law and facing the consequences that follow. They remind us that to advance in life, we must honor its flow. They represent the hidden movement of life, order, principles, and laws that govern the universe.

Individuals represented by the second letters as name leaders or in groups of letters are sensitive to the feelings of others, and their sensitivity to others' opinions and reactions can lead them to imagine slights when none are intended. Because the moon's influence governs oceans as well as public tides, its influence behind these letters tells us that individuals with such letters are often pulled into diverse types of public life. The absence of these letters points to a limited understanding of one's feelings and the feelings of others. While they are often helpful to others, they are also unaware of how much help is needed and the limits they need to place on giving help.

The Contestant and Achiever Type Letters—CLU

The third enneagram letters are represented by the sun, the planet that represents the source of all energy, harmony, warmth, movement, growth, expansion, and the center of all activity. The third letters are symbols of the eternality and continuity of human potential forever and ever expanding. They contain the energy of mediation and conflict but are neither mediation nor conflict. These letters are associated with achievement, the motivating power behind all activities, and the energy that enables groups, communities, and societal activities to exist. They typify people with dramatic and flamboyant personalities who express their emotions as a way of gaining social recognition.

The influence of the sun's vitality and youthful nature personify the third letters' optimism, confidence, positive characteristics, and desire to express one's individuality. The third letters represent the element of fire and the intuitive insight that precedes thinking. While they have sunny, happy dispositions and attract many friends, at times they seem to be naively childish and egocentric. Individuals whose name or names begin with one of the third letters are often creative in the ways of business and perhaps the arts. They find ways to express who they are and seek to make an impact in terms of their own identity. They prefer to be in the forefront of any activity where they can be recognized and dislike working behind the scenes. Third-letter-type personalities are not especially modest, and they are able to make others notice them by their demeanor. Self-expression is the major goal of these letters, and they often overestimate their own worth and do not feel it's necessary to do anything to justify their high self-opinion. The presence of third letters as name leaders or in letter groups often points to people who are totally wrapped up in themselves and arrogant and have strong needs for admiration and uncompromising personal integrity. Individuals represented by these letters enjoy being the center of attention and must have the spotlight, and once in it, they must shine.

Those represented by the CLU or sun letters cannot operate meaningfully except through their relationships with others and the form in which they are located. Sun types have strong attachments to the family and establish themselves in society through a personalized environment. They want people to think well of them and have strong attachments to the family. They direct a great deal of energy toward these goals, project themselves in the most dramatic way possible, tend to be very aware of the effect they have on others, and study what to do to create a better effect. Missing third letters suggest an inability to attract attention to oneself. Individuals with this situation are uncomfortable being the center of attention, being on stage, or being dramatic. They prefer to work behind the scenes and dislike being in the spotlight or forefront of any activity.

The Romantic and Individualist Type Letters—DMV

The fourth enneagram letters are represented by Neptune, the most distant and mysterious planet. The fourth letters are associated with bringing together the numerous opposing energies and contradictions represented by the four directions in ways that can serve concrete reality. They provide the integrated elements and structure needed for consciousness and the reality of all forms to exist. The goal of unifying the extremes represented by the seen and unseen, the known and unknown, and the material and spiritual tell us that the enneagram letters DMV are highly idealistic. Because these letters are associated with aspects of the universe that are unclear, illusory, ill-defined, and even imaginary, they are the most difficult to understand. Individuals with these letters are known for being way out and weird, escapists, artists, or creative people who often dislike physical work and feel constrained by established rules.

While many individuals with these letters are interested in psychic phenomena, see visions, and look for signs, those who ignore them are likely to turn to drugs or alcohol to shut out these unusual feelings. Until individuals with fourth letters as name leaders or in groups of letters learn to respond to the extrasensory qualities associated with these letters, they are inclined to remain unrealistic dreamers. More than other enneagram letters, fourth letter types are open to the temptations of their lower nature or to the glories of their spiritual nature. They are usually loveable, sympathetic, and comfortable to be with if you just want to relax. They can be dignified, benevolent, and warmhearted and have intuitive foresight and the ability to interpret human feelings. They have the urge to reach out to help and serve the weak and helpless and demand no external rewards for the humanitarian services through performance.

As symbols, the letters DMV represent the formless void before structure is imposed upon it, and they are associated with giving us a glimpse of ultimate reality itself and the urge to accept all things at once. The Neptune influence associated with these letters inclines them to represent the subtle and illusive energy in the universe. The unlimited possibilities and exaggerated imaginations associated with these letters often makes it difficult for people led by these letters to be successful in the mundane universe. These letters are associated with the inspirations that show up before things can be brought into the physical world. Much of their success is tied to dealing effectively with dualities and concrete realities.

The absence of fourth letters in a name is a sign of people who tend to question their imagination, avoid mysteries and psychic phenomena, and seeking direct connections with the transcendent. They struggle to understand dreams, visions, and symbols and express their creative and artistic potential.

The Innovator and Investigator Type Letters—ENW

The fifth enneagram letters are represented by the planet Uranus, a symbol of one's liberation from the bondage of personality and urge to become an individualized soul. Those represented by these letters are extremely independent, self-willed, and reluctant to be dominated or controlled by external rules and regulations. Like the fourth letters, the fifth letter types often embody the sixth sense and are associated with new ideas, inventions, and social doctrines. They represent a blending of intuitive insights, practical sensing, the wisdom of feelings, and the rational nature of thinking that communicates new things. They tend to be idealistic and revolutionary by nature and work for the improvement of humanity. They are known for having intuitive flashes that lead to new discovery and the overturning of old ideas. Those represented by these letters are driven to break out of patterns that have become too rigid, even though they may wish to stay within them.

The enneagram letters ENW as name leaders or in groups of letters contain unexpected elements that show up as sudden bursts of energy to shed light on and explain those parts of the universe that have remained hidden. They operate like an invisible pressure cooker that explodes into existence with new awareness that's been held down. The submarine that emerges from the ocean depths is a metaphor for how these letters function. While those with these letters may follow traditional canons of logic or reason, they do operate in ways that reason can relate to. Those who pursue higher education often have the capacity to understand spirituality energies and religious concepts, and many have great scientific and inventive talents. They are less emotional and more objective and less likely to follow hopes, fears, or ego defenses to distract their observations.

The Uranus influence associated with these letters produces bohemian-type individuals and groups that enjoy experimentation into things that seem strange and outside the established order. Those with these letters in significant position are detached, rarely wedded to the status quo, and motivated to continue growing through life. They tend to have strong social ideals about how people ought to be and do not relate easily to how people are. These socially oriented letters produce radical or innovative thinkers who are individualistic and self-sufficient and do not need the approval of society at all. Many people with these letter types want to challenge society's outworn structures and bring about change. It is rare for someone to have a name without fifth letters. An absence of these letters points to shortcomings in their ability to make needed changes or release outdated ego patterns. People without these letters find it difficult to embrace their intuition and explore those parts of the universe that seem strange or hidden from ordinary view.

The Skeptic and Loyalist Type Letters—FOX

The sixth enneagram letters are represented by the planet Saturn, a symbol the planet of learning the rules of how to make life on earth successful. They represent those aspects of reality that come from a consensus of the collective. Instead of representing the truth or absolutes, they represent a reality that is socially created. Individuals of this type are careful and cautions, and they are well known for being doubters, questioners, skeptics, and agnostics. They are associated with law and order, boundaries, and everything that contains or puts a limit to growth. Those who willingly accept the nature of these letters will find a friend upon which they can depend to guide them safely. They learn to accept responsibilities with a serious emotional intensity but may harbor deep resentments when they feel they have been dealt with unjustly.

Much more than other types, they are steady, committed, traditional, and responsible. They are thorough, persistent, determined to achieve their goals, and almost fanatic in their adherence to principle. Those with sixth letters as name leaders or in groups of letters learn that life is associated with difficulty when the law is not followed or known. They understand that it takes time to learn the deepest, hardest, and most important wisdom of life. These individuals are often overly emotional because they are rigidly involved with defending their sensitive feelings from the threat of the outer world. This type often encounters many emotional lessons that bring pain and suffering until they learn to master and control their tendency to be unforgiving when hurt. Although these individuals rigidly defend their sensitive feeling from threats of the outer world, as they learn to let go of resentments, they gain greater emotional stability in life. A good match for this type is someone who can share optimistic ideas with them.

While those with the letters FOX are often difficult to understand because of their reserved exterior and secretiveness, they are among the safest when it comes to a faithful partner. The Saturn influence associated with these letters gives them the urge toward being safe, secure, fiercely loyal, and devoted to loved ones and family. The older they get, the more secure they become, and their relations with others usually become better over time. They adore family and often grow more sentimental with time. While they are associated with complaining, they are responsible and committed and go about their business without advertising themselves or their achievements. An absence of the letters FOX in a name is a sign of instability, difficulty in keeping one's commitments, or accepting responsibilities. Those without these letters tend to ignore established rules and traditions in efforts to advance their agenda.

The Seeker and Enthusiast Type Letters—GPY

The seventh enneagram letters are represented by Jupiter, the planet that stands as a symbol of the development of one's higher mental attributes, humanity's contact with the universal mind, and the individual's tool for comprehending the meaning of life. Those with these letter types often have a strong fondness or love of religion, depth psychology, and philosophy as a consciousness-expanding system and system for describing their relationship with the universe. These letters represent the potential to expand one's understanding of human life through philosophy and become conscious of their spiritual nature. In addition to their love for growth, most people associated by the seventh letters want to be a part of something greater than themselves. They have a deep interest in the social and philosophical ideas that have shaped history.

While the Mercury letters AJS are associated with people learning how to communicate with one another, the Jupiter letters GPY are associated with individuals learning how to communicate with God. The presence of seventh letters point to the goal of learning, growing, and exploring the universe of knowledge beyond the boundaries of earthbound realities. The sixth letters, by contrast, focus on learning how to play by the rules to make life on earth successful. The seventh letters represent the achievement of compassion gained through wisdom. They are associated with seekers of truth and new experiences. These people tend to be idealistic and never satisfied with life as it is. Those with seventh letters as name leaders or in groups of letters are enthusiastic about learning and have a great need for self-exploration. The more progressive individuals with these letters seek to acquire as much education as possible, make diligent students and teachers, and often associate themselves with institutions of higher learning.

The Jupiter influence associated with these letters often provokes people to be wasteful, irresponsible, and extravagant in their generosity. Those associated with seventh letters are rarely satisfied with life as it is and want to move on to new experiences. Many want to own everything, become more important than anyone and grander, and have an exaggerated self-opinion. They reach out to people to incorporate as much of the external world as possible into themselves to grow both physically and psychologically. They have a powerful desire to be free to experience life in their own way. While they are free, unconventional, and self-righteous in their youth, they tend to settle down and identify with higher consciousness. These letters present the message that traditional teachers, nontraditional teachers, and other sources of wisdom and learning are unlimited. Names without seventh letters indicate a lack of interest in expanding one's understanding of the purpose of human life. People without these letters have little interest in pursuing new ventures, going beyond life as it is, or exploring the universe of knowledge beyond the boundaries of earthbound realities. They tend to have no interest in philosophy or becoming conscious of their spiritual nature.

The Defender and Challenger Type Letters—HQZ

The eighth enneagram letters are represented by Mars, the planetary symbol of courage, energy, and the ability of individuals to survive and meet their needs. Individuals in this group are impatient and impulsive, have an aggressive outward expression, and often express themselves without consideration for other people's wishes. As Challenger types, the HQZ letters are associated with the destruction of old forms so that more highly evolved aspects of one's selfhood and the material world can take their place. They are associated with the impetus for moving energy into the material world and making short-term changes in life. They are highly independent, competitive, and assertive but need to learn to express more love and patience. Even though individuals with these letters take the lead through force and push their way to the top, they should learn to cultivate the attributes of cooperation and sharing. While they are admired for their courage and youthfulness, they have little tolerance for opposition or interference and often act before thinking.

The goal of eighth letters HQZ, like the goal of sixth letters FOX, is to attain success in material matters, such as making things, making progress, and being competitive. The difference is that the HQZ group approaches their goals through direct and forceful means, and the FOX group approaches their goals through learning the laws that make material success possible. Unlike sixth letters, which represent the earth element, the established order, and material success, the eighth letters represent the element of fire, youthfulness, growth, expansion, and forward movement.

Most eighth letter types tend to be good natured and warm and can get to the heart of a matter without getting bogged down with details. The Mars influence associated with these letters tells us that the individuals with the eighth letters as name leaders or in groups of letters usually act with little concern for whether their action is reasonable, prudent, timely, or even effective if self-expression is achieved. Many of these people seek someone who is very dependent on them and yet independent. To provide for their family, they require an occupation that involves them totally and allows them the freedom to constantly express themselves. Because they have too much passion and too little compassion, they often misjudge the extent of people's situations in life. Despite these shortcomings, they are themselves on their own terms and often need less social reinforcement than other types. An absence of eighth letters in one's name represents a diminished ability to be assertive in a forceful and direct manner. While people with significant eighth letters can be brash and insensitive in leading a social cause and pushing their way forward, those without these letters prefer to remain in the background and support those who are more aggressive.

The Mediator and Peacemaker Type Letters—IR

The ninth enneagram letters are represented by Venus, the planetary symbol for love, spiritual vitality, harmony in relationships with people, mediation, unification, and peacemaking. This planet and the ninth letters have a big hand in any relationship that causes people to become more fully realized. They reflect divine love in material form and the force that pulls things together and holds them by attraction like the sun. For individuals with ninth letters as name leaders or in groups of letters, giving people a sense of harmony in their world is just as useful as making sure they have material resources. The unions produced by those with ninth letters are stable because such relationships allow people to express who they are better than they could if the union were absent. Wherever they operate, harmony is often produced by something moving in accordance with nature and itself. They will do a great deal to ensure happiness to those around them as they feel best when others are happy.

Those with the presence of ninth letters as name leaders or in groups of letters usually have active participation in social affairs because this satisfies their need to be among people. Close personal bonds and harmonious social relationships are of extreme importance to those represented by the ninth letters. They are usually well liked and have an innate ability to understand the feelings of others. Many people with an emphasis on these letters make a living by their pleasing manners and aptitude in dealing with the public, which can be applied to business, counseling, and public relations. They know how to keep the peace and negotiate in times of stress and unresolved differences. They recognize that the power of love and connection nurtures a healthy heart and extends the life span. They tend to operate in a lighter, less serious manner than other types, but they do not need to be subservient.

Since the Venus symbol, which has its influence on nine, is an inverted Mars that has its influence on eight, we can understand the Mediator and Peacemaker as an inverted Defender and Challenger. In cases where the eighth and ninth letters operate together, e.g., as leading letters in one's first and last name, the eighth and ninth letter groups' qualities take many elements from each other. Those represented by the eighth letters get things started and often break things because of their aggressive nature, and those associated with the ninth letters bring things to fruition and mend broken things because of their harmonious nature. The masculine hardness of eights is fulfilled by the feminine softness of nines. Those represented by eights want to initiate and make changes, whereas those represented by nines want to bring things to completion and plant seeds for the future.

Missing ninth letters point to a lack of interest in efforts to mediate disputes, bring people together, and go out of their way to keep the peace. Those without these letters have little interest in public relations, social affairs, or humanitarian work.

The examples that follow include readings of the first letter of a name, missing letters in a name, the sum of letter numbers in a birth name or adopted name, and the trinity sections represented by body, mind, and soul.

The table that follows presents the trinity arrangements of forces and stages of development for the nine letter groups in the alphabet. These arrangements provide an additional understanding of the universal trinity principle behind the letters. In the first row of development stages, we have AJS, BKT, and CLU as the beginning letters; DMV, ENW, and FOX in the second row are middle stage letters; and GPY, HQZ, and IR in the third row are the completion or ending stage letters. As seen among the planets, types, and numbers, the beginning, middle, and ending letters also represent our individual development stage; the development stage of our close relationships; and the development stage of our relationship to society and the collective respectively.

Among the nine letter groups as trinity forces, the first column consists of the letters ASJ, DMV, and GPY as the affirming or active trinity forces. The second column consist of the letters BKT, ENW, and HQZ as the denying or receptive trinity forces; and the third column consist of the letters CLU, FOX, and IR as the reconciling or facilitating trinity forces.

Trinity Forces and Stages in the Alphabet

	Affirming	Denying	Reconciling
Beginning	AJS	BKT	CLU
Middle	DMV	ENW	FOX
Ending	GPY	HQZ	IR

Missing Letters in a Name

The presence, frequency, and absence of individual alphabet letters or letter groups in a name represent the building blocks of the name. As a group, they also represent the united vision of one's first, last, and middle birth name and the full birth name, known as the expressive self. Although there are many ways to study the letters in a name, this chapter only considers the first letter in names and missing letter groups and the sum of letter in a name. Missing letter groups indicate both underdeveloped potentials and the greatest opportunities for growth.

In my full birth name, I have no letters in groups two and eight. Empty letter groups are like psychological shadows and areas of one's personality that have not been integrated into the whole. They represent areas of uncertainty, weakness, and low confidence, areas where it is difficult to see things for oneself or get things done. As a result, these are areas in which we tend to follow the lead of others until they are developed. My name will serve as an example of how missing letters within it assisted in shaping my life and soul personality.

ALLEN DAVID YOUNG

1 33 55   4 14 94   7 6 3 5 7

The absence of second-group letters indicates a limited understanding of one's feelings and the feelings of others. They tend to stuff or ignore their feelings because they do not really understand or trust them. Even though they are often sensitive to others and helpful to those in need, they tend to be unaware of how much help to give and the limits they need to place on helping. They are less attached to tradition and things from the past than those with letters in this group. In addition, these people often have a distorted moral compass and are not in touch with the need to be aligned with universal laws or principles than those with letters in the second group.

Missing second letters present an excellent opportunity to learn about and develop one's multisensory perceptions and spiritual awareness. They point to opportunities for learning to express one's feelings, regulate the extent to which they can help others, and use their intuition. Because intuition, like feeling, is subjective, the use of intuition can supplement the shortcomings of not being fully in touch with the subjective nature of feelings. Perhaps the main advantage of missing letters is that one has a greater level of emotional detachment and, as a result, is less biased by the intrusion of feelings. In my case, I only became interested in developing my intuition when I had my first psychic reading at age thirty and became aware of its power to shed light on my subjective world. It was this opening that lead to my interest in spirituality, dreams, and learning to develop my ability to better experience emotions and express them.

The absence of letters in the eighth group is a symbol of an underdeveloped ability to assert oneself in a forceful and direct manner. Although individuals with an emphasis on the eight letters can be brash and insensitive in pushing their way to the top, those without these letters prefer to remain in the background and support aggressive leaders. In most cases, they only fight and take the lead when they are backed into a corner and it becomes necessary. While people with an emphasis on the eighth letters need to learn how to cooperate and share with others who oppose them, those without eights don't have this problem.

Individuals with missing eight letters have an opportunity to build up their confidence and go after what they want. Their learning opportunities deal with becoming more self-centered and being an advocate for those who cannot defend themselves. They should learn to become independent and rely less on social reinforcement and what other people think of them. My first experience with missing eighth letters came out of the time I ran for a seat on the Oakland city council. A few months before entering this race, I had no thought of doing so. Had I really looked into it, I would not have done so. I collected 45 percent of the citywide vote and learned that I could assert myself in the public arena and be an advocate for the less fortunate if I didn't think deeply about what I was doing. This experience led me to abandon my short-term political quest in favor of becoming a long-term spiritual warrior and leader.

The First Letter in a Name

The first letter of a name announces and reflects new directions being pursued or developed by the name. First letters are like guides, teachers, and leaders of a group whose purpose is represented by the name, such as a department, division organization branch, staff, and so forth. They represent the beginning stage or first steps in any undertaking. They are the guiding principle or mission of one's personality that leads or integrates a department of one's personality or their total personality.

The first letter of an individual's first name indicates their unique interests in relation to their purpose, external elements, and focus in life.

The first letter of an individual's last name represents the motivation and experience inherited from their family of origin. The last name is a symbol of the tangible things built and manifested by the individual's family of origin—the individual's inheritance. The first letter of the last name plays an important subordinate and support role to the first letter of the first name.

The first letter of a person's middle name is associated with additional areas of interest. The motivations and gifts represented by this letter or letters tend to be more hidden from those who rarely identify with their middle name. The middle name or names represent potentials and talents within the unconscious or creative mind and can remain unmanifested and underdeveloped.

The first letter of a name is often called the cornerstone of the name. The first letters of the first, last, and middle name(s), if any, describe the foundations of an individual's soul potential and personality. These enneagram letter types have a huge influence on the way a person tends to express himself or herself in situations and challenges that come up in their life.

The first letter of a name indicates specific dimensions of experience. In general, the numbers associated with these letters symbolize basic psychological functions, desires, needs, and motivators. The first letter is the leader, motivation, and direction of the name. First letters represent universal principles that regulate how the energy of the name functions. They point to the major principles that form a person's character and lifetime motivation. Each first letter represents an energetic part of our being and how that part is manifested. The well-known name given below will serve as an example of how the initials direct one's life and soul personality.

BARACK   HUSSEIN   OBAMA
2 1 9 1 32   8 3 11595   6 2 1 4 1

President Obama's first, middle, and last initials give us a window into the direction of his potential and soul personality. The second enneagram letter B as the president's first letter in his first name tells us that the leading focus of his authentic personality expresses feelings and the emotional energy that connects and nurtures others. It points to his interest and ability to attract and relate to people in his private and public life. As a member of the first third of the alphabet, the letter B is associated with increased understanding, communication through words, starting things, and planning.

The sixth enneagram letter O as the president's first letter in his last name tells us the main inherited focus from his family of origin is associated with law and order, boundaries, and everything that contains or puts limits to growth. This letter points to his inherited urge toward being safe, secure, fiercely loyal, and devoted to loved ones and family. As a member of the first third of the alphabet, the letter O shares these qualities with the letter B.

The eight enneagram letter H as the president's first letter in his middle name implies that his hidden and underdeveloped talent and potential is represented by taking the lead through force and pushing their way to the top. To provide for their family, they require an occupation that involves them totally and allows them the freedom to constantly express themselves. As part of the first third of the alphabet, this letter shares these qualities with the letters B and O.

President Obama's trinity group letters show up as six body letters, three mind letters, and six soul letters. This pattern suggests that his authentic personality has a balanced opposition between body-centered feelings and soul-centered spiritual interests. His lesser mind-centered interests imply that he tends to rely far more on his instincts and intuitive side than on thinking and objective analysis. However, when his body and soul forces are in opposition, he turns to intellectual sources to reconcile the conflict. Because his body and soul interests carry more weight than the mind interests, conflicts between body and mind or soul and mind are unlikely. Although President Obama is often referred to as "no-drama Obama" and a deep thinker, his main piece of legislation nicknamed Obamacare is a testament to his compassionate body- and soul-centered focus.

The Birth Name or Authentic Personality

The sum of the letter numbers in the one's first name represents an individual's first personal growth number or lesson. The first name is the one by which we are known and called and relates to the mind and the senses. The first name is the most conscious part of a person's identity, full name, and total personality. The number that represents the first name describes the nature of the group that supports and follows the first letter. Ultimately, the number of the first name will lead the way toward one's growth and expansion and the manifestation of their enneagram sign and soul potential. This numbers lays out the pattern to assist them in attaining the growth and development represented by this number.

The number derived from the sum of letters in one's last or family name represents the person's hereditary number. It points to their inherited influence from common ancestors on the family tree and the genetic material inherited from their ancestors. The family name is important but plays a subordinate and supportive role to the first name. The hereditary number allows a person to know about their family characteristics and often gives insight into ways to better understand their relations with themselves and others. This number lets us in on the traits inherited from our family of origin. This number represents the lessons that one's family as a group is here to experience and learn.

The number or numbers derived from the middle name or names, if any, represent hidden or unconscious potential and talents that may be developed or ignored. Those who have no middle name will also have hidden talents, but they are not identified by the middle name. The middle name number or numbers represent the greatest area of undeveloped potential and opportunities for expressing one's total personality.

Of the many personality components represented by one's birth name, the most dominant component is the authentic personality, which is indicative of the way one expresses their individuality. An individual's full name at birth determines the face they show the world. The sum of the letters in one's full name provides the authentic personality number (a number from one to nine). With the first breath, the birth name represents the nature of an individual's soul personality. The birth name is a person's authentic self and represents the outer characteristics of their total personality as seen by others, even though these character traits may not give an accurate portrayal of one's soul personality. The authentic personality number may reveal personal traits that are at variance with one's more inward orientations. The number for this part of one's personality represents the way in which individuals naturally approach and actively merge with life in the outer world. This expressive part colors how a person sees their environment and their attitude toward the outer world in general. The well-known name given here will serve as an example of how one's first, middle, last, and full name describes their potential and expresses their soul personality.

CARL   GUSTAV   JUNG
31 93   7 31 2 14   13 5 7
16   18   16
7   9   7
             23
              5

By adding the first row of numbered letters together for each name, we get 16, 18, and 16. By adding the double-digit second row of numbers, we get the single digit numbers 7, 9, and 7 for his first, middle, and last names. Upon adding the third row of numbers, we get 23, and upon adding this double-digit number, we get 5 for his authentic personality. The human body and its parts are a metaphor for understanding an individual's full name. The meaning of Jung's first, middle, last, and total name numbers are given here.

One's first name represents the head, their consciousness, stored memories, way of thinking, speaking, imagining, dreaming, and making observations to experience reality. The number seven for Jung's first name, Carl, tells us that his main and leading focus and expression is his love of studying the human soul through depth psychology as both a consciousness-expanding system and a system for describing his relationship with the universe. The seventh letter group implies that he was focused on learning how to communicate directly with the transcendent, the soul, or what he calls the self.

The last name represents one's inherited physical body, social and economic conditions, circumstances, environment, etc. Since the seventh letter group also represents Jung's last name, we can conclude that he is highly focused on seven and considered a specialist in the qualities associated with this number. Because Jung's father made his living as a priest and Jung considered following in his footsteps, his decision to pursue the field of psychiatry and depth psychology is highly related to his father's career interests in the human soul.

One's middle name operates like the unseen inner organs that support the mind and body and give birth to their continued existence. The ninth letter group for Jung's middle name, Gustav, tells us that his hidden talent was an innate ability to understand the feelings of others, promote inner harmony, and assist others in becoming more fully realized. This hidden potential also includes an attitude for dealing with the public in ways that can be applied to counseling. The talent represented by his middle name was likely more developed than most people with middle names because he identified with his middle name on a regular basis.

The authentic personality number is the sum of all letters in an individual's full birth name. The resulting single-digit number represents the midpoint between the individual's unconscious inner world and their conscious outer world. The function of its number offers the best opportunity to keep these two major players in a state of timeless balance. Although the enneagram sign indicates how we understand and assimilate experience as much as the birth name, the role of the full birth name provides a greater understanding of how the enneagram sign is expressed. The expressive self is modified by a person's first, last, and middle names and, to a lesser but important degree, the first letters of these names. Carl Gustav Jung's birth name is represented by the fifth letter group. This letter group tells us that he brings together a blending of intuitive insights, practical sensing, and rational thinking to communicate new things. The fifth letter group is associated with radical and innovative thinkers who are individualistic and self-sufficient and do not need the approval of society at all.

Names and Personality Changes

Name changes produce personality changes. They have some effect on how an individual is seen by others and how they project themselves toward others. Name changes are common and range from those adopting a completely new name, adopting a last name, which often happens with marriage, and adopting a new first name or nickname. Below are some popular name change examples:

Birth Name	Adopted Name
Cassius Marcellus Clay	Muhammad Ali
Marion Mitchell Morrison	John Wayne, nicknamed Duke
Peter Gene Hernandez	Bruno Mars
Margaret Mary Emily Anne Heyra	Meg Ryan
Eric Arthur Blair	George Orwell
Demetria Guynes	Demi Moore
Martin Michael King	Martin Luther King
Anthony J. Mahavoric	Anthony Jay Robbins

While the meanings assigned to names are not limited to those associated with the enneagram letters, these letter groups provide invaluable readings into one's soul- and ego-centered personalities. Unlike the enneagram sign and type, the meaning of names defined by enneagram represent the face one shows to the world, how they are perceived by others, one's general impression on people, and their spontaneous reactions. The name changed to Muhammad Ali will serve as an example of how first letters, authentic personality, and adopted name are expressed.

Cassius	Marcellus	Clay	Muhammad	Ali
4 111931	4 19353331	3317	4 3 81 4 4 14	139
19	32	14	29	13
10	5	5	11	4
1	5	5	2	4
	11			
	2		6	

Because the first letters in Cassius and Clay are identical, their power is increased. They tell us that his inherited past and personal focus are both related to this letter. These letters tell us that the leading focus in his authentic personality expresses energy, flamboyance, movement, achievement, and the need for social recognition. Since he is a junior, he has many of the performer traits as his father, who was a painter and musician. These letters tell us that he had a high self-opinion, enjoyed being the center of attention, and went out of his way to make others notice him and remain in the spotlight. The first letter of a middle name is less dominant than the first and last names' leading letters and, as such, tends to represent hidden qualities. The letter M, the leader of his middle name, tells us that he was drawn to spirituality, mysticism, ESP, and unrealistic dreams.

The sum of all letters in his birth name add up to two, which tells us that his authentic personality is about understanding the world through feelings and emotions more than by rational means. Twos need to feel wanted and need to have a meaningful home life. His type-two full name tells us that he was perceived by others as a person attracted to those who required protection and to matters that required attention. Despite being a boxer, he was also a minister, social activist, poet, and man of peace.

Cassius Marcellus Clay changed his name to Muhammad Ali in 1964 when he converted to the Nation of Islam. His interest then switched to the Sunni version of Islam and again to Sufism. He referred to his birth name as his slave name and insisted that people use his new name when speaking to him. He pointed out that he didn't choose his birth name and that his new name, Muhammad Ali, is a free name that means "beloved of God." In Arabic, Ali means "high and elevated." He once said that he was given the name because it was the most common name in Arab countries, the rest of the Muslim world, and since it was the most well-known name, it makes him the most well-known person.

The first letter in Muhammad tell us that his new name represents a personality that leads with a focus on spirituality, mysticism, big dreams, and ideals and being independent of culture and environment. It is interesting to note that his name change came with announcing that he was a Muslim minister, having his boxing license revoked for not entering the military during the Vietnam War, and a deepening of his religious studies and social activism. The first letter of his new last name points to an interest in being a reformer who confronts problems head-on. When combined with the letter M, the leading letter of his chosen last name, A, increased the expression of his intelligence, exacting standards, and desire to make the world a better place. While these new first letters did not replace the first letters in his birth name, they broadened the dimensions of his life experience and expression.

The sum of the enneagram letters in Muhammad Ali add up to six, which tells us that his ego-chosen personality expresses the qualities of commitment, persistence, responsibility, and loyal devotion to loved ones and family. His authentic personality, represented by two, is modified by his adopted six personality in ways that add discipline to the emotional nature represented by two. The combination of the loyal skepticism represented by six and the helpful guidance represented by two suggests an increased reticence to express the personal needs symbolized by his authentic birth name. The two-six combination between his authentic and adopted personalities or names implies a tendency to keep others at arm's length and express less affection and interaction than the more people-oriented two alone.

Related Bibliography

This book is an outgrowth of my work with clients as an intuitive counselor, astrologer, and Science of Mind minister for decades. I am providing related bibliography sources from the enneagram, astrology, spirituality, depth psychology, and the occult to assist interested readers in understanding the new enneagram concepts presented in this work. Because the enneagram and its relationship to the planets is not restricted to one form and rarely discussed, there are few sources for the material presented in this work. Gurdjieff did not present a model of the enneagram or explain how the system works. However, he taught that the enneagram must be thought of as a system in motion and that a motionless enneagram is a dead symbol. The concepts of the zodiac-based enneagram signs, stages of life, and enneagram letter groups represent new directions for the enneagram. When they are added to the traditional enneagram model, the enneagram becomes a system in motion and reveals more of its insights.

In addition to the standard nine personality types based on survey results, the nine soul-centered personality signs are based on birth dates and times. The enneagram signs serve as benchmarks for the nine stages and nine cycles of life. The enneagram letter groups complement the enneagram signs and provide a deeper assessment of the soul-centered personality than signs can provide alone.

I. The Enneagram

Keyes, Margaret Frings. *Emotions and the Enneagram: Working through Your Shadow Life Script*. Muir Beach: Molysdatur Publications, 1993.

———. *The Enneagram Relationship Workbook*. Muir Beach: Molysdatur Publications, 1993.

Palmer, Helen. *The Enneagram in Love and Work: Understanding Your Intimate and Business Relationships*. San Francisco: HarperCollins Publishers, 1996.

Ouspensky, P. D. *In Search of the Miraculous: Fragments of an Unknown Teaching*. Fort Washington: Harvest Book Co., 2001.

Speeth, Kathleen, and Ira Friedlander. *Gurdjieff, Seeker of the Truth*. New York: Harper & Row, 1980.

Riso, Don Richard. *Discovering Your Personality Type: The New Enneagram Questionnaire*. Boston: Houghton Mifflin Harcourt, 2003.

Riso, Don Richard, and Russ Hudson. *The Wisdom of the Enneagram: The Complete Guide to Psychological and Spiritual Growth for the Nine Personality Types*. New York: Bantam Books, 1999.

II. Astrology

Arroyo, Stephen. *Astrology, Psychology and the Four Elements: An Energy Approach to Astrology and Its Use in the Counseling Arts*. Sebastopol: CRCS Publications, 1984.

———. *Relationships and Life Cycles: Astrological Patterns of Personal Experience*. Vancouver: CRCS Publications, 1993.

Hand, Robert. *Horoscope Symbols*. Atglen: Schiffer Publishing, 1997.

———. *Planets in Transit: Life Cycles for Living*. Gloucester: Para Research, 1976.

Oken, Alan. *Alan Oken's Complete Astrology*. Lake Worth: Bantam Books, 2006.

Ruperti, Alexander. *Cycles of Becoming: The Planetary Pattern of Growth*. Vancouver: CRCS Publications, 1978.

III. Spirituality

Hoeller, Stephan A. *Gnosticism: A New Light on the Ancient Tradition of Inner Knowing.* Wheaton: Quest Books, 2002.

Holmes, Ernest. *The Science of Mind.* New York: Penguin Group, 1998.

———. *The Science of Mind: Original 1926 Text.* Encino: HI Productions, 1998.

Mitchell, Stephen. *Tao Te Ching.* New York: Harper Perennial, 2006.

Wilhelm, Richard, and Cary F. Baynes. *The I Ching or Book of Changes.* New Jersey: Princeton University Press, 1977.

Young, Allen David. *I Ching Wisdom from the Soul.* New York: Page Publishing, 2015.

VI. Depth Psychology and the Occult

Fadiman, James, and Robert Frager. *Personality and Personal Growth.* 6th ed. New Jersey: Prentice Hall, 2005.

Goodwin, Matthew Oliver. *Numerology - The Complete Guide, Volume 1: The Personality Reading.* North Hollywood: Newcastle Publishing, 1981.

Jung, C. G. *Psychological Types.* New Jersey: Princeton University Press, 1976.

———. *Psychology and the Occult.* New Jersey: Princeton University Press, 1977.

Metzner, Ralph. *Know Your Type: Maps of Identity.* Garden City: Anchor Books, 1979.

Myers, Isabel Briggs, and Peter B. Myers. *Gift Differing: Understanding Personal Type.* Palo Alto: Davies-Black Publishing, 1995.

Tart, Charles T., ed. *Transpersonal Psychologies: Perspectives on the Mind of Seven Great Spiritual Traditions, 3rd Edition.* New York: HarperCollins, 1992.

Index

A

achiever, xiv, 59, 74, 82, 101–3, 134, 161, 251–52
Aquarius, 15, 45–46, 78
Aries, xvi, 36–37, 39, 78
astrology, xiv–xv, xviii, 12, 49–50, 210
authentic personality number, 234–35
awareness, xv, 5, 7, 22, 43, 69, 89, 97, 102, 116, 154, 170, 187, 191, 193, 199, 201, 213–14, 229, 249, 255, 257
  spiritual, 118, 229

B

birth date, xvi, 1–2, 11–12, 15, 18, 36–37, 75, 77, 87, 94, 210
birth name, xviii, 87, 210–11, 215, 227, 233–35, 237–38
body-mind-soul trinity, 33
Brahma, 31

C

Cancer, 41, 78, 85
Capricorn, 45–46, 78
challenger, 69, 74, 82–83, 89, 115–17, 193, 225, 227

Clay, Cassius Marcellus. *See* Muhammad Ali
combination
  stage-cycle, 121, 159, 199
  three-one-two, 205
consciousness, xv, 9, 14, 21, 32, 34, 52, 60, 62, 68, 91–92, 97, 114, 116, 156, 168, 186–87, 196, 213, 216, 219, 234
contestant, 89, 102–3, 157, 165, 174, 192, 198, 204
cosmic year, 13
cosmos, xiv, xvi, 2, 5, 13, 18, 32, 36, 47, 49, 150
creation, xvi, 3, 5, 9, 13, 17, 21, 31, 38, 56, 96

D

defender, 45, 115–17, 164, 182, 190, 192, 194–95, 200
destruction, 17, 31, 70, 100, 153, 225
detachment, 44, 103, 109, 111, 167, 185–86
development
  first cycle of, 84, 150, 213
  individual, 89, 96, 99, 154
  second cycle of, 213
  third cycle of, 85, 95, 214

Discovering Your Personality Type (Riso), 75
DNA (deoxyribonucleic acid), 2, 66
dualism, 6
dualities, xiii, xviii, 3, 6, 18, 24, 29–30, 52, 101, 106, 220, 251

E

Einstein, Albert, 26
Emotions and the Enneagram (Keyes), 75
energy
    emotional, 32, 58, 99, 214, 217, 232
    mental, 126, 161, 205
    negative, 65, 111
    optimistic, 135, 137, 165, 174
    warm, 148, 196, 201
enneagram, xiv–xvi, 10, 36, 49–51, 80–81, 86–87, 211
enneagram letter groups, xvii–xviii, 95, 215
enneagram letters, 83–84, 211–12, 216–17, 220, 222, 232, 236, 238
enneagram letter types, 215, 231
enneagram model, 18, 49, 86, 124
enneagram numbers, 4, 124, 212
enneagram signs, xiv, xvi–xvii, 1–4, 8, 11, 14, 16–17, 21, 25–26, 36–41, 44, 50–51, 76–78, 83, 86–94, 123, 125, 149, 151, 162–63, 171, 176, 189, 194, 211–12, 233, 235–36
    zodiac-based, 11, 75
enneagram stages of development, 11, 150
enneagram system, xiv, 43–46, 49, 124, 247
enneagram types, xiv–xvi, xviii, 19, 28, 33, 36–37, 47, 50–51, 75, 77, 81–84, 86, 88–90, 94–95, 121–25, 211–12, 247, 251
enthusiasts, 74, 82–83, 113

F

first law of thermodynamics, 16
forces
    affirming, 8, 21–22, 78, 152
    denying, 8, 21–22, 78, 167
    independent, xiii, 9
    reconciling, xv, 8, 21–22, 78, 184

G

Gemini, xvi, 37, 40–41, 78
guidance, 35, 99–100, 103, 169, 197, 238
guide, 15, 39, 41, 99–100, 123, 130, 156, 161, 168, 187, 192, 197, 203, 205
guide and helper type letters, 217
guide archetype, 157, 179, 202–4
guide sign, 39, 154, 159, 203
Gurdjieff, Geroge Ivanovich, xiii, 8, 49, 78

H

harmony, xiii, 8, 46, 50, 52, 60, 71–72, 83, 101, 112, 118–19, 130, 134, 137–38, 140, 145, 147–48, 156, 160–63, 169, 173–74, 178–79, 182–83, 190–91, 196–200, 218, 226, 249
helper, 57, 74, 82, 99–100, 196
Hindu Trinity, 31
Holmes, Ernest, 33
Hudson, Russ, 51, 79

I

Ichazo, Oscar, xiv
I Ching, 22
individualist, 61, 63, 74, 82–83, 104–5
individuation, 18

initiator, 44, 96, 168, 179, 197, 199, 203

innovator, 42, 107–8, 142, 158, 174, 176, 208

intuitive flashes, 64, 136, 164, 188, 190, 221

investigator, 63, 74, 82–83, 90, 107–8, 123

J

Jung, Carl Gustav, 18, 28, 37, 86, 234–35

Jupiter, 29, 44, 50–53, 68, 74, 129, 133, 136, 140, 142, 144, 146, 223

K

Keyes, Margaret Frings, 75

Know Your Type (Metzner), 22

L

Law of One, 5

Law of Three, xiii, xv–xvi, 7–9, 20–21, 24

Law of Two, 6

Leo, 42, 78, 85

letters
   cycle of, 84, 211
   groups of, 212, 216, 218–22, 224–28, 236, 251

Libra, 43–44, 78

life cycle, xvi–xvii, 3, 10, 21, 25, 76, 88, 109, 125, 149–50, 152, 166–67, 185

M

manifestation, 2–3, 8, 24–25, 31, 34, 52, 55–56, 72, 74, 78, 89,

96–97, 212, 215, 233, 248, 250–51

Mars, 30, 32, 45, 50–53, 70, 72, 74, 225

Maslow, Abraham, 74

mediator, 46, 82, 160, 165, 191, 198–200, 227

Metzner, Ralph, 22

mind
   conscious, 7, 34–35, 78, 202, 215
   creative, 7, 34–35, 52, 63, 68, 78, 169, 172, 193, 198, 231

moon, 58

Muhammad Ali, 236–38

N

Neptune, 29, 41, 50–53, 62, 74, 219

Newton's third law, 18

nines, 11, 118–19, 122, 140, 147–48, 227

nine-year cycles, xvii, 13, 77, 88, 90–91, 98, 106, 114, 117, 120, 151, 165, 172, 197–98, 202–3, 254

nonphysical universe, 8, 62, 73, 76, 127, 129, 138, 150, 164, 170–71, 187–88, 207

O

Obama, Barack, 232

P

peacemaker, 71, 74, 82–83, 100, 118–19, 227

performer, 82

personality, xviii–2, 13–14, 18–19, 22, 34, 36, 47, 58, 61, 83, 87, 89–90, 92–93, 96, 101, 106,

113, 130, 197, 208–10, 215, 217, 229–31, 234, 238
authentic, 232–34, 237–38
soul-centered, xvi, 36–37
personality types
  affirming, 21
  denying, 21–22
  reconciling, 21–22
philosophy, 68, 92, 108, 113–14, 136, 146, 164, 186, 188, 223–24
Pythagoras, 24

R

Reformer, 39, 55, 74, 82, 96, 238
Riso, Don Richard, 51, 75
romantic, 42, 44, 82, 104–5, 119, 140, 157, 162, 193, 198, 205
romantic and individualist fourth cycle ages, 104
romantic and individualist type letters, 219
Roosevelt, Teddy, 113

S

Sagittarius, 45, 78
Science of Mind, The (Holmes), 33, 35
Scorpio, 44, 78
seeker, 44, 83, 113, 187, 189, 195, 200, 207
Shiva, 31
skeptic, 15, 43, 110–11, 142, 179–83, 194, 200, 222
spring equinox, 4, 13
sun, xvi–xvii, 1–2, 4, 11–13, 16–17, 30, 32, 35–37, 40, 50–52, 54, 58–60, 70, 72, 74, 83, 87, 94,

127, 131, 134–38, 161, 211, 218, 226

T

Tao, xiii, 8–9, 30, 35, 78
Taurus, xvi, 37, 39–40, 78
trinities, xiii–xvii, 3–4, 7–10, 21–25, 27–30, 32–35, 37, 50, 56, 77–79, 84–85, 102, 149, 152, 166, 184, 213–14
Trump, Donald J., 89
type compatibilities, 122, 125

U

Uranus, 30, 42, 50–53, 64, 74

V

Venus, 30, 32, 46, 50–53, 72, 74, 226
Virgo, 42–43, 78
Vishnu, 31

Y

yang, xiii, 3, 5–6, 8–9, 22, 24, 30–31, 50, 52, 78
yin, xiii, 3, 5–6, 8–9, 22, 30–31, 50, 52, 58, 78

Z

zodiac, 14–15, 36–39, 41, 43, 45, 47, 77
zodiac signs, 1, 11, 36–38, 50, 85, 87, 153, 156

The Nine Stages of Manifesting

Throughout this work the enneagram system has been presented as nine personality types, nine soul types or signs, and nine stages of development in the form of a circle. As already mentioned the meaning the nine enneagram types are based of the nine planets and the enneagram signs or soul types get their meaning from two complementary opposite and adjacent astrology signs. Although enneagram personality types are based on self-assessment surveys, and soul types and cycles of development are based on birthdates they can all be understood as the nine individual stages required to bring any new arising into existence.

Trinities are straightforward and easy to comprehend. Enneagrams can be understood as detailed versions of trinities because each portion of a given trinity contains a trinity within in it. In the manifestation process, stages 1, 2 and 3 represent the beginning segment of the circular journey or cycle; stages 4, 5 and 6 represent the middle segment; and stages 7, 8 and 9 represent the completion segment. Stages 1, 4 and 7 are in the group of active, positive, and motivating trinity forces; stages 2, 5 and 8 are in the group of receptive, negative, and passive trinity forces; and stages 3, 6 and 9 represent the group of reconciliation, mediation, and facilitation forces and result of uniting the first two groups.

While the nine enneagram types, soul types and cycles of development are identified by objective measures, the nine stages are also individual roles played in the subjective inner observation process that take place from conceiving to manifesting all forms through imagery, visioning, meditation, contemplation, planning, and so forth. Since everything in the inner world of the unconscious seeks outward manifestation, those who receive and understand its message will attract what they need to assist them in becoming the manifestation they seek. Taken apart and examined the nine stages and roles played by the types can be described as you experience each of nine steps.

Stage 1: You define things and ask questions that set the stage for gaining new answers and knowledge. Here you explain what you are seeking and help others to understand what you are seeking. Roles played by the Reformer and Initiator types.

Stage 2: You Keep your focus on the question or subjects from the first stage in a way that is open and receptive to answers or the knowledge requested. Here you encourage others to remain open and receptive as well. Roles played by the Helper and Guide types.

Stage 3: You combine the first two stages in ways that increase your focus and help you catch as many details as possible. Here you are expressing what has been called forth and brought into the light of day. Roles played by the Achiever and Contestant types.

Stage 4: You become so unified or one with your inner world established in the third stage that you completely forget yourself. Here your ego is suspended for a moment or long enough to get the insight. Roles played by the Individualist and Romantic types.

Stage 5: You catch the vision, insight or revelation and its basic meaning from the fourth stage. Here you record or describe your insight, and initial interpretation. Roles played by the Investigator and Innovator types.

Stage 6: You analyze, consider, and question other possible meanings to interpret the insight from stage five. Here you continue to raise questions until you really understand what has been revealed. Roles played by the Loyalist have and Skeptic types.

Stage 7: You verify your stage six interpretation by getting a reality check or validation from independent source(s). Here you are then eager to share your findings or knowledge to expand the awareness of others. Roles played by the Enthusiast and Seeker types.

Stage 8: You act to make things happen and manifest your view of heaven on earth. Here you are confident, assertive and determined to give concrete reality to your stage seven understanding. Roles played by the Challenger and Defender types.

Stage 9: You interact with others to create harmony and acceptance of promising ideas. Here you look for ways to peacefully integrate all elements of the previous eight stages. Roles play by the Peacemaker and Mediator types.

From Four to Three Seasons

In every year, the four seasons known as spring, summer, fall, and winter contain trinities that consist of approximately three 30-day months. This four-three combination gives us the twelve calendar months from January through December and the astrology signs from Aries in the spring through Pisces in the winter. The seasons and months are objective and subjective signs or symbols used by the people of our world to measure time. The four seasons and twelve months are the continuous cycles or stages that serve to guide and define all life on earth. They represent the ongoing stages from inner concepts, seed potentials, and birth to manifestations, completions, and death.

In every year, the three seasons known as beginning, middle, ending stages of the year contain trinities that consist of approximately three 40-day periods. This three-three combination gives us nine sacred enneagram periods to represent the types or signs and stages from the Reformer in the spring through the Peacemaker in the winter. As in the twelve-month year, the seasons and stages are objective and subjective signs or symbols that measure time. While the nine-fold division of the year is not used as widely as the twelve-month division, it is just as real. The three-three perspective of the enneagram offers a greater natural connection to the spiritual side of human life than the four-three or square-trinity arrangement. As an upgraded or advanced version of the trinity, enneagrams help us to investigate trinities at a deeper level.

The universal cycle of life is an ongoing and recurring process. Throughout the circle of life, inner concepts and manifestations, seed potentials and concrete reality forms, all births and deaths are linked together in oneness. Whenever manifestations and completions take place the seeds of renewal and birth are present. No matter how things appear, change is the only constant throughout life. Even though we are born into a world where knowledge and thinking separates things into different seasons, time and space, dark and light, mind and matter, etc., in oneness, everything exists in the same place at the same time, and there is no division. In the circle of oneness, there is no up and down, no here and there, no now and then, no time and space. In oneness, all things exist together side by side as one thing.

From the biblical perspective, the second chapter of Genesis essentially tells us that oneness is represented by the Tree of Life and living inside the Garden of Eden. In addition, the Genesis narrative tells us that duality, thinking, and separation from the oneness is represented by the Tree of Knowledge of Good and Evil and life outside the Garden.

The table that follows presents the trinity arrangements of forces and stages of development for the nine enneagram types. These arrangements provide an additional understanding of the trinity principle behind the types. In the first row of development stages, we have the Reformer, the Helper, and the Achiever as the beginning types; the Individualist, we have the Investigator, and the Loyalist in the second row as middle stage types; and the Enthusiast, the Challenger, and Peacemaker in the third row are the completion or ending stage types. As seen among the planets, letter groups, and numbers, the beginning, middle, and ending types also represent our individual development stage; the development stage of our close relationships; and the development stage of our relationship to society and the collective respectively.

Trinity Forces and Stages Among the Types

	Affirming	*Denying*	*Reconciling*
Beginning	Reformer	Helper	Achiever
Middle	Individualist	Investigator	Loyalist
Ending	Enthusiast	Challenger	Peacemaker

Among the nine types as trinity forces, the first column consists of the Reformer, the Individualist, and the Enthusiast as the affirming or active trinity forces. The second column consist of the Helper, Investigator, and the Challenger as the denying or receptive trinity forces; and the third column consist of the Achiever, the Loyalist, and the Peacemaker as the reconciling or facilitating trinity forces.

Life Events, Stages, and
Your Biography

Knowing the life cycle and its stages gives us a treasure trove of insights and meanings of our past, present, and future life experiences. Even though people often think of age as linear, the life cycle timeline is a circular, spiraling, and ascending journey. By recording the biographical events in your life, you can view it in an informative and entertaining manner. At the end of your biography, any readers should feel that they know you on a personal level. Unfortunately, this feat is unachievable because it is not possible to collect and report on every fact in a comprehensive and unbiased manner while making it entertaining.

Understanding your biography and future begins with knowing your history and the meanings of your life stages and cycles as enneagram signs and fulfillments through your experience in connecting the two. You may see no connections, some connections, or many connections. Understanding your stages and cycles to date will help you understand future cycles and make the most of them.

Documenting your biography will help you discover your purpose for existence and assist you in keeping track with your authentic self. By reflecting upon your history, you can better understand your life's purpose and predict your future. Since every year represents a new and recurring stage of development, understanding your experience in past stages will help you align yourself with their presence in the future. The easy part of writing your biography is that you have personal knowledge of the subject. Because facts can be lost, forgotten, suppressed, and distorted over time, many biographies will not be complete.

Although you may not be able to change the significant events in your life, you will live through them, and you can influence them. Even though people believe that life is a random mix of life events, there is a pattern to how life unfolds. Knowing what life events have in common can help you anticipate, prepare for, and survive them. More importantly, they can give you the foresight to focus upon and bring about the events you want and minimize the influence of the ones you don't.

You can get started by checking off which relevant areas of experience and listed life experiences apply to you for the relevant time. For instance, you might check off items under Job, Career, or Business; Personal Possessions and Places Lived; and Personal Relationships as the main experiences in your midlife cycle from ages thirty-six to forty-five. You can then expand this checklist by including more areas of interest. By listing or identifying more key points and perhaps dates or the order in which the events occurred, you address the questions given here.

The biographical checklist that follows applies to all the nine-year cycles separately and to the nine annual stages within them. You can start the checklist from the first nine-year cycle (birth to nine years old) and work toward the present, start with the present nine-year cycle and work backward to the first, recall the timing of special events in your life, or start in the middle and work outward. There is no need for great details as you start because you can add them later if wanted. After noting the events within your selected nine-year cycle, go back and identify the age in which you experienced the event. The month or date of the event is optional.

Ages included (from_____to_____)

Enneagram sign_____

[ ] Job, Career, or Business

[ ] Business Ventures
[ ] Significant New Learning
[ ] Accepting More Responsibility or a Promotion
[ ] Hobbies or Avocation
[ ] Main Job or Career
[ ] Military Service
[ ] Outgrowing or Leaving a Job
[ ] Positions Held
[ ] Subjects Given or Taught
[ ] Volunteer Activities

[ ] Personal Growth and Development

[ ] Connecting with Nature
[ ] Developing Multisensory Perceptions and Awareness
[ ] Learning about Where You Belong
[ ] Learning about Who You Are or Your Purpose in Life
[ ] Major Teacher or Influential Individuals
[ ] Settling your Affairs
[ ] Significant Dreams, Visions, or Reading
[ ] Transforming Life Change
[ ] Significant Benefit or Gain

[ ] Decisions Made, Financial Gains and Losses

[ ] Awards Earned
[ ] Mistakes or Wrong Decision(s) Made
[ ] Good Decision(s) Made
[ ] Major Challenges or Obstacles Met and Overcome
[ ] Major Lessons and Learning
[ ] Significant Financial Gains or Losses

[ ] Health

[ ] Death of Parents, Children, or Loved Ones
[ ] Death of Relatives, Siblings, or Friends

[ ] Health Issues or Crises
[ ] Preparing for Retirement
[ ] Physical Limitations
[ ] Physical Fitness
[ ] Significant Injuries
[ ] Significant Illnesses
[ ] Joining an Important Social or Spiritual Group

[ ] Personal Possessions and Places Lived
[ ] Significant Places Lived or Visited
[ ] Business or Financial Investments
[ ] Cars Owned or in My Possession
[ ] House(s) or Property Owned
[ ] Major Assets and Liabilities
[ ] Renting an Apartment or Buying a House
[ ] Other Important Possessions

[ ] Personal Relationships
[ ] Beginning a New Love Relationship
[ ] Ending an Important Love Relationship
[ ] Bringing New Life into the World
[ ] Falling in Like or Falling in Love
[ ] Getting Attached
[ ] Getting Back Together
[ ] Getting Disappointed or Hurt
[ ] Getting Married or Remarried
[ ] Dealing with Major Relationship Problems
[ ] Making a Commitment or Getting Serious
[ ] Relationship with Close Associates, Friends, or Clients

[ ] Education and Vocational Training
[ ] Learning About and Using Multisensory Awareness
[ ] Choosing and Attending a School or College
[ ] Choosing and Working on a Major or Area of Study

[ ] Middle and High Schools Attended
[ ] Graduating and Earning a Degree
[ ] Self-Development Learning and Awareness

[ ] Other Events Not Indicated Above

With the assistance of the checklist, your answers to the next three questions will help you further record your biographical themes. To get started, you can answer these questions starting with any nine-year period and work backward or forward. By recording patterns and recurring themes, you can get many insights into how you have experienced past stages and how you may likely experience future stages.

- List your accomplishments, activities, and positive experiences for the nine-year period under study.

- List your setbacks, involvements, and negative experiences for each nine-year period of study.

- After your list of nine-year events, record, if possible, one or more happenings for every year within the nine-year period of study.

CPSIA information can be obtained
at www.ICGtesting.com
Printed in the USA
LVHW08*2057200718
584493LV00004B/23/P

9 781543 446142